MW01626369

Studies in

The Book of Acts

VOLUME FIVE

TRIUMPHANT CHRISTIANITY

MARTYN LLOYD-JONES

CROSSWAY BOOKS

A PUBLISHING MINISTRY OF
GOOD NEWS PUBLISHERS
WHEATON, ILLINOIS

Triumphant Christianity

Published by Crossway Books
A publishing ministry of Good News Publishers
1300 Crescent Street
Wheaton, Illinois 60187

Cover design: David LaPlaca

Cover photo: © Photo Disc

First U.S. edition published 2006

Printed in the United States of America

All Bible quotations are taken from the *King James Version.*

Italicized text in Scripture quotations indicates emphasis added.

Library of Congress Cataloging-in-Publication Data

Lloyd-Jones, David Martyn.
Triumphant Christianity / Martyn Lloyd-Jones.
p. cm. — (Studies in the book of Acts : v. 5)
ISBN 13: 978-1-58134-784-5
ISBN 10: 1-58134-784-7 (hc : alk. paper)
1. Bible. N.T. Acts VII, 29-60—Sermons. 2. Sermons, English—20th century. I. Title. II. Series: Lloyd-Jones, David Martyn. Studies in the book of Acts ; v. 5.
BS2625.54.L59 2006
226.6'077—dc22 2006002983

RRDH 15 14 13 12 11 10 09 08 07 06
15 14 13 12 11 10 9 8 7 6 5 4 3 2 1

Contents

1

The God Who Intervenes

> *Then fled Moses at this saying, and was a stranger in the land of Madian, where he begat two sons. And when forty years were expired, there appeared to him in the wilderness of mount Sina an angel of the Lord in a flame of fire in a bush.*
>
> —Acts 7:29-30

These verses are part of a great statement made by Stephen, the first Christian martyr, in his self-defense, in his explanation of his conduct to the members of the great court, known as the Sanhedrin, in Jerusalem. He was on trial because he was a Christian, because he said that Jesus of Nazareth was the Son of God, because he said that the Son of God came into the world to save men and women and did so supremely by dying for them on the cross on Calvary's hill and rising again in the resurrection to justify them. Stephen and all others who believed and preached this message not only said that Jesus was the Son of God and the Savior, they also said He was the *only* Savior: "Neither is there salvation in any other" (Acts 4:12).

Stephen was on trial, and his defense, as I have been showing you,[1] was a brief survey or review of the long story of the children of Israel. These people in the Sanhedrin were Jews, and they were very proud of their story. So Stephen took it up just to show them that they had entirely misunderstood it, and that in rejecting this message concerning the Son of God as the Savior, they were simply doing what their forefathers, alas, had done on so many previous occasions. We have seen [in earlier volumes] how Stephen showed this by taking up the cases of Abraham and Joseph, and we continue now with his third case, which is that of Moses.

We have found that the story of Moses passed through different phases. First of all, we spent some time considering how his very birth took place. Then we looked at him at the age of forty. There he was, brought up as the son of Pharaoh's daughter, with wonderful prospects, but God spoke to him and put something into his heart. God disturbed him and told him that He had chosen him to be the leader of his people and said he was to take them out of the bondage and serfdom of Egypt. Moses realized that it was God who was speaking, and he was ready to listen; he sacrificed everything and went to his people.

We have considered further how these foolish people rejected Moses. We are told, "For he supposed his brethren would have understood how that God by his hand would deliver them: but they understood not" (Acts 7:25). They were muddled in their thinking, and they were still worse in their hearts and showed antagonism to him. One of them "thrust him away, saying, Who made thee a ruler and a judge over us? Wilt thou kill me, as thou diddest the Egyptian yesterday?" (vv. 27-28). As the result of this, Moses' life was in danger. He realized that these countrymen of his, whom he had come to deliver, and for whose sake he was ready to sacrifice so much, were about to report him to Pharaoh and the court. Knowing that he would undoubtedly be arrested and probably put to death, he fled for his life: "Then fled Moses at this saying, and was a stranger in the land of Madian, where he begat two sons" (v. 29).

If you go back to the Old Testament, to the book of Exodus, you will find, in detail, this whole story concerning Moses. Stephen was only summarizing it, picking out what suited the particular point that he was so anxious to make. But there was Moses, this great man, brought up as the son of Pharaoh's daughter, "learned in all the wisdom of the Egyptians," "mighty," we are told, "in words and in deeds" (v. 22), now because of the hostility of his people reduced to being a shepherd. And that was the life he lived for the following forty years.

And then we come suddenly to the thirtieth verse: "And when forty years were expired"—forty years as a shepherd—"there appeared to him in the wilderness of mount Sina an angel of the Lord in a flame of fire in a bush."

Then we read:

> *When Moses saw it, he wondered at the sight: and as he drew near to behold it, the voice of the Lord came unto him, saying, I am the God of thy fathers, the God of Abraham, and the God of Isaac, and the God of Jacob. Then Moses trembled, and durst not behold. Then said the Lord to him, Put off thy shoes from thy feet: for the place*

> *where thou standest is holy ground. I have seen, I have seen the affliction of my people which is in Egypt, and I have heard their groaning, and am come down to deliver them. And now come, I will send thee into Egypt. This Moses whom they refused, saying, Who made thee a ruler and a judge? the same did God send to be a ruler and a deliverer by the hand of the angel which appeared to him in the bush.*
> —*vv. 31-35*

Now this was obviously a new phase in the story of Moses, not only as it was told by Stephen but as it actually took place. But Stephen here was not only reviewing the story of Moses and the way in which the children of Israel treated him. He was doing that, and that was, in a sense, his main purpose from the standpoint of his self-defense, but he had another, and a much more important, motive. He was above all teaching them about God's great purpose of salvation, of God's ways with respect to the human race.

Now this is a point that is summarized and brought out with special clarity in verse 30. This verse reveals to us God's way of salvation, which, of course, reaches its climax and its acme in our Lord and Savior Jesus Christ. What a wonderful verse it is! Were it not for the truth taught us in this verse, there would be no such thing as the Christian church, and we would all be left to ourselves. I do not think the world would even be in existence—it would have brought itself to extinction long ago. This is the sort of verse that saves us all; it is a verse that gives us hope. It is the very essence of the gospel message.

So Stephen reminded the Sanhedrin of the great event that took place there in the wilderness of Mount Sinai in order to press home upon them again this extraordinary characteristic of the human race—namely, the way in which it reacts to the kind of statement recorded here. There is nothing about human perverseness and sinfulness that is more terrible than this—men and women in all their trouble, in all their confusion and unhappiness, in all their need and wretched failure, reject the offer of deliverance and do so with scorn and with sarcasm, thinking, as they do so, that they are clever.

That was what Stephen was pointing out to the members of the Sanhedrin; and it is because, alas, that humanity still behaves in the same way that I am calling your attention to it now. Stephen was giving the members of the Sanhedrin ancient history. But just as he was able to show that ancient history is an indication of what they were still doing, so I am able, unfortunately all too easily, to demonstrate the same thing now. Men and women do not change; that is where history is of such great value. We go on repeating the errors of our forefathers right back to the very beginning. The whole story is of one piece, and the tragedy of the human story is that men and women reject this message at its most glorious points. That is what is so amazing. They do not merely reject certain details, certain incidentals. Their most bitter objection to the Gospel concerns the most vital truths, the saving truths, the most wonderful truths of all. That is what Stephen brings out.

What, then, are the points at which men and women go most completely and grievously astray? There are three: the first is with regard to God Himself, the second is with regard to man himself, and the third is with regard to the way of salvation and of deliverance. Now can anything be more important than those three points? God! Man! The way of deliverance—the way of salvation! And all three come out here in the story of Moses. "When forty years were expired, there appeared to him in the wilderness of mount Sina an angel of the Lord in a flame of fire in a bush"; and the whole story goes on. God speaks! God tells Moses His plan, His purpose, and sends him to carry it out, and the great story of the exodus follows. I say again that it is astounding that it is just this kind of statement that is most rejected and resented by men and women at the present time.

This rejection is such an important matter that I want to put it as plainly and as succinctly as I can. Perhaps the simplest way for me to do that is to put it in terms of something I read recently in *Reader's Digest*. I am anxious to speak concerning this, not only to Christians, but especially to those who are not Christians. That magazine included an interview with a very famous old man and preacher, Dr. Harry Emerson Fosdick. He was interviewed on a fashionable modern craze in America—"the death of God movement." According to this teaching, the God who has always been worshiped is nonexistent—He is dead. This view is being propounded by some prominent theologians who teach something entirely opposed to the old belief; they ridicule it, saying that God as a person has disappeared completely.

So Fosdick was interviewed on this very matter, and in his reply he says he does not agree with the "God is dead" teaching. He ridicules it, in fact, pointing out how this really fails to deal with certain obvious facts in nature and creation. He stated:

> The only alternative to mind behind the universe—*that is [the God-is-dead theologians'] view of God*—is blind protons and neutrons—*portions of the atom*—accidentally colliding in space to produce the universe. This is the choice, one or the other. You cannot have it both ways. Do people really think that the cosmic scheme of things is mindless and purposeless, without meaning or destiny? I believe there is a

> mind behind the universe, purpose running through it, ultimate meaning in it, and destiny ahead of it. Denial of God is the denial of all four, leaving the universe mindless, meaningless, a dead-end street.

In other words, Fosdick very rightly shows us how ridiculous is this modern fashion that presents itself in terms of "God is dead." So far, excellent; but, alas, he goes on to say things that are quite as bad and that make his first statement, therefore, more or less meaningless and useless. He says, for example, "I think there are many concepts of God that should die."

What are these? Here is one of them: "God as a kind of pillow to lie down on—the God who will take care of everything!" That God, he says, should die.

Secondly: "God as a kind of venerable bookkeeper who takes note of everyone's good and bad deeds—he must die."

And thirdly: "Certainly the King of Glory ruling the universe from a golden throne is dead."

He continues:

> The God that walked in the Garden in the cool of the day is dead, too. The "God of the gaps" is quite dead—that was the one who accounted for everything that man could not comprehend or control, from dreams to thunderstorms.

He is dead, Fosdick says. "In our modern world, the God who is on our side has to die."

And then he says: "But perhaps the God most difficult to bury is the one who makes things come out right. It takes real maturity to get rid of him!" The God who answers prayer, the God who makes things come out right for His people, must be buried. It takes "real maturity" to get rid of Him, but we must. Then Dr. Fosdick asks what that leaves us with.

> I believe we come close to God wherever there is beauty, love, integrity, truth. So often if you ask people where God is, their thoughts go shooting up among the stars; but it is deep down within human life that we find God. The simple truth is that we discover the divine wherever love illumines life.

In other words, there is no God, really, apart from us. You find God in yourself, not out in the stars, not in the heavens, not beyond all thought and comprehension. God is within you, wherever there is love and beauty and goodness and truth. Of course, Fosdick contradicts himself; he has already told us there is a mind behind the universe and above it and beyond it. This is his teaching, however. Then he says: "It is very difficult to realize that God's word does not come to man through magical handwriting on the wall, or spelt out on stone tablets, but from the inner counsel of the heart."

God never speaks from the outside—never, according to this man. What, then, is Fosdick's view of man? He agrees that man is in terrible trouble; so what is he to do? Of course, men and women are not sinful or depraved. They just need teaching and instruction; they need help; they need an example. Fosdick puts it like this: "If you want anything physical, then you have to obey physical laws."

And then he goes on:

> If we want spiritual results, we must fulfill spiritual conditions. This is the law of life, and it is both stern and magnificent. Modern religion says: Go out into God's world and fulfill his conditions. If you want health, fulfill the conditions of health—physical, mental and spiritual. What a man sows he indeed reaps. Sow friendliness and reap friendship. Sow unselfishness and reap an enlarged life. Sow goodwill and reap a better world for our children. Sow worship, which is the uplift of the heart towards the Highest, and reap open-hearted responsiveness to things Eternal.

Now that, I think, is as good and as eloquent a statement as you will ever have of this modern attitude toward God and toward the whole message of the Bible and of religion. What it comes to is this: God is inside us, and if you want to find God, you must look into yourself. God speaks in the heart, never outside. You find Him in others, in goodness, beauty, and truth, in various manifestations of love, and so on. He is not a God to whom you can pray. Fosdick's very definition of worship is "the uplift of the heart towards the Highest," and as you do that, as you try to "uplift [your] heart," you "reap open-hearted responsiveness to things Eternal."

So the message is that we must do it all; it is all left to us. We must save ourselves: go out into the world, think beautiful thoughts, and so on. That is what we are told to do! With the modern world as it is, with wars, immorality, vice, and the breakdown of marriage, we must go out and sow goodwill, and then we will reap a better world for our children.

It is amazing to me that a man of ninety years of age can go on talking such nonsense. This is the sort of thing that is being preached and propagated *ad nauseam.* This is the old liberalism that denies a supernatural Gospel of salvation and says that people must save themselves by thinking beautiful thoughts and doing good deeds. Poor Dr. Fosdick—he has forgotten that he had to write a book years ago that he entitled *Beyond Modernism.* He had been preaching modernism all his life, but the last war convinced him that modernism was not enough. But he has gone back to it again. All that we are offered with the world as it is today is that our salvation is within us.

When I come across a verse like the thirtieth verse in the seventh chapter of the book of Acts, I am filled with praise and rejoicing. "When forty years were expired, there appeared to him in the wilderness of mount Sina an angel of the Lord in a flame of fire in a bush." Thank God, that is the truth. If it were not, there would not be a single hope for anybody whatsoever—good, bad, or indifferent—in the whole of the universe. That other view leaves us to ourselves. We are told there is some mind behind the universe, but we are told specifically that we must not look to Him to do things for us and to deliver us. That is the sort of God we must bury, we are told. We must not believe any longer in this God who is for us, the God who is on our side, the God who intervenes, the God who solves our problems. Men like Fosdick tell us, "You must reject such nonsense; you are making God into a pillow."

Now I am ready to grant—it would be foolish not to do so—that many Christian people oftentimes have had unworthy thoughts of God and of the Lord Jesus Christ and of His great salvation. We do not claim to be perfect as Christians, and Christians have often confused magic with miracle, and sentimentality with the love of God. I am not here to defend anything of that kind, and there is still a lot of it in the modern church. I am not interested in a Gospel that just tells stories and preys on people's feelings and is so anxious to get a decision that it does not care very much how it gets it. But the Gospel is truth, and we must be interested in truth.

The tragedy of teaching like Fosdick's is that it leaves us absolutely to ourselves in all our helplessness; it does not even tell us anything about judgment, about death and what lies beyond it. It does not seem to believe in that. It believes only in this world and says that you and I, by doing certain things, are going to make this world a better place for our children. But that is not the Gospel—that is a lie.

What, then, is the gospel message? Let me start again with the three points that I have put before you, the most important questions of all. Start with God! What is the teaching of the Bible, what is the teaching of this verse, with regard to God? First of all, God is someone who is outside us, someone who is outside the whole universe. He has not only made it, He is not merely a mind behind it, God is the living God. "When forty years were expired, there appeared unto him in the wilderness of mount Sina an angel of the Lord." Who sent the angel? The Lord! This whole approach is entirely different. I have a message to preach because of what God has done—not because of what man has been trying to do and cannot do. The whole message is that "[God] hath visited and redeemed his people" (Luke 1:68). He is the living God; He is the thinking God. God is personal.

Now we do not understand God—who can understand Him? By definition He is entirely beyond our understanding; He would not be God if He were not. That is why these people are so arrogant in expressing their opinions as they do. I am amazed that they are not afraid of blasphemy, speaking as they do about "burying God" and so on. No; God is. "God is light, and in him is no darkness at all" (1 John 1:5). He is a God who has made the universe and who sits above the universe.

We are but human beings, and we must use anthropomorphic language; we cannot speak in any other way. The Bible does this; it speaks of God in human terms—it uses anthropomorphisms. But that is because of our lack of understanding; these are designed to help us. But God is beyond us! "Great is the mystery of godliness" (1 Tim. 3:16). That is our confession. But, thank God, He has revealed certain things about Himself to us, and He has told us that He has not only made the universe, but He is the controller of the universe. He can control bushes—there is nothing He cannot control. He is all-powerful; He is all-mighty! He is omniscient—there is nothing that He does not know. He sees the end from the beginning. All things are under His hands.

Not only that—God is the Judge of the universe. He made the universe, so He is entitled to judge it. Now these clever men object to this idea of God above us, judging us. Of course, they object to that, but they object to all law. I do not believe that is true of Fosdick, but it is true of many of his followers. They do not believe in any law at all; many of them do not believe in morality. Every man does as he likes. They say, "Why not? Why shouldn't he? Have a good time. Let yourself go. Be like animals; obey your lusts and passions!" But this is God's world, and He has made it, and He is in control of it, and every one of us will have to stand in judgment before Him and give an account of the deeds done in the body, whether good or bad (see 2 Cor. 5:10).

But, you say, that is a terrifying message. Of course it is! The law of God is alarming; it is terrifying. Who can dwell with a burning fire? We have all known what it is to feel unworthy in the presence of some particularly saintly human being. They did not condemn us—they were the kindest, gentlest people we had ever met. But in their presence we felt we were unclean, we felt we needed to go out and have a bath, we wanted clean clothing—their purity condemned us. Multiply that by infinity, and you see yourself in the presence of this eternal, holy God! That, I say again, is terrifying. But this is the message, this is the Gospel—that same God has a plan and a purpose for delivering humanity.

Now the children of Israel whom Stephen was talking about were slaves. God raised up this man Moses in a very wonderful way in order to deliver them, but we have been seeing how they rejected him and thrust him away. They were so annoyed with him that they would have been glad if they could have killed him. In spite of that, God had a plan of deliverance for them. After forty years He sent this angel to speak to Moses about His purpose of redemption. He said, "I am the God of thy fathers, the God of Abraham, and the God of Isaac, and the God of Jacob." He is the covenant-keeping God. He is the God of the children of Israel. He is the God who had made a nation out of a man for a definite purpose. The whole universe is interested in this because, through this people, the whole universe will be reconciled to God. That is who He is.

God is the living God, the true God, a thinking God, and He is a loving God. Out of His own love and mercy and compassion He prepared a plan for the deliverance of these recalcitrant, rebellious people. And He not only prepared this plan—He acted. God acts! If this is not true, I have no message, and there is no Gospel. If Fosdick is correct and it is wrong to say that God intervenes in the lives of men and women and has a plan for delivering them—if that is wrong, then there is no Gospel, there is no hope whatsoever.

But, thank God, this is the message: "When forty years were expired, there appeared to him in the wilderness of mount Sina an angel of the Lord." God is concerned about you; He is interested in you and knows all about you. He is a God who intervenes in our lives. Let me use a stronger word—He *erupts* into them! Thank God that He does. We, like the foolish children of Israel, dislike this; we try to shake God off, as it were—we try to get rid of Him in various ways. But He keeps coming back. He will not let us go, and He suddenly intervenes and comes to us. The whole message of the Bible is a record of the activity of God, not of some "mind behind the universe" that apparently, having made the universe, gave it all up and left it to us so that all we do now is think beautiful thoughts and somehow or another try to "uplift the heart towards the Highest, and reap open-hearted responsiveness to things Eternal."

In the name of God, is it not about time we asked, "What is the meaning of such verbiage?" We are fooling ourselves if we are just thinking beautiful thoughts, treating ourselves to a bit of Couéism.[2] That will never save anybody and never has; that will not make the world safe for our children. That has been tried for a very long time, and if anything has been utterly discredited, it is that sort of nonsense. Thank God, that is not the message. Here *is* the message: this God is outside us, and He acts, He comes in, He does things. Read the Old Testament, and you will find that He has been doing this right through the whole story. The children of Israel would have disappeared long since, the whole story would have come to an end, if God had not kept on coming in, taking hold, interfering, dealing with their enemies, dealing with them, putting them into captivity, bringing them out—always God acting.

And here we see a point that we have already emphasized several times in going through this sermon of Stephen in this book series. God not only acts and intervenes in our affairs, but he always does it in his own time—"after forty years"! We, in our cleverness, want to ask questions, do we not? Why did He wait forty years? All I know is that it does us good to be kept waiting forty years—this brings us to our senses. Why did God take so long before He sent His Son into the world? Why did He not send Him immediately after the fall? One reason—and this alone is enough for me—was this: to teach man how small he is. God allowed some 4,000 years or so just to teach men and women that all their wisdom and cleverness and philosophy and science could not do the job. God very often delays in order to bring us down to the level that we really occupy and to make us see ourselves as the foolish worms that we are. "Forty years"! But God knew what He would do when he sent Moses to Midian. He had kept him forty years as the son of Pharaoh's daughter and now had him wait for forty years in Midian. God was timing it. He sees the end from the beginning.

In the same way, astoundingly, at this moment God knows when He is going to end the story of this universe. I do not know when it is, and I have not wasted any of my time, as some of my friends have, in trying to determine that. Do not waste your time trying to fix times and seasons. The Lord Jesus Christ said that even He did not know what the date was, but He said, "The Father knows." He said that even the angels did not know. God the Father has kept this as His own secret, but He knows. There is an appointed end to everything. The world is not out of control; God is still on His throne, and the timing is in His hands.

And, of course, God not only acts in His own time, but in His own way. He has His own method.

God moves in a mysterious way
His wonders to perform.
William Cowper

He suddenly touches you; He interferes, so to speak, in your life. Why are you where you are at this time? You think you know, but you do not. God suddenly appears, touches, interferes, erupts; he does it in 1,001 different ways. Thank God, He is outside us, and He intervenes. He acts among us, and He does things for us that we cannot do for ourselves.

When does God do this? "When forty years were expired, there appeared to him in the wilderness of Mount Sina . . ." Forty years had gone by, forty years of slavery and misery and unhappiness for the poor children of Israel, who in their blindness had rejected Moses as their leader and emancipator. There they were, powerless, helpless in the hands of a cruel foe, a terrible taskmaster.

That is a picture of every one of us in the grip of sin and evil and the devil. We are slaves, every one of us, by nature. There is not a person who was not born a slave. We are not only slaves to evils such as drunkenness and adultery and fornication, but also slaves to passion, slaves to jealousy and envy and malice and bitterness and spite and hatred. Each one of us was born a slave, and we know it. "We're going to do better," we say. "We're going to give up certain things." But we *cannot* give them up; sin is slavery. We are all helpless slaves, and we cannot do anything to free ourselves. We have tried. We have turned to civilization for deliverance, but it cannot deliver us; nor can education, nor can moral exhortation—all this nonsense about "sowing beautiful thoughts." These have all been tried, and they are absolute failures, a complete waste of time and energy.

We cannot do anything. If we could think those beautiful thoughts and save ourselves, we would do it. If only the drug addict could stop, he would. Many have reached the stage where they are miserably unhappy. I have known many a slave to drink who has said to me, "I wish I had never started." He would give anything to stop, but he cannot. Think of your own sins: you are a slave to them. "Whosoever committeth sin," says Jesus Christ, "is the servant [slave] of sin" (John 8:34).

But remember the Gospel! God comes to us just when we are in utter slavery and are powerless to do anything to redeem ourselves. Salvation is altogether and entirely of God. The Gospel is not an exhortation to people to save themselves; that would be mockery. It knows we cannot save ourselves. It is the record, the proclamation, the account, of God acting and arising and coming and setting in motion a way, the *only* way, of salvation.

And I emphasize again the way God intervenes and the time when He does it and the method of it all. Where did this happen? Well, this happened to Moses "in the wilderness." Every word in the Bible is important. Do you realize what all this means? Look at this man Moses, with all his shining ability and qualities, reduced to the position of an ordinary shepherd for forty years. How often did thoughts come to him of what he once had been, what he might have been, and then thoughts of his people and their suffering and their agony and their shame and their slavery? But what could he do? What could a shepherd do? Nothing! His life was wasted, he was obviously going to die in this position, and there were his people in utter helplessness. This had gone on for forty long years, and he must have arrived at the point when he was virtually giving in, when he had almost ceased to hope. At first he had thought that it would not be long, that soon he would be able to get back. But after forty years it was completely hopeless.

Oh, my dear friend, listen! This is an essential part of the Gospel. Have you begun to feel hopeless about yourself? Are you feeling hopeless about someone who is dear to you, for whom you have been praying for years, but instead of getting better they seem to be getting worse? Are you near the point of despair? Do you say, "I've tried, but I cannot get free. I'm hopeless; throw me away. Perhaps I'll do away with myself"? I have a message for you! Your condition is not hopeless! And it is not hopeless for one reason only, and that is God—the God who is outside of us, the God who acts, the God of all power, the God who intervenes—and He comes to us.

Notice the correspondence between what we read here and what we read in the first verses of the third chapter of the Gospel According to St. Luke: "Now in the fifteenth year of the reign of Tiberius Caesar," and then comes the list of those men who were "tetrarchs"—of Abilene and Ituraea and all the rest. "What is it all about?" you say. Let me tell you.

For many years there had been no prophet in Israel. The last prophet had been the prophet Malachi, and he had prophesied and taught 400 long years before the birth of John the Baptist. There had not been a word from God, there had been a dead silence, and the children of Israel seemed to have been abandoned. Had God been defeated? Was it the end? No! "In the fifteenth year of the reign of Tiberius Caesar" this man was doing this and that man was doing that—kings, princes, potentates, important people, the things that the newspapers are excited about. But that is not important. Here is the important thing: "The word of God came unto John the son of Zacharias."

Where? In London? In the academies and the porches of Greece? Not at all: "in the wilderness"!

This is always the story. God's word comes suddenly, in a most unexpected manner to the most unexpected person. I will sum it all up by putting it like this—it always comes in spite of us. We have nothing to do with it. We are hopeless, at the point of despair. It is God who sends an angel, raises up a man, causes a child to be born. God! It is always God acting. God delivering! The Gospel tells of His plan of deliverance; it tells of the power that enables Him to deliver—the angel, the burning bush!

The apostle Paul expresses all this in these great words in the Epistle to the Romans: "I am not ashamed of the gospel of Christ." Why not? This is his answer, and it is a complete contradiction of Dr. Fosdick and company: "for it is the power of God unto salvation to every one that believeth" (Rom. 1:16). It is what *God* has done. "I am declaring," says Paul, "to the Jew first, and also to the Greek"—what? There is a righteousness from God by faith. "The just shall live by faith" (v. 17). God has done something. God has intervened. God has acted. As Zechariah, the father of John the Baptist, put it, "[God] hath visited and redeemed his people" (Luke 1:68). This is the message: the God who sends an angel into the bush after forty years of utter hopelessness has gone on intervening, and "when the fulness of the time was come, God sent forth his Son, made of a woman, made under the law, to redeem them that were under the law" (Gal. 4:4-5). This is the whole message. It is God sending His own Son into the world, "in the likeness of sinful flesh, and for sin" (Rom. 8:3).

Again, God does it all in spite of us—in spite of our folly, in spite of our shame, in spite of our unbelief. If it depended upon us, we would all be lost and undone, and there would be no hope for anybody. But in this message there is hope for all.

Jesus sought me when a stranger
Wandering from the fold of God.
R. Robinson

He came after me! The Hound of Heaven, who chased me "down the nights and down the days" and "down the labyrinthine ways of my own mind," will not let me go. This is the message. He comes back when I have given up hope, when I am defeated by sin and filled with shame, when I am feeling it is useless to struggle anymore, and when everybody else equally feels it is useless—but God still does not give up on me, even after forty years!

When forty years had passed, God began to move, and there was hope for the wretched children of Israel in the hopeless bondage and serfdom of Egypt.

This is a picture of the Gospel. We see it finally and perfectly in the Lord Jesus Christ. This is the Son of God! "God so loved the world, that he gave his only begotten Son, that whosoever believeth in him should not perish, but have everlasting life" (John 3:16). This is the message—thank God for it. God is the God of the impossible, and the fact that He is interested, that He is concerned, and that He intervenes is our only hope.

But this is not only the only hope—this is a hope for all, for anybody. You may have spent a lifetime in sin and rebellion against God; you may have sunk so low that you have lost your willpower; you have perhaps been taken captive by drink, drugs, or something else. I say to you, there is as much hope for you as for the best man in the world today. Our Lord said it Himself: "They that be whole need not a physician, but they that are sick . . . for I am not come to call the righteous, but sinners to repentance" (Matt. 9:12-13).

What is the use of going to a poor man who has lost his integrity and everything else and asking him to "sow beautiful thoughts"? The idea is ludicrous! Nobody can do it; even moral, respectable people, religious people, cannot do it. They are full of bitterness and backbiting. And if they cannot do it, fancy saying that to a man in the gutters of life! It is mockery! It is nonsense!

It takes the power of God to save a man or woman, and the message is that the Gospel of Jesus Christ is "the power of God unto salvation to every one that believeth" (Rom. 1:16). It does not matter what your past has been; that does not matter at all.

> *However long from mercy we may have turned away,*
> *Thy blood, O Christ, can cleanse us,*
> *And make us white today.*
>
> Oswald Allen

I have already made a reference to the poem "The Hound of Heaven" without mentioning the author, Francis Thompson. The Hound of Heaven is the God who will not let us go, the God who chases us "down the nights and down the days," the God who comes from without and intervenes and interferes.

Poor Francis Thompson. Do you know his story? He had sunk so low in the grip of sin and evil that he had become a tramp. To get a few pence to have a little more drink and a little food, he was reduced to selling matches outside Charing Cross station. But he had a very wonderful experience. God came to him, interfered in his life, and his whole position was changed. So later on he could write words like these—thank God, they are true because God is outside us, and Christ is outside us, but interested in us and able to help us.

But (when so sad thou canst not sadder)
Cry,—and upon thy so sore loss
Shall shine the traffic of Jacob's ladder
Pitched betwixt Heaven and Charing Cross.

Yea, in the night, my Soul, my daughter,
Cry,—clinging to Heaven by the hems;
And lo, Christ walking on the water
Not of Genesareth, but Thames!

Francis Thompson,
"The Kingdom of God"

Standing in your rags, in your shame, in your penury, in your utter failure, He will come to you. He has already come from heaven to earth to death to a tomb to Hades for you. He will come to you just where you are. He does not say, "Think beautiful thoughts, and then perhaps you will have some feelings for Me or some consciousness of some responsiveness to the Eternal." No! He will come; He will take hold of you; He will lift you up; He will give you a new nature, a new mind, a new heart, a new outlook, new strength. He will make you more than conqueror (Rom. 8:37). Cry unto Him, "And upon thy so sore loss shall shine the traffic of Jacob's ladder." Even while Jacob was asleep, God spoke to him and came to him.

Just where you are in your failure, in your shame, in your hopelessness, cry out to Him. He is there, and He will hear. He has said, "Him that cometh to me I will in no wise cast out" (John 6:37).

2

THE MIRACLE OF SALVATION

> *And when forty years were expired, there appeared to him in the wilderness of mount Sina an angel of the Lord in a flame of fire in a bush. When Moses saw it, he wondered at the sight: and as he drew near to behold it, the voice of the Lord came unto him, saying, I am the God of thy fathers, the God of Abraham, and the God of Isaac, and the God of Jacob. Then Moses trembled, and durst not behold. Then said the Lord to him, Put off thy shoes from thy feet: for the place where thou standest is holy ground.*
>
> —Acts 7:30-33

We continue with these verses from Stephen's account of the story of Moses. We saw in the last study that salvation is possible because God is outside us. He is God, the living God, and He is personal. He is not mere sentiment, not a mere general feeling of love and goodness. No; God *is*. He says, "I AM THAT I AM" (Exod. 3:14). And He acts, He intervenes, He suddenly appears, as we see here, and, thank God, He appears to us when we least expect it—"in the wilderness." After forty years of frustration and disappointment and hopelessness and near despair for Moses, God came into the wilderness of Sinai, and He spoke his great and His glorious word.

That is what we have seen so far, but we must go on because that is only the beginning. The second important question that is to engage us is: What is our response, what is our reaction to this? We are dealing here in a very practical way with the reason why most people are not Christians and why so much that passes as Christianity is nothing but a denial of it. The reason why the masses are outside is that they are confused because of the confusion among those who call themselves Christians while denying the Christian faith at its most glorious points. Why do so-called Christians do this?

The answer is that their whole approach is wrong. It follows, of necessity, that if your approach to any subject is wrong, you will never be able to understand it and can never be helped by it. If your initial approach is wrong, there is no hope whatsoever. If you come with prejudice, then you cannot understand. Prejudiced people are not open to enlightenment. They put themselves in a position where nothing can happen to them. That is why the members of the Sanhedrin were putting Stephen on trial, and that is why these same people crucified the Son of God. They could not see the truth because their whole attitude, their whole approach, was wrong. This is a very important point, and it is the essence of the modern difficulty and the modern tragedy with regard to this whole matter of the Christian faith and its great salvation.

Are we aware of this tragedy? We see the world as it is in its trouble and in its agony, but what makes this a tragedy is that here is a message that offers to deliver us. It is a message of salvation, deliverance, emancipation, hope, and liberty. This is what the world in its blindness is rejecting, and it does so because its whole approach to it is so grievously and entirely wrong.

What do I mean by this? Again, in a very interesting way, these things are constantly repeated and put before us, and so once more I am able to put it to you in one of the typical modern expressions of this whole fallacy. A book has been published, and this is its title: *The God I Want.* One of the writers, an ordained member of a certain church, a teacher of theology at the University of Cambridge, puts it like this: "The God I want is a God who is not mixed up with infantile phantasy of omnipotence." Did you get that? To this man, the idea of an omnipotent God is "infantile," just the sort of thing that a child thinks of. "No," he says, "the God I want is a God who is not mixed up with that." And this is a perfect statement of the modern attitude that I was trying to describe to you when I quoted from the *Reader's Digest* interview with Dr. Fosdick earlier. Indeed, these views are all part of the same movement.

Let me put it succinctly like this: There is no need for anybody to read that book—the title tells you all about it. *The God I Want*—do you see where the emphasis lies? It is on *I. I* am the important one. I say, "I am not ready to take just any sort of God. I want a certain type of God." So you get these blasphemous statements as to what people want or do not want.

Let us therefore look at this great statement that we have here in Acts 7 in the light of this modern approach to the whole question of God and religion and the Christian faith and its message of salvation. As I am going to show you, it is because men and women approach Christianity in that way, instead of the way that is taught here in the Bible, that they reject it. The true way that we are shown here is the exact opposite of that other view.

> *And when forty years were expired, there appeared to him in the wilderness of mount Sina an angel of the Lord in a flame of fire in a bush. When Moses saw it, he wondered at the sight: and as he drew near to behold it, the voice of the Lord came unto him, saying, I am the God of thy fathers, the God of Abraham, and the God of Isaac, and the God of Jacob. Then Moses trembled, and durst not behold. Then said the Lord to him, Put off thy shoes from thy feet: for the place where thou standest is holy ground.*

This is Stephen's recapitulation or reminder to the Sanhedrin of the account that is given in the third chapter of Exodus, where you find these additional details:

> *Now Moses kept the flock of Jethro his father in law, the priest of Midian: and he led the flock to the backside of the desert, and came to the mountain of God, even to Horeb. And the angel of the* LORD *appeared unto him in a flame of fire out of the midst of a bush: and he looked, and, behold, the bush burned with fire, and the bush was not consumed. And Moses said, I will now turn aside, and see this great sight, why the bush is not burnt. And when the* LORD *saw that he turned aside to see, God called unto him out of the midst of the bush, and said, Moses, Moses. And he said, Here am I. And he said, Draw not nigh hither: put off thy shoes from off thy feet, for the place whereon thou standest is holy ground. Moreover he said, I am the God of thy father, the God of Abraham, the God of Isaac, and the God of Jacob. And Moses hid his face; for he was afraid to look upon God.*
>
> —*Exod. 3:1-6*

There is the account in greater detail, but Stephen, as you see, gives us the essence of the story. So what is the lesson, what does this story tell us? Here is the Christian, the biblical, message. What are its characteristics? The first thing that is true of it is that it is a matter of revelation: "And when forty years were expired, there appeared unto him . . ." This is not of man at all. Moses had been reduced to the position of a shepherd. He was not in the wilderness trying to work out a philosophy of life and searching for God. He was just doing his job, feeling pretty hopeless. But suddenly there appeared . . . !

Now this is entirely of God—it is all *given*. It is not the result of human thought or human ability; nor is it the result of human investigation and inquiry. We are all so taken up with the idea of the quest and the search and the research, and we are so accustomed to reading about discoveries and inventions as the result of discoveries that we tend to think that everything comes to us as the result of our own effort and striving and that all we have is the result of our searching. This notion has become second nature to us, and that is why, when we hear this biblical message, we instinctively react against it. We tend to reject it because it is the absolute antithesis of everything we have ever known. The gospel message is something that comes to us as a great surprise.

I want to emphasize this. There is no mixture of divine provision and human wisdom and reason and understanding here, none at all. It is all of God. Moses made no contribution to this crucial event in his life. This did not happen to him as the result of a long period of preparation. Not at all! It all came to him, and he was taken completely by surprise.

Just when we are safest, there's a sunset-touch,
A fancy from a flower-bell, someone's death,
A chorus ending from Euripides,
And that's enough for fifty hopes and fears.

That's how Browning puts it in "Bishop Blougram's Apology." Similarly, "just when we are safest," when we least expect it, God comes, and we have made no contribution whatsoever.

This Gospel, I repeat, is altogether from the outside; it is altogether from God. Many have misunderstood it in that respect. They say that people go so far, but then they come to a dead end and God supplements their investigations. But that is not what we are told in the Bible; here we are told that human thinking is all wrong. That is why the Lord Jesus Christ said to that learned teacher Nicodemus, "Ye must be born again" (John 3:7). Christianity is not a supplement to human philosophy; it is altogether different. It does not base anything upon human philosophy, human thinking, human endeavor, human anything—nothing at all.

This is vital. I know that I am saying something that is particularly obnoxious and objectionable to the modern man and woman. I am sorry, I cannot help that. I was born a natural man myself, and I know the reaction. But I do not want to please men—I want to proclaim the Word of God because I know that is the only thing that can do men and women any good. I can please people. I think I might have been a politician if I had wanted to! But I want to proclaim this Gospel, to expound the Word of God, and no consideration of pleasing comes in. It is what is good for the souls of men and women that matters—nothing else. I therefore must emphasize that the Word of God is revelation, which means not only that it comes altogether from God but also that it is a complete system—a system that must be taken as it is and in its entirety.

God did not call Moses into consultation and say, "Now, Moses, what do you think about this problem of rescuing your fellow countrymen who are in the bondage of Egypt? What are your ideas?" And Moses did not say, "Well, I've been thinking a lot about this, and here is my idea, but I would like a little help, if you do not mind." That is the exact opposite of what took place! And that is still the simple truth about the Gospel. In the Bible we find a complete scheme of salvation, and it is all from God. It is God's plan, God's purpose, and He has worked it out in detail.

Salvation is, as I shall show you, something that God has worked out from beginning to end. It is presented to us as a whole, and we must receive it as a whole. It is one great, complete message to which we make no contribution whatsoever. There it is—Moses doing his work, taking these sheep around the backside of the mountain and looking at them and wondering how they are going to get on there because it is a wilderness. Suddenly he is confronted by this, and the whole course of his history, and of human history, is changed because of what God did and what God said.

We find, second, that the outstanding character of this action of God is that it is supernatural. "What?" says somebody. "In these modern times are you talking about the supernatural?" The condition of humanity is such that nothing less than the supernatural will make the slightest difference.

But let me be yet more bold and show you what you are asked to believe as you listen to this Gospel. If you want to become a new man or a new woman, this is it. This is the supernatural message. "There appeared . . . an angel." Is it possible for the modern, sophisticated, scientific person to believe in angels? This is something that is laughed at, one of the fantasies that learned people talk about. Children, of course, believe in angels, primitive man believes in angels, but not the man of today.

But wait a minute, why not? Why should you not believe in angels? The Bible is full of angels—angels appearing, angels bringing messages. The author of the Epistle to the Hebrews says that angels are the ministering spirits of God (1:14) and that He uses them to speak to people, to bring messages, even as He did in the case of Moses. This is a frankly supernatural message, and it tells us of the everlasting and eternal God existing in three Persons—Father, Son, and Holy Spirit. It tells us that no one has seen God at any time, and yet God *is* and has made everything, and the universe would collapse without Him. God is spirit (John 4:24). "No man hath seen God at any time" (John 1:18). There it is—the supernatural.

We see here not only the three Persons in the blessed holy Trinity, but myriads of angels and archangels also. Seraphim! Cherubim! The unseen realm is peopled by these majestic beings. An essential part of the biblical message is that we are surrounded by an unseen spiritual world and that occasionally these others visit this world in visible form and do their work. You cannot begin to understand the message of the Bible unless you believe this.

And on top of that is this whole element of miracle. Miracle! Again, the modern sophisticated person says, "You surely don't believe in miracles; not now, in this scientific age?" Yes, I do! A bush was on fire and yet was not consumed. It was flaming, and yet it went on flaming. It did not suddenly disappear; the flame did not go out. It was a miracle. And then a voice spoke out of the bush and addressed Moses.

The miraculous is an essential part of this message, and it is essential in the sense that if this aspect of it is not true, we have no Gospel at all, and there is no hope for anybody. The Gospel is frankly miraculous and supernatural. It is a message of God's mighty acts, and they are supernatural acts. Indeed, as the people put it on the Day of Pentecost: "We do hear them [the apostles] speak in our tongues *the wonderful works of God*" (Acts 2:11)—and they are wonderful, they are amazing. We are told in Acts 7, "When Moses saw it, he wondered at the sight." This is the characteristic of all the works of God as they are recorded in the Bible. This is the first fact you must start with. You may say, "The God I want." But this is the God you need, and the only God who can save you.

What are we told about Him? Well, this is the whole message of the Bible. Take the Old Testament: "In the beginning God created . . ." That is miracle. "God said, Let there be light: and there was light" (Gen. 1:1-3). There was nothing there—God produced it. That is miracle; that is supernatural action.

On it goes: the Flood and the destruction of Sodom and Gomorrah and more. All these are miracles. Jacob, running away from his brother, laid down to sleep at a place called Bethel. He had a vision, and God appeared. He woke up, and he was afraid and said, "Surely the LORD is in this place; and I knew it not. . . . How dreadful is this place! this is none other but the house of God, and this is the gate of heaven" (Gen. 28:16-17). God appearing! Always supernatural.

It was the same when Jacob went back years later to meet his brother Esau. An event took place at Peniel when a person came and struggled with Jacob and lamed him; but, oh, it was the biggest thing that ever happened to him! Another appeared to him and dealt with him and made a new man of him—and Jacob became Israel. Who did this? God!

Then here it is in the case of Moses, and as you go on with this story of Moses and read about how he brought the children of Israel out of the captivity of Egypt, what are you confronted by? You are confronted by a whole series of miracles; ten happened before they even left Egypt. Then they came out of Egypt in a marvelous manner. As they went on their way, suddenly there was a dead stop: the Red Sea, a mountain here, a mountain there, and the hosts of Pharaoh behind—an impossibility. But the sea divided!

Now this is history—salvation history. These are God's acts of history. If this is not true, I say again, I have no message for you. This is the God of salvation! The Red Sea divided! It was a miracle. Then there was the giving of the law and the mountain quaking, on fire. Then the crossing of Jordan in a miraculous manner, the destruction of Jericho in a miraculous manner, the miracles of Elijah and Elisha, the miracles at all the crucial moments in the history of these people. Miraculous interventions, supernatural interferences. You cannot understand the history of the Jews except in those terms. This is the essence of the story.

And when you come to the New Testament, the supernatural is even more plain and obvious. If you read the introductions to the Gospels of Matthew and Luke, do you know what you will find? You will find angels. A man called Zechariah goes to the temple to do his turn of duty one day, as he has been doing for so many years; he is an old man now, on the point of retirement. Suddenly an angel appears to him. That is how the Gospel is introduced into the Gospel of Luke: an angel appears and speaks to this man. He is struck dumb, and then he is given his speech back. If you take angels out of the Bible, what do you have left? You do not have the Gospel; you have no real message. And then in the case of Mary, the mother of our Lord, suddenly an archangel appears to her and speaks to her, saying, "Blessed art thou among women" (Luke 1:28), and he gives her the message. An archangel! This is the very essence of this gospel message. It is altogether supernatural and miraculous.

It is the same with the virgin birth of Christ. You must be clear about these things. Jesus of Nazareth had no human father. Mary herself stumbled at this. When the archangel said to her, "Thou shalt conceive in thy womb, and bring forth a son," Mary said, "How shall this be, seeing I know not a man?" The thing was impossible.

And the archangel replied, "The Holy Ghost shall come upon thee, and the power of the Highest shall overshadow thee: therefore also that holy thing which shall be born of thee shall be called the Son of God. . . . For with God nothing shall be impossible" (Luke 1:31-37). The very birth of our Lord was a miracle. He was not just a man, thrown out suddenly and unexpectedly by a race of people. No; He was the eternal Son coming into the world out of the eternal glory and being born as a babe in a miraculous manner. This is the essence of the New Testament message. They all preached this. ". . . made of a woman, made under the law" (Gal. 4:4); ". . . made of the seed of David according to the flesh; and declared to be the Son of God with power, according to the spirit of holiness, by the resurrection from the dead" (Rom. 1:3-4).

And then we read on, and what do we find? We find that He worked miracles. He was only a carpenter, He had not been trained in the schools of the Pharisees, He would not have been a member of the Sanhedrin—He did not have the qualifications. And yet there He was, dominating the whole scene, gathering the people after Him. What was His secret? Well, He did speak amazing words. Everyone was astounded at the gracious words that came from His lips. But it was the miracles that really shook the people. Nicodemus said to Him, "We know that thou art a teacher come from God: for no man can do these miracles that thou doest, except God be with him" (John 3:2). What was it, do you think, that made people listen to this carpenter, this unknown person, about whom they said, "How knoweth this man letters, having never learned?" (John 7:15). What was it? Oh, it was the miracles! And on one occasion He remonstrated with the Jews and said, "For the works which the Father hath given me to finish, the same works that I do, bear witness of me, that the Father hath sent me" (John 5:36). Look at the facts—the miracles. Take the miracles out of the life of Christ, and what is left? John says they are "signs": "This sign did Jesus." These are the attestations of His person.

And then there is the greatest miracle of all: the resurrection of Christ. Our Lord was the first to rise from the dead: He burst asunder the bands of death, "the firstborn from the dead" (Col. 1:18). This was the great miracle, the conquest of death. It is a part of the preaching of the Gospel. There would have been no Christian church but for this. Stephen would not have been on trial were it not for the fact that he was asserting this great event. And on top of it all, there is that great fact of the coming of the Holy Spirit on the Day of Pentecost. And once these men were filled with this power, they began to work miracles.

Read these early chapters of the Acts of the Apostles. The apostles had already been thrown into prison more than once before Stephen was ever arrested. Why were they in trouble? It was because as Peter and John went up into the temple one afternoon at the hour of prayer, they were confronted by a poor fellow sitting on the pavement outside the Beautiful Gate of the temple. He had never walked in his life. He was over forty years of age, and nobody could do anything for him. He expected to receive a gift, to receive alms from Peter and John, as he had from so many others. But Luke writes: "And Peter, fastening his eyes upon him with John, said, Look on us." And he looked. "Then Peter said, Silver and gold have I none; but such as I have give I thee: In the name of Jesus Christ of Nazareth rise up and walk" (Acts 3:4, 6). And he rose up, and immediately he was "walking, and leaping, and praising God" in the temple (v. 8). There would have been no church but for this power. There would have been no Christianity. This is the essence of the message—"there appeared . . . an angel"; "the bush burned with fire, and the bush was not consumed." Miracles! The supernatural!

This is equally true of the way of salvation that is offered to us. What does Christianity offer? Is it an exhortation to live a better life? Is it the business of preaching to tell you, "Stop drinking. Stop committing adultery. Don't do this and that. Try to pull yourself together. Read good books. Get a little moral uplift. Gradually make yourself a better person"? A thousand times no! That is not the message; we cannot do it.

What is it, then? Our Lord put it so plainly to Nicodemus: "Ye must be born again." This is the message, and it is about a miracle. We cannot be improved. We need the miracle of a rebirth, a regeneration, a new nature, a new creation. The God who created all at the beginning wants to create us anew, to make new people of us. This is the only hope. The Gospel is not the proclamation of a moral reformation, but of regeneration and life in the Spirit. It offers us a new start, a new beginning; it offers us a new power, which is "the power of God unto salvation" (Rom. 1:16). It offers us power to live the remainder of our lives in this world, and at the end it promises us victory over death, a glorious resurrection, and an eternity in the presence of God. It is not an educational scheme or a moral, ethical scheme; it is not a political scheme; it is nothing but the re-creating work of Almighty God. It is a miracle. It is supernatural. It is divine action from beginning to end. This is the message of the Christian Gospel of salvation.

So the next vital question is: What is our attitude and reaction to this message? The Sanhedrin rejected the Son of God and His preaching; now we see them rejecting His deacons, of whom Stephen was one. This also is where the world goes so wrong today, and, alas, as I say, where the church, to her eternal shame, goes so wrong too. If theologians and church teachers think that by diluting this Gospel they are going to appeal to men and women who are outside, if they think that by taking out the miraculous and the supernatural, by taking out the divine, they are going to win people, they are seriously mistaken, because by denying the essence of the Gospel they are actually driving people from the churches.

So what is this wrong reaction? Unfortunately, Moses himself went wrong at first. Moses was not divine—he was human like us, and when he saw this phenomenon of the burning bush, he said, "I will now turn aside, and see this great sight, why the bush is not burnt" (Exod. 3:3). Typical of modern scientific man, you see! A phenomenon! Ah, this calls for an investigation. What is this? So I bring all my ability to it. Moses was moved by curiosity; so he had a desire to understand, he wanted an explanation. He was exactly like Nicodemus. When our Lord said to him, "Ye must be born again" (John 3:7), Nicodemus said, "How can a man be born when he is old?" He was trying to understand. He was using his own critical apparatus. "How can these things be?"

Nicodemus came with typical human confidence, as Moses did when confronted by the burning bush, filled with a confidence in human ability and human understanding, the human attitude that says, "The God I want." You investigate God. You begin to examine Him. You say, "I don't want this, and I don't want the other. I don't want that infantile fantasy. This is the God I want, and I'm not accepting any God unless he conforms to my dictates and demands." That is typical of the modern attitude. Man is the final judge and arbiter in all matters. Man has the capacity to pronounce judgment, even on God!

Oh, my dear friend, learn the lesson that Moses had to learn. He was shown how completely wrong he was. Here he was, about to advance and to investigate, when suddenly a voice came to him out of the bush and said, "Moses! Moses! Stand back!" What was he being told? He was being told that his whole attitude was wrong. He should have seen this. "He wondered at the sight" (Acts 7:31). You could translate that, "He marveled at the sight." Should not that in itself cause us to be humble? Whenever we see anything extraordinary, we do not rush forward in self-confidence—we stand back in astonishment. That was what Moses should have done. Confronted by something so unusual, he should have held back.

And when we go on to consider further reasons why this should be our attitude, we see it still more plainly. What are we concerned about here? We are concerned about the nature of the everlasting and eternal God. God *is*. Can you conceive of God? "No man hath seen God at any time" (John 1:18). Can you measure God? Can you think of absolute qualities? Can you think of omniscience, omnipotence, omnipresence? Of course not. Our minds boggle. "Great is the mystery of godliness" (1 Tim. 3:16). And yet modern men and women in their folly seek to investigate God! They try to put their little tape measures on Him! Here they are, confronted by the infinite, the absolute, the eternal God, and they want to understand. What fools they are! The very word *God* should show them the utter impossibility. If I could measure and understand God, He would not be God—He would be smaller than my mind. There is the first major reason.

But then consider the second, which is man himself, the utter inadequacy of man. Man is very finite, very small. "Ah, but," you say, "look at all we have learned and discovered!" But think of what you do *not* know, especially in the matter of your knowledge of yourself and how to live. What is the use of boasting about sending people into outer space and talking about millions and millions and millions of miles and of innumerable years if it does not make you see your own finite condition and your smallness and your insignificance? How contradictory we are in our proud boastings.

But we are not only finite, we are sinful. There is something about us that vitiates all our best efforts. We are biased; our minds are not open. There is no such thing as free thought. All our thinking is blinded by prejudices and preconceived notions. We are sinful, even perverted. We are liars; we twist and turn; we will do anything to wriggle out of things. As the Common Prayer Book says, "There is no health in us." And yet, in spite of that, we, like Moses, go on to investigate, and it is because we are foolish enough to do this that we continually go away rejected and rejecting, and we go on in our misery and failure and shame. That is the wrong way of reacting to God's supernatural intervention.

What is the true way? Thank God, we are told this here quite clearly. But notice this: we are in such a terrible condition as human beings that we even need to be taught how to approach this matter, how to listen to it. Since we do not even know that, how much less can we understand the miraculous and the supernatural and the divine. We are so completely hopeless that we need to be instructed as to how we should conduct ourselves and behave ourselves even as we listen. We come confident in our knowledge. We are scientific inquirers, believing ourselves able to measure all things. We are ready for the great inspection and the great analysis. "The God *I* want!" And as we begin our investigation, He shouts at us, calls us, commands us: "Stop!" He says, "Man, do you realize what you are doing?" "Moses, Moses" (Exod. 3:4). Moses was commanded to stand still. That is the great imperative of the New Testament as well. On two different occasions a voice came from heaven attesting the claims of Jesus of Nazareth, and the voice from heaven said, "This is my beloved Son: hear Him." Listen to it! God commands every one of us now in the same way.

What does God say to us? He says, "Your whole attitude is completely wrong. Stop! Stand back! Who are you to advance and to examine and to investigate and analyze? Stand back! You must be born again." Moses recognized the voice of authority, the voice of God, and he listened.

There are two kinds of wondering about spiritual truth—a wondering that is wrong and a wondering that is right. The wondering that leads to curiosity and investigation is wrong. It is of that of which our Lord says, "Marvel not at this" (John 5:28). But there is a true wondering, the wondering that Moses now began to feel. He heard the voice, and then "Moses trembled, and durst not behold" (Acts 7:32). He put his hands over his face; he dared not look at God. Here is the true response. You realize that you are in the presence of the everlasting and eternal God. "Moses trembled"! He was filled with a feeling of fear and awe and reverence. He was humbled. "Put off thy shoes from thy feet: for the place where thou standest is holy ground" (v. 33). Our pride must be broken; our spirit must be broken; we must approach God "with reverence and godly fear" (Heb. 12:28). Why? Because God is who and what He is. He is the God of glory. He is the God of holiness. He is the God of power.

My friend, do you not realize that you are in the hand of God? The God whom you are proposing to investigate is the God who has not only given you life and being—He is the God who can destroy you in a second if He chooses to do so. Your breath is in His hands. You can do nothing about it. You can no more control God than you can control the lightning and the thunder and the raging of the sea. God is over all, and you are nothing. "Put off thy shoes from thy feet." You are going to judge God? You say, "The God I want. I'm not going to believe in a God who is mixed up in any way with that infantile fantasy of omniscience." Are you not? Whether or not you say that, your times are in His hands, and we must all die and stand before Him.

Before you go further with your examination and your investigation and your postulating of what you want in God, realize what you are—that you are nothing, that you are a dying, vanishing worm, and that you will have to stand in the presence of Almighty God.

It is not your opinions that matter finally—it is your whole attitude. It is your self-righteousness, your self-confidence, your self-assurance in the presence of God that condemns you. "Stand back! Put your shoes from off your feet: for the ground on which you stand is holy."

Then imitate and emulate the example of Moses: he was ready to listen. He was now afraid to look; he felt the presence of God. This is what makes a man or woman a Christian. No one has ever become a Christian without going through this in some shape or form. It is not always as dramatic as in the case of Moses, but no one can be a Christian who does not know what it is to tremble in the presence of Almighty God, to see his or her own smallness and insignificance, his or her vileness and utter hopelessness.

So here was Moses—what could he do? He was ready to listen. He knew he could do nothing; here was a message, and he was ready to listen to it. Whether or not he understood it was no longer the question; what mattered was that he was face to face with God. And the moment you become conscious of the presence of God, you do what Moses did—you put your hands over your face. You dare not look—not because God is cruel, but because he is kind, because he is pure, because he is holy, and you feel vile.

Do you remember what we are told about Job? Poor old Job! A good and a godly and a righteous man, but he was afflicted and he was tried. He grumbled and complained, and he criticized God, and he said many things that he should not have said—though he was a much better man than those miserable friends of his. And then God suddenly appeared to him, and poor Job said, "I will lay mine hand upon my mouth" (Job 40:4). He said he had spoken unadvisedly with his lips. "I have heard of thee by the hearing of the ear: but now mine eye seeth thee" (Job 42:5), and he put his hand upon his mouth.

There is no hope for any of us until we are silenced, until we are utterly ashamed, until we become like the tax-collector depicted by our Lord in His parable of the publican and the Pharisee who both went up into the temple to pray. The proud Pharisee goes to the front and says, "God, I thank thee, that I am not as other men are." He can speak to God as an equal, he is such a good man. But he goes home unblessed; he goes home condemned, as he richly deserves to be.

Who is the man who is blessed? The poor publican who is so aware of his sinfulness and his shame that he beats his breast. He cannot lift up his face; he can only cry out in his agony, "God be merciful to me a sinner" (Luke 18:10-13). He is not investigating; he knows that he has been investigated and that the judgment has been pronounced. He has no excuse, no plea; he knows nothing, and he is silent. That is repentance. It is acknowledgment of your sin, your shame, your utter unworthiness to receive anything from God, and then you just cast yourself on Him as you are and listen to Him. And the moment you do so, He will say what He said to Moses through the angel at the burning bush in the wilderness of Sinai. He will tell you the message of deliverance. He will tell you that He has loved you with an everlasting love, that He so loved you that he sent His only begotten Son into the world to die for you, so you would not perish but have everlasting life.

3

God Has Come Down

And when forty years were expired, there appeared to him in the wilderness of mount Sina an angel of the Lord in a flame of fire in a bush. When Moses saw it, he wondered at the sight: and as he drew near to behold it, the voice of the Lord came unto him, saying, I am the God of thy fathers, the God of Abraham, and the God of Isaac, and the God of Jacob. Then Moses trembled, and durst not behold. Then said the Lord to him, Put off thy shoes from thy feet: for the place where thou standest is holy ground. I have seen, I have seen the affliction of my people which is in Egypt, and I have heard their groaning, and am come down to deliver them. And now come, I will send thee into Egypt. This Moses whom they refused, saying, Who made thee a ruler and a judge? the same did God send to be a ruler and a deliverer by the hand of the angel which appeared to him in the bush.

—Acts 7:30-35

We have seen that Stephen uses the story of Moses in his address to the Sanhedrin. I am trying to do the same thing because the world is still as it was in the time of Stephen in the first century; the world is still rejecting the Savior of the world. As Christians we observe Palm Sunday, which begins what people call Holy Week, ending with Good Friday. What do these days stand for? What do they mean to the average person? Do they mean anything at all apart from a public holiday, an opportunity for more pleasure, more enjoyment? What do those terms represent, and what is their significance? To most, these days mean nothing.

Yet these days have been commemorated throughout the centuries. They go right back to the New Testament, and they remind us of things that happened before that. They are not something conjured up by men in their imagination; they are records, reminders of historic events. They are solid, belonging to history. Whether we like it or not, that is simply the fact.

Palm Sunday reminds us of the day when Jesus of Nazareth rode into Jerusalem on the back of a donkey. It reminds us how the people cut down branches from palm trees and put them on the road and threw down their clothes, and acclaimed him, saying, "Hosanna to the Son of David." But we remember that the same people, at the instigation of the chief priests and Pharisees and scribes and others, were equally ready in a few days to shout out, "Away with Him. Crucify Him."

We are dealing with historical happenings and their significance. But I repeat, the central tragedy of the human race is that these things mean nothing to the vast majority of men and women—nothing at all. The whole trouble with humanity is that people are unaware of the most important issues of all. They give great time and attention to other things, but the biggest things, the most glorious things of all, they are unaware of. They are not interested in them; they do not understand them and do not see their significance.

This has always been true. Read again the accounts that are given at the beginning of the Gospels of the birth of Jesus. They typify this fact and sum it up perfectly. We are told that Joseph and his betrothed wife Mary arrived at Bethlehem. They had to go there because there was an edict from the imperial government in Rome that all the provinces conquered by Rome should be taxed. So everybody had to register in the particular places to which their families had always belonged. The Romans were great planners—we could not teach them anything in the matter of local government. So everybody was traveling, and Joseph and Mary had to go to this little place called Bethlehem. But when they arrived there, you remember, they were unable to find accommodation—"There was no room for them in the inn" (Luke 2:7)—so they had to sleep in a stable.

Now that is the perfect picture. You can just see the people in the inn, can you not, all talking with great animation about the taxing. They did not like this; they felt it was unfair. They had a political grievance, and this was the topic of conversation, the great excitement. Nobody said anything about what was happening in the stable. It was the most momentous, the most stupendous event that the universe had ever known or ever could know, yet nobody knew about it. They heard there was a poor woman about to give birth to a child, but why should they give up their rooms? They had a perfect right to hold on to their accommodations. She must look after herself. So they were unaware of what was happening, and they were not talking about it.

And the world is still not talking about these things. Everybody is talking and reading and expressing opinions. But these other great events are not understood; they are not spoken of, and their significance is not realized.

Why is it that these events that matter above everything else are forgotten, ignored, and not understood? Here we come to the very essence of the problem of humanity, and the problem of your world and mine. Why are students so restless? Why are young people taking drugs? Why are we building up horrible armaments? Why is there constantly some kind of crisis in the international realm? Why all the pain and the agony and the suffering that is in the world—what is the matter? Is there no hope? Can nothing be done?

In the Bible we are given the only true answer to all this. The real trouble with humanity is that it is not truly aware of its condition; men and women are not aware of their deepest problem, their deepest need. They are playing away on the surface and tinkering with symptoms and odd manifestations without ever facing the real, hard, central problem. That is the difficulty. And it is because they have never realized the depth of their problem, their desperate condition, that they are not interested in these glorious, amazing, momentous events and facts that have literally taken place in the history of the human race. They have never seen the need of them! These two things go together. It is only when you realize that your case is desperate that you send for the specialist. You are content to go on medicating symptoms until you realize there is something vitally wrong. Then you become alarmed and say, "I must have the best treatment." And it is exactly the same with the human race. Its failure to understand its need and its problem accounts for its unawareness of what God in His infinite grace has done about us and about our salvation.

That is the consideration I want to put before you, and I shall again do so through the medium of this story of Moses. Stephen knew that this was a very good way of putting it to the members of the Sanhedrin, and I cannot think of a better way now because this Christ is still being rejected by heedless men and leaders. The Sanhedrin consisted, let me remind you again, of the greatest men in the nation. Here were the religious and political leaders, all mixed together. These were the men who rejected their Messiah, and people like them are still rejecting Him today. Let us see, then, exactly what they were doing and why they were doing it.

Stephen, in handling the case of Moses, was able to show God's great plan and purpose for the salvation of his people. In this paragraph that we have been considering, we find this extraordinary, climactic turning point, as it were, in the whole story of Moses, the point at which he was commissioned and when God gave him the message explicitly. We have already seen how God had spoken to him when he was regarded as the son of Pharaoh's daughter, in all the pomp and the ceremony of the Egyptian court, being looked upon as a military genius and a wise man, with the world at his feet. God had already spoken to him and had reminded him of his people, and he had been ready to forsake all the glittering prizes in order not only to do the commands of God but to deliver his people.

But Moses had been rejected and had to flee for his life to the land of Midian, and we are told that he had been there for forty years performing the menial task of a shepherd. Then one afternoon—a dull, drab afternoon, when he had not been expecting anything at all—he had taken the sheep in his care to the back of a certain mountain. Oh, the humdrum ordinariness of life! But there he had been confronted by a phenomenon, a burning bush, a bush aflame and yet not being consumed. So he had gone forward to investigate, and then he had been addressed by the voice of an angel out of the bush.

As we have considered this burning bush, we have seen that the essence of the biblical message of deliverance and salvation is that it is God's action, and it is miraculous, it is supernatural, it is divine. And now we come to the point at which we are face to face with the message that was delivered to Moses: "I am the God of thy fathers, the God of Abraham, and the God of Isaac, and the God of Jacob." And what did God say? "I have seen, I have seen the affliction of my people which is in Egypt, and I have heard their groaning, and am come down to deliver them. And now come, I will send thee into Egypt."

Moses prefigured what God has done supremely in the person of Jesus Christ, His only begotten Son. So what do we find here? First of all, God has not forgotten or abandoned this world. If I did not believe that, I would have no message, I would be the pessimist of pessimists. But my message is that God Himself announces that He has not abandoned the world.

And this is how God describes Himself: "I am the God of thy fathers, the God of Abraham, and the God of Isaac, and the God of Jacob." Moses was familiar with the history and knew exactly what God meant. These words meant that God was the God of the covenant, the God of the promise—and this is the whole message of the Bible. Here we are in this world in trouble—what is the explanation of it all? Has it always been like this? Are we just gradually emerging out of some agony and arriving at perfection by some evolutionary process?

No; it is the exact opposite. God made a perfect world; then man by sin and rebellion brought disorder and chaos into it, and unhappiness to boot. And if it had been left at that, we would not be here now; the world would have long since festered into the oblivion of nothingness. But we are here for one reason only: the great God who made this world, and whose it is, is still interested in it, is still concerned about it, and has pledged Himself to redeem the whole cosmos. He has promised this. He promised it first in the Garden of Eden, but then He made the promise particularly clear to Abraham, to his son Isaac, and to his son Jacob; and here God is renewing this promise with this man Moses and reminding him of it.

God has a plan and a purpose for this world, but the world does not know about it. The world listens to the philosophers or to the statesmen. At one time the statesmen were our idols, until we began to see through them as we read their autobiographies. We idolize the philosophers today. Well, the philosophers are writing their autobiographies also, and I think that after we have read them we shall think a little less of them. Who shall we turn to then? Here we are, with no hope. But God has a purpose and a plan for redemption and for the salvation of the universe; that is the message of the Bible. And God was telling Moses, "That is who I am; I have not forgotten." He is the unchanging God. He is the same as He was in the days of Abraham and of Isaac and of Jacob— the everlasting, the eternal God.

Furthermore, God called Himself and revealed Himself to Moses by the name Jehovah. He said that He had not spoken by this name before (see Exod. 6:3). "Jehovah" means, "I am that I am." It also means, "I am what I shall become." In other words, it means, "I am always eternally the same, the everlasting and eternal God." What a comfort it is with a world like this to know that over all is the eternal, unchangeable, and unchanging God, and that He has pledged Himself to us; He has given His word and will keep His promises. That is what He is saying, though God may delay: "when forty years were expired"! Moses was allowed to be a shepherd for forty years.

"What was God doing?" you ask. "God had forgotten him. It's all very well to have promises, but forty years had gone by, and that's a long time."

People often say that. The Bible is a very honest book. You will find the psalmists now and again turning to God in agony, saying things like, "Hath God forgotten to be gracious?" (Ps. 77:9). But what an insult! In His permissive will God allows many things to happen, but He never forgets His purpose; He never forgets His promise. His word is everlasting and eternally sure, and in His own time He will bring it to pass. And here is the amazing thing: He said to Moses, "I have seen, I have seen the affliction of my people." What was He speaking about? He was speaking of those miserable children of Israel in Egypt who had rejected Moses and had treated him harshly when he had appeared before them as their deliverer. Yet He calls them "my people"!

Were this not true, we would not be considering these words now. God has His purpose of salvation for us in spite of us. Though we have rebelled against Him, though we have spat into His holy face, though in our arrogance we have expressed our opinions about Him and what He should and should not do, though we richly deserve nothing but hell and eternal torment and destruction, in spite of all that, He says, "My people"! "God so loved the world"—the world as it is, the world of His people—"that he gave his only begotten Son, that whosoever believeth in him should not perish, but have everlasting life" (John 3:16).

The truth that thrilled the apostle Paul from the depths of his being was this: "When we were enemies, we were reconciled to God by the death of his Son" (Rom. 5:10). Paul had hated Christ; he had denounced Him as a blasphemer. But when he was going down from Jerusalem to Damascus "breathing out threatenings and slaughter" (Acts 9:1) in order to exterminate that little body of Christians meeting there in secret, suddenly Paul saw Him. Paul never got over that. "Saul, Saul," the Lord asked, "why persecutest thou me?" (Acts 9:4). And so, writing years later to the Christians in Galatia, Paul spoke of "the Son of God, who loved me, and gave himself for me" (Gal. 2:20). Writing to Timothy, he said in essence, "I have changed—I cannot understand it." "Who was before," he says, "a blasphemer, and a persecutor, and injurious: but I obtained mercy" (1 Tim. 1:13). "He looked upon me in mercy. He saved me in spite of myself."

That, then, is the great initial statement—God has not abandoned the world—and immediately that gives us hope. This is our *only* hope. God has promised this redemption in spite of us, in spite of the worst that is true of the worst person in our churches. There is eternal hope in Christ. What a Gospel!

But the second point that is made abundantly clear in this passage is that God made this promise and purposed this great plan of redemption solely as the result of His love, His pity, and His compassion. What heart-moving words these are: "I have seen"—as the eternally self-subsistent God—"I have seen the affliction of my people." The Hebrew can be alternatively translated like this: "I have surely seen," or "seeing, I have seen." And not only that, He says, "I have heard their groaning." It is almost incredible that God—who has existed from all eternity, who does not need us at all, who can live without us—should be interested and concerned and that He should watch, that He should look and listen and hear. This explains the great drama of redemption as we see it in Jesus of Nazareth, the Son of God. This is the explanation of it all. It is that God looked down, as it were, from heaven and saw what sin and evil had done to men and women as He had originally created them. He looked, and He saw, and He heard "the groaning," He heard "the still, sad music of humanity," in the words of William Wordsworth.

In other words, God saw what sin has done to humanity. What has it done? It has produced "affliction" (v. 34). What does that mean? It means oppression. We are told about our Lord Himself that in the days of His flesh He looked at men and women—people like ourselves in the world today—and saw them "as sheep not having a shepherd" (Mark 6:34). In those days when sheep did not have a shepherd, they were at the mercy of marauding dogs, violent, vicious dogs that were to be found in the Near East at that time, roaming about, ever ready to attack and harass these poor sheep. Sheep without a shepherd did not know where to find the food they needed. They were hunted, hounded, panting, thin, exhausted, collapsing.

That is the full meaning of the term "affliction," and that is how the Lord saw men and women, and He had come into the world because He had seen that. God saw the tyranny and the slavery of sin. God knows that every one of us is a slave by nature, driven by lusts and drives and passions. There is not a single person who is free. I am not only talking about the lusts of the flesh. The apostle Paul talks also about the lusts of the mind, and perhaps the lusts of the mind are even worse than the lusts of the flesh. The lusts of the flesh, at any rate, can claim to be more or less natural, but these others—jealousy, envy, malice, self-importance, hatred—these are the evils that hold humanity in thralldom, and the world is full of such slaves. Of course, people do not know it; that is the tragedy. They think they are free—free, especially, from the tyranny of religion, free not to go to church on Sunday, free to read the great Sunday newspapers and the marvelous, sophisticated articles that give an understanding of life! But *are* they free?

Well, now I am going to do an odd thing—I am going to encourage you to read those papers. Read what these great thinkers are saying. If you want to know what intellectual bankruptcy means, and moral bankruptcy to boot, read these writers. Let me pay a tribute to them for their honesty. There is always hope for people as long as they are honest. But they are all testifying to what the Bible has always said: life without Christ is slavery, bondage, men and women driven, controlled; we are unable to free ourselves. "The way of transgressors," says the Bible, "is hard" (Prov. 13:15). And God has looked down and seen this; He has seen human beings as slaves of the world and the flesh and the devil.

Oh, humanity has never been in such slavery as today. We said of a certain political leader that he was impossible to work with, that nothing could be done with him at all. But in a few years people were almost worshiping him as a god. The same man, remember. That is utter slavery. People are slaves to what they read, to what others say or do. The advertisers know this. They do not understand the real essence of what they are dealing with, but they see its manifestations; so they play upon it and use it, and they are successful. But the Bible has already explained the problem: people are slaves to sin and cannot set themselves free.

And this affliction produced by sin is not only slavery—it is misery. God has not only *seen*—He has *heard* the groaning. Oh, the unhappiness in the world, the suffering, the misery, the heartbreak. You can dress respectably, you can dress fashionably, but beneath is a broken heart, an unhappiness that is agonizing. And the universe, humanity especially, is groaning. But this is the glory of the message of the Gospel—God can hear it, and He has heard it. He has heard the groaning, the misery, the shame, the unhappiness, the suffering; He knows the fear, the pain, the hopelessness. He has seen it all, He has heard it all, and He has had pity upon us.

The heart of the Eternal
Is most wonderfully kind.
F. W. Faber

And then, having seen and heard, God said that He was going to do something about it: "I have heard their groaning, and am come down to deliver them. And now come, I will send thee into Egypt." This was the message. And today this is the message of the Gospel of Jesus Christ, the *only* hope. This is the message the Sanhedrin rejected, and this is the message people are still rejecting. They say, for example, "Palm Sunday—what does it mean? What nonsense! Don't try that rubbish. Don't talk about such a horrible thing, saying one man can die for another." That is the attitude of the world still, and it is missing this glorious message of what God has said and done.

Let me summarize this message for you. If you let this control your thinking, you will find that you are face to face with the most glorious news the world has ever known or can ever know. It is this: God is going to deliver. He says, "I have seen the affliction of my people . . . and am come down to deliver them." That is it—God, in the glory, in the heavens, is coming down. He has not forgotten; He has not abandoned; He has not given up.

Oh, my dear friend, in your distress, in your despair, in your failure, if only you could see the hope there is for you! God knows about your unhappiness; He has "come down." And He has been doing this ever since man went astray. Read the third chapter of the book of Genesis. Adam and Eve sinned when they rebelled against God, and then suddenly "They heard the voice of the LORD God walking in the garden in the cool of the day" (v. 8). He had come down. He knew what they had done; He knew their unhappiness. The moment they sinned, they were unhappy. You cannot sin and remain happy—it is impossible. It is an absolute law that you will suffer if you sin. And the world is unhappy because of sin. But God has come down; He knew.

Adam and Eve were hiding behind the trees, and God cried, "Adam, where are you? I have come down to speak to you." And that is the beginning of the Gospel—God coming down and speaking. Read the Old Testament, and you will find that God kept coming down in different ways. When His people were in trouble and in distress, He sent an angel—"the angel of the covenant," who was in fact the Lord Jesus Christ Himself appearing before His incarnation. He came down to deliver. He came down before the destruction of Sodom, and He came down when the armies of Israel were in trouble. One night Joshua was faced with a terrible problem. Annihilation was staring him in the face, and he did not know what to do. Suddenly he was aware of a presence—God, who said, "As captain of the host of the LORD am I now come" (Josh. 5:14). God had come down, He had appeared, and He brought about a great victory.

We see God's deliverance in perfection in the Lord Jesus Christ. Listen to Paul's way of expressing God's coming down to deliver us:

> *Let this mind be in you, which was also in Christ Jesus: who, being in the form of God, thought it not robbery to be equal with God: but made himself of no reputation, and took upon him the form of a servant, and was made in the likeness of men: and being found in fashion as a man, he humbled himself, and became obedient unto death, even the death of the cross.*
>
> —*Phil. 2:5-8*

"[I] am come down." Here is the eternal Son of God, the one of whom John writes: "In the beginning was the Word, and the Word was with God, and the Word was God" (John 1:1). "God in three Persons, blessed Trinity," wrote the hymn-writer Reginald Heber. Father, Son, and Holy Spirit enjoyed the pure glory of eternity. But at a given point the Son "came down on earth to dwell," as the children's hymn puts it:

I love to hear the story
Which angel voices tell,
How once the King of glory
Came down on earth to dwell.
Emily Huntingdon Miller

That is the meaning of the babe of Bethlehem. This is God the Son, who has come down into the world, leaving the courts of heaven.

From the highest throne in glory
To the cross of deepest woe.
Robert Robinson

That is what happened in the birth of Jesus of Nazareth in the little town of Bethlehem. God the eternal Son came down in the likeness of man, "in the likeness of sinful flesh" (Rom. 8:3). He humbled Himself; He divested Himself of the signs and insignia of His everlasting glory. Oh, look at what that means! God said to Moses, "I am going to send you to Egypt," and God sent His only begotten Son into our world, the place of torment and shame, of serfdom, agony, and trouble. God sent His only Son into the Egypt of our life.

Look at Him; look at His weakness, a helpless little babe. All things were made through Him, and He sustains everything; yet He was born in abject weakness and was laid in a manger, completely helpless. Look at the poverty into which He was born. Mary and Joseph could not afford a lamb for a sacrifice—two turtle doves only. Born in a stable! Laid in a manger! The Son of God! Here it is, His self-humbling: He identified Himself with us. "I will send thee into Egypt," said God to Moses. And He said the same to His Son. "Go down, live among them, be one of them."

And our Lord did it. He identified Himself with us. He worked with His hands as a carpenter; He lived an ordinary life. He heard all the gossip and backbiting, all the cruel and unkind things that people say about one another and even about Him. He has known it all; He has been in it all; He has shared it all. He came deliberately into the Egypt of our lives, and He has shared all our burdens and problems.

What happened to Moses in Egypt? Read the book of Exodus, read of his conflict, his fight with Pharaoh and the magicians of Egypt, the terrible struggle that went on. When God sent His Son into this world, He sent Him to a place of conflict. What did He have to struggle with? After He was tempted forty days and forty nights in the wilderness, the devil tested Him and did everything he could to drag Him down. And look at the struggles with the Pharisees and the scribes and the Herodians; look at the space given to all that in the four Gospels. There they were, wrangling with Him, asking their skeptical questions—all the folly and the shame! But He submitted to it. He went through with it all. He knew that this is what is happening to us, so He identified Himself with us; He shared our lives.

And not only that, look at the dullness and the stupidity and the slowness of His own followers, the obtuseness of these disciples who could not see the point and kept on asking the same old foolish questions. They did not understand it all, and they especially misunderstood the most glorious thing of all—namely, His death upon the cross. Then there was the treachery of Judas, one of the innermost circle, a man to whom Jesus had opened His heart—Judas betrayed Him, sold Him merely to get money, and used Him to serve His own nefarious ideas and projects. Treachery! Shame! Disloyalty! Christ has borne it all. He came deliberately; He came in order to go through all this because He knew that these people of His had to endure and suffer this kind of thing. And then He went through one of the most terrible things of all when the disciples "all forsook him, and fled" (Mark 14:50). Even His closest friends left Him, and Peter denied Him with oaths and curses. This is history; these things have literally happened, and it was the Son of God who was suffering all this.

But we have not come to the final crisis, and it is at this point that Moses pales into insignificance. Moses is a type of Jesus Christ, but when you come to this next point, Moses disappears off the map altogether. Moses was instructed to tell the people of Israel that on that crucial, dramatic Passover night, God was going to punish the Egyptians because of their treatment of His people. A pestilence would destroy all the firstborn of the land, but how were the children of Israel to be saved? Each family was to kill a lamb, collect the blood, and then dip a bunch of hyssop into the blood and paint the blood on the lintels and doorposts of their houses. Then when the angel of destruction passed through the land, he would see the blood and pass by those houses. That was the message, and that was what happened. The children of Israel were brought out of Egypt on that dramatic, momentous night.

That is a picture of what God has done for you and for me in the person of His only begotten Son. The Son of God not only came into this world, He not only came "in the likeness of men" (Phil. 2:7), He not only humbled Himself and became a servant—it goes beyond that. He "became obedient unto death, even the death of the cross" (Phil. 2:8). He came in order to die on that cross: his blood was to be shed. Why? Oh, for this reason: that the person on whom this blood is painted might be passed over in the judgment, might be forgiven, set at liberty. The Son came down in order to do this. He Himself is the Lamb of God!

The apostle Peter, in his first epistle, reminded the Christian people to whom he was writing of this in these words:

> *Forasmuch as ye know that ye were not redeemed with corruptible things, as silver and gold, from your vain conversation received by tradition from your fathers; but with the precious blood of Christ, as of a lamb without blemish and without spot: who verily was foreordained before the foundation of the world, but was manifest in these last times for you, who by him do believe in God.*
>
> —*1 Pet. 1:18-21*

This is God's way of salvation. He sent His Son into this world to bear our sins in His own body on the tree. That is the meaning of the Communion service. On that last night before He was crucified, our Lord took a loaf and broke it and said, "This is [represents] my body, which is broken for you" (1 Cor. 11:24). "I am going to give My life for you; I am going to give My body." Then He poured out the wine and said, "This is [represents] my blood of the new testament, which is shed for many" (Mark 14:24)—that is, "for your transgressions, in order that you, believing this, will not be punished. I am going to bear your punishment. I am making Myself a sacrifice for you. I am God's Lamb, slain in order that you might be delivered. My blood is what ransoms you, redeems you, purchases you, and sets you free from the bondage, the slavery, the misery of Egypt so that you may go out and inherit Canaan, the land 'flowing with milk and honey,' that you may know God's promises, God's love, God's mercy, God's compassion, God's receiving you as His children, adopting you into His family, and showering His blessings upon you."

That is the message. "He stedfastly set his face to go to Jerusalem" (Luke 9:51). This was not the death of a pacifist; He could have escaped it all—He said so Himself. He did it deliberately. He had come in order to do this. This is the whole point—God had sent Him to provide deliverance, salvation, redemption for all who believe in Him. His blood was shed so that we, covered, as it were, by the blood, are accepted by God, are spared the judgment and eternal misery and wretchedness that we so richly deserve, and on the contrary enter into the inheritance of the children of God and the saints in light and can look forward to life with Him forever. "Blessed are the pure in heart: for they shall see God" (Matt. 5:8).

His blood can make the foulest clean,
His blood availed for me.
Charles Wesley

It does not matter what you have been in the past, it does not matter how deeply you have fallen into sin, it does not matter what your shame is, it does not matter what your degradation is, it does not matter what is true of you, bodily, mentally, in any sense—it does not matter at all. No man can save himself. The most moral person in the world is no better off than you are. "For all have sinned, and come short of the glory of God" (Rom. 3:23). "There is none righteous, no, not one" (Rom. 3:10). The idea that religious people are better than others is nonsense; it is pharisaism, a contradiction of Christianity. No; we have nothing, nothing at all. But God is offering us free salvation, pardon and forgiveness for all our sins, reconciliation unto Him, and all the promises that He has made to his children. He is offering it all to you just as you are at this moment, with no conditions, with nothing that you have to do.

Only believe, and thou shalt see
That Christ is all in all to thee.
John Samuel Bewley Monsell

This was the message of Paul and Silas to the Philippian jailer of old. There he was in his trouble, his agony, his alarm, and he cried out saying, "Sirs, what must I do to be saved?" There was only one answer: "Believe on the Lord Jesus Christ, and thou shalt be saved, and thy house" (Acts 16:30-31).

Is it not marvelous, is it not wonderful to know that the everlasting and eternal God, who plays with the constellations as if they were nothing, is interested in us, that He sees us, that He knows all about us, our failures, our sins, our shame, our hopelessness, our despair—that He has heard our groanings? Only believe that and turn to Him and thank Him and tell Him that though you do not understand fully, you believe the message that He has sent His Son into the world and to the death of the cross in order that you might be forgiven and reconciled to Him. Tell Him that you believe it and that you want to understand it more and more, and He will receive you just as you are. That is the message.

This will give you immediate peace, immediate rest, immediate satisfaction, and it will begin to open into a life of understanding and strength and power and will finally lead you through death to the glory everlasting, to the vision of the God of Abraham, the God of Isaac, the God of Jacob, the God and Father of our Lord and Savior Jesus Christ.

4

Complete Victory

This Moses whom they refused, saying, Who made thee a ruler and a judge? the same did God send to be a ruler and a deliverer by the hand of the angel which appeared to him in the bush. He brought them out, after that he had shewed wonders and signs in the land of Egypt, and in the Red sea, and in the wilderness forty years.

—Acts 7:35-36

We have seen how God spoke to Moses and gave His great message: "I have seen, I have seen the affliction of my people which is in Egypt, and I have heard their groaning, and am come down to deliver them. And now come, I will send thee into Egypt" (v. 34). Now we turn to verses 35-36 of Acts 7, in which Stephen, in his address to the Sanhedrin, summarized the great deliverance that God brought about through Moses.

But why did Stephen say all this? You may say, "What did all this have to do with the Sanhedrin? This had all happened 1,400 years earlier—so why was he going over it?" But can you not see the purpose? "You," said Stephen to the Sanhedrin, "in rejecting the Son of God, the message that we are preaching, are simply reenacting what your forefathers did, but remember that the message is still the same. It is God who always acts; it was God who acted in the time of Moses, and it is the same God who is acting now. Moses merely prefigured Christ. Here is the Savior and His great salvation. This is what you are rejecting."

So Stephen was preaching the Gospel of salvation in order to show these Jewish leaders the folly and the blindness of their rejection of it. And I am using this story, this incident, in exactly the same way; that is all I am anxious to do. You see, this great salvation was all prefigured in the time of Moses. We have seen that it is all of God, that it is God's message, God's activity, and that it is always miraculous and supernatural. And we have seen, too, how the Passover was a picture of Christ dying on the cross. He is "the Lamb of God, which taketh away the sin of the world" (John 1:29). But we have not finished. There is a further, wonderful element, another crucial aspect to the story of Moses, and that is this great element of victory, this defeat of their enemies and the setting at liberty and the freedom of the children of God. It is all put perfectly in these two verses that we are now considering together.

Look at Moses as the picture and see that he is but a very pale adumbration of what God has done once and forever in the person of His only begotten Son, our Lord and Savior Jesus Christ. We are told, "This Moses whom they refused, saying, Who made thee a ruler and a judge? the same God did send to be a ruler and a deliverer." Though they had rejected him, he was still the one who had been chosen by God to do the work, and after forty years God called him again, gave him his commission, and sent the angel with him to give him power and strength. So Moses was sent off to Egypt to do the work to which God had appointed him.

Read the book of Exodus for yourselves. Start reading at chapter 1 and go right through to the fourteenth chapter; it is worthy of your perusal. God sent Moses. Moses, a very modest, meek man who was not a good speaker, was sent to do this impossible task—to confront Pharaoh and all his soldiers, his chariots, and his horsemen. Moses had nothing, not even a sword; he was given a rod or staff, just a stick. The very idea seems quite ridiculous, does it not? But that was how it was. He was told to go, and he was told what to say, and he constantly protested. "What can I do? Who am I? How can I go and face this mighty Pharaoh? It's impossible!" But God said, "Go on! Do what I tell you."

So on Moses went and did it. And the outcome, of course, was a tremendous struggle—a struggle with Pharaoh himself, with his magicians, his astrologers, his seers, and his wise men.

How was Moses able to do this? What could he do in those circumstances? We are given the answer: "He brought them out, after that he had shewed wonders and signs in the land of Egypt." If you read those chapters in the book of Exodus, you will find that there were ten altogether—ten signs. Moses was given miraculous powers. He could create lice out of dust, produce frogs from the river, turn the river into blood. Read about all ten of them, the "wonders and signs." Up to a point the magicians of Egypt could enter into a competition; they were not without power. The forces confronting us are very, very powerful, and this was a tremendous contest in which Moses was constantly losing heart and losing hope. But God sent him back and gave him more power, and at last Moses was able, by the signs and wonders, to hold Pharaoh in check and get him to liberate the children of Israel, or at least to allow them to go and perform their act of worship. The power given to Moses proved to be greater than all the power of Pharaoh and all the power of Egypt put together. The "wonders and signs" enabled him to win this concession, as it were, out of the hand of Pharaoh.

If you do not feel, whenever you read the fourteenth chapter of the book of Exodus, that you are reading one of the greatest and most dramatic incidents in the whole of literature, then I must confess that I feel sorry for you. I shall never forget reading that chapter in the pulpit on the Sunday morning after the fall of France in June 1940, and I think the small company that was with me on that occasion felt that it was the voice of God speaking again. Everything seemed to have gone wrong, and we were in a crisis! But God was still with us, just as he was with Moses.

Let me try to reconstruct this tremendous story for you. Can you see it happening? The children of Israel had come out of Egypt, and they had no staves, no swords, no spears, no chariots, nothing at all; they were slaves. They had to leave in a hurry—even the bread was unleavened, and there they were, escaping. They knew that Pharaoh and his hosts were coming after them, and suddenly they arrived at this point of tremendous crisis. They reached a place where there were obstacles on both sides—Pi-hahiroth and Baal-zephon. Exodus 14:3 says, "For Pharaoh will say of the children of Israel, They are entangled in the land, the wilderness hath shut them in." They could not go one way, they could not go the other way, and behind them were Pharaoh and his hosts and his chariots and his horsemen. They could not go back, so they had to go forward, but in front of them was the Red Sea. What could they do? They were absolutely hemmed in; their position was completely hopeless.

As usual the children of Israel began to complain. They said, "Because there were no graves in Egypt, hast thou taken us away to die in the wilderness?" (v. 11). "Did we not tell you that it was madness to come out of Egypt, that it was utter folly, that we would be caught in disaster and would be overwhelmed? Why did we listen to you! Now it is too late. Here we are, absolutely hemmed in."

Poor Moses! It was all on his lonely shoulders, this impossible task. He was, remember, a very meek and modest man. What could he do? He surely fell on his face before God; there was nothing left for him to do but that. And we are told that God spoke to him and said, "Wherefore criest thou unto me? speak unto the children of Israel, that they go forward" (v. 15). So he spoke the word, and the miracle happened. As they moved forward, the sea divided, and they walked through on dry land, as described in that dramatic fourteenth chapter of the book of Exodus.

And what did this lead to? On that tremendous night, as the children of Israel walked forward, the Egyptians thought, *We've got them now*, and they began rushing after them. But there was utter confusion; the wheels of the chariots got stuck in the sand and in the mud. Then God gave Moses a command to hold out the rod again, and the sea came back. The Egyptians were drowned and destroyed, every single one of them; and the story ends with these words: "And Israel saw the Egyptians dead upon the sea shore" (v. 30). The old enemies, the old tyrants, the old taskmasters, the people under whom they had groaned and had sweated and had cried through all the years, were dead upon the seashore! The Israelites were free! Their enemies had all been conquered in a miraculous manner, and God's people were free to go on with their journey to the promised land of Canaan.

That is the story of Moses. Stephen put it in a few words, he gave the essence of the event, because these leaders, these members of the Sanhedrin, knew this story backwards. But why was Stephen saying it at all? He was doing so because that story was nothing, it paled into insignificance, when you consider what it prefigured.

Now we come to the tremendous story of our blessed Lord and Savior, the Son of God, Jesus of Nazareth! Why has He come into this world? What is the meaning of the incarnation? What is the meaning of this great story that we can read in the pages of the four Gospels? This is the most marvelous thing in the universe! Our Lord came into this world to set us free; He came to liberate us. Notice the wonderful parallel. As Moses was the liberator of the children of Israel under the hand of God, so the Son of God came into the world to set us free.

What are we told about Him? "He is despised and rejected of men; a man of sorrows, and acquainted with grief" (Isa. 53:3). "He came unto his own, and his own received him not" (John 1:11). He was rejected by the world, just as He was rejected by the members of the Sanhedrin. But here is the message: in spite of man's rejection of Him, He is God's own appointed Savior. Peter had already made this point in addressing this same Sanhedrin. He and John had been arrested and put on trial, and Peter had ended his speech on that occasion with these words: "This is the stone which was set at nought of you builders, which is become the head of the corner. Neither is there salvation in any other: for there is none other name under heaven given among men, whereby we must be saved" (Acts 4:11-12).

The children of Israel had rejected Moses, but that did not make any difference—he was God's appointed deliverer, and in spite of themselves, God sent him to deliver them. In the same way, though the world has rejected the Son of God, He is still the Savior of the world. But remember this: it is in spite of us, in spite of our blindness, in spite of our folly, in spite of our recalcitrance, in spite of everything that is so true of us, that God sent Him, just as He sent Moses—"The same did God send to be a ruler and a deliverer." And the whole message of the Bible is this: "When the fulness of the time was come, God sent forth his Son"—"sent forth" into the Egypt of this world—"made of a woman, made under the law"—what for?—"to redeem them that were under the law" (Gal. 4:4-5).

Follow the parallel. When Moses was sent to Egypt, he had a great struggle: he struggled with Pharaoh and his hosts and powers. And it was precisely the same with the Son of God when He came into the world. Read the four Gospels again and see the battle He had to fight! Look at the world into which He came, a world that never understood Him, a world that was utterly opposed to Him. The whole organization of this world is against God, it is against Christ, and it is against each one of us. Look at it in its newspapers and in its films; look at it on the television; look at it in everything that is regarded as wonderful today. The Son of God came into a world like that. The whole mind and outlook of the world was the exact opposite of everything that He was and everything that He stood for. The apostle Paul sums up the mind and outlook of the world when he says that all who belong to the world and follow "the course of this world" are simply living according to "the lusts" of the flesh, "fulfilling the desires of the flesh and of the mind" (Eph. 2:2-3); and our Lord is the eternal opposite of all that. So He came into a great struggle with the world.

And then, of course, there was the opposition of the devil. "[He] was in all points tempted like as we are, yet without sin" (Heb. 4:15). You remember how for forty days and forty nights our Lord was tempted by the devil in the wilderness. We remember the three most notable temptations, but they were only three out of a great number. The devil did everything he could to entrap Him. He tried Him; he sifted Him; he offered Him the kingdoms of this world; he took Him to the pivotal point of the temple and told Him to throw Himself down so that God might save Him. Oh, the subtlety, the cleverness of it all. The devil did not merely send an underling to fight our blessed

Lord and Savior—he always came himself. Our Lord met him in single combat, and the devil brought out all his reserves. That is the kind of life that our Lord lived.

Notice that as in the case of Moses, so with our Lord, there were miracles and signs and wonders. Do you not see that as you read the four Gospels? What was our Lord doing? All the time He was doing miracles and wonders. If He had not done that, there would be no Gospel to preach. He "went about doing good," said Peter later on (Acts 10:38). He was always setting people free.

We read of a certain miracle that our Lord worked on a poor woman who was doubled up and could not straighten herself. Luke, who was a physician, tells us that our Lord said she had been bound like this by Satan for eighteen years (Luke 13:16). Bound by Satan! And nobody could help her, nobody could heal her, nobody could liberate her, nobody could enable her to stand upright. And, too, there was the man with the withered arm. He could not move it, he could not raise it—he was helpless. Our Lord went about freeing people like this. He delivered men and women possessed by devils.

I accept medically that there is a difference between demonic possession and insanity; and there is a difference between possession and epilepsy. You say, "But I have never seen a case of demonic possession." The fact that you have not recognized it does not mean it does not exist. There is a periodicity about this, but as the West goes back, as it is doing more and more, to devil worship and to spiritism, we will see more and more cases of devil possession—men and women whose personalities are governed by some unseen personality who can enable them to do extraordinary things, to speak languages that they do not know, and at times to use a kind of superhuman power.

Our Lord was constantly dealing with such men and women. With His almighty power he was driving devils out of people. This was part of his conflict with the world and the devil and all the minions of the devil, these "principalities and powers" that brought such havoc and misery into life and brought in even disease itself. Disease is ultimately the result of sin. There should never have been any such thing as disease. When God made the world, it was Paradise, it was good, there was nothing wrong. There was never meant to be suffering; there was never meant to be sighing; there was never meant to be death. All these things have come in as the result of sin. Now that does not mean to say that every particular case of disease is due to a particular sin. All I am saying is that the whole teaching of the Bible from beginning to end is that there would never have been disease and there would never have been death had it not been for man's rebellion and sin.

The apostle John tells us that our Lord came into the world "that he might destroy the works of the devil" (1 John 3:8). The devil does his nefarious work. He influences people's minds, making them creatures of lust and passion, slaves to drink, slaves to drugs, slaves to fashion, slaves to the thing to do, slaves to temper and pride and jealousy and envy and malice. All this is the work of the devil, who came into God's perfect creation to produce the chaos that resulted. And our Lord came to fight all this in order to set us free from it and to enable us to live again as the children of God. He came for that purpose, and while He was here He overcame the devil through signs, wonders, miracles, and amazing deeds. He said, "I with the finger of God cast out devils" (Luke 11:20), and when they saw His miracles, people were filled with amazement and said, "We have seen strange things to day" (Luke 5:26). And often they were filled with a kind of terror and alarm at His miraculous power as He showed His mastery over all the enemies of the human race.

But our Lord also came to a supreme crisis, as did Moses at the Red Sea. On either side were Pi-hahiroth and Baal-zephon. Behind, the hosts of Pharaoh. Ahead, the Red Sea. They were completely hemmed in! What could they do? But that is nothing when you put it by the side of what I may call the Red Sea of the Son of God. What am I talking about? It is all in the four Gospels. Read about the machinations of our Lord's enemies, the plotting and the conclaves of the miserable Pharisees and scribes and Sadducees. Read how they agreed together to trick him with their questions. Oh, the devilish subtlety of it all; they were merely dupes of the devil! Then read of the treachery of His friends, for even His chosen disciples all "forsook him, and fled" (Matt. 26:56). Also see the terrible onslaught of the devil, letting all his powers loose upon Christ, telling Him that all His claims had come to nothing.

Read about His agony in the Garden of Gethsemane—this was a part of that terrible battle. Not only was our Lord facing what He knew was going to happen, but the enemy brought out all his evil powers, and there at the back of them all our Lord could see the law of God. He had been born "under the law" (Gal. 4:4). He knew that He had to fulfill this law; He had to bear the penalty of this law. He bore "the handwriting of ordinances that was against us" (Col. 2:14). The Ten Commandments tell us what we ought to be, but we cannot do it, and so they are against us. All these were surrounding Him, and there in front of Him was death. This could not be avoided. He could not go to that side or to this side—Pi-hahiroth, Baal-zephon, the hosts of Pharaoh, the Red Sea, death—he was alone, surrounded by it all, hemmed in—the end had come.

Moses prefigured Him in a very remarkable manner. The author of the

Epistle to the Hebrews tells us of Jesus' "strong crying and tears" (5:7). That was the agony of the Garden of Gethsemane: "O my Father, if it be possible, let this cup pass from me" (Matt. 26:39). Crying! Strong tears! These impossible enemies on every side! What could He do? He died, and they took His body from the tree and laid it in a tomb, and they rolled a stone before the entrance and sealed it and put soldiers to guard it. He was finished, was He not? He had entered the Red Sea; He was overwhelmed; it was the end.

No! Then came His glorious resurrection! He came through the other side. He went through the Red Sea! He emerged triumphant, bringing "life and immortality to light through the gospel" (2 Tim. 1:10). As Peter put it in his sermon on the Day of Pentecost, "It was not possible that he should be holden of [death]" (Acts 2:24). He is the Holy One of God, and the malignity of devils and of hell were apparently bringing His end, but He triumphed over all and emerged alive forevermore. Later on He addressed John on the Isle of Patmos and said, "I am he that liveth, and was dead; and, behold, I am alive for evermore" (Rev. 1:18).

Do you know what that means? It means that all your enemies have been defeated once and forever—the world, the flesh, the devil, the law, death, the grave—every one of them is defeated. Do you remember what this same Lord said after He had risen and ascended to heaven? He gave a commission to a man called Saul of Tarsus as he met him one day on the road to Damascus. He revealed Himself to Saul and told him that he was sending him as a preacher to the people of Israel, and also to the Gentiles. What was the commission given to Paul? It was:

> *To open their eyes, and to turn them from darkness to light, and from the power of Satan unto God, that they may receive forgiveness of sins, and inheritance among them which are sanctified by faith that is in me.*
>
> —*Acts 26:18*

Paul was commissioned "to turn them from darkness"—the ignorance of the world and all its mentality and its wisdom—"to light"—the light of God—"and from the power of Satan"—which had held them all and the whole world in its thralldom and bondage—"unto God," to "the glorious liberty of the children of God" (Rom. 8:21).

The apostle John puts it like this: "We know that whosoever is born of God sinneth not"—does not go on sinning, does not live a life of sin—"but he that is begotten of God keepeth himself, and that wicked one toucheth him not. And we know that we are of God, and the whole world lieth in wickedness [literally, "the wicked one"]" (1 John 5:18-19). The devil has the whole world in his embrace, but he cannot touch us, says John. We no longer belong to him; we have been translated into the kingdom of God's dear Son. And this is because "for this purpose the Son of God was manifested, that he might destroy the works of the devil" (1 John 3:8). He came to do that. The devil had tyrannized the whole human race as "a strong man armed" who "keepeth his palace, his goods are in peace" (Luke 11:21). The devil had defeated all the patriarchs, all the prophets, all the great kings of Israel—none of them could touch him. But here was One who met him and refuted him, who robbed him of his armor wherein he trusted and set his goods at liberty.

And not only is the devil defeated, the world is also. Listen to John shouting out at the top of his voice, "This is the victory that overcometh the world"—what is it?—"even our faith" (1 John 5:4). "Our faith"! We who are Christians are not slaves to the world. We overcome the world. I am not dependent upon the Sunday newspapers or the entertainment on television. I have seen through the world; I have seen beyond it.

What of sin? "For," says Paul, "sin shall not have dominion over you: for ye are not under the law, but under grace" (Rom. 6:14). Therefore, says Paul, "Likewise reckon ye also yourselves to be dead indeed unto sin, but alive unto God through Jesus Christ our Lord" (Rom. 6:11). And what of the law of God? "For the law of the Spirit of life in Christ Jesus hath made me free from the law of sin and death," says Paul (Rom. 8:2).

The terrors of law, and of God
With me can have nothing to do;
My Saviour's obedience and blood
Hide all my transgressions from view.
Augustus Toplady

He has conquered my every enemy: the world, the flesh, the devil, the law, sin.

"But wait a minute," says somebody, "you still have to die! The last enemy is death!"

But remember Easter Sunday! Death has been conquered. In His name I can look at death and the grave and say, "O death, where is thy sting? O grave, where is thy victory?" (1 Cor. 15:55). He has burst asunder the bands of death; He rose triumphant over the grave. The last enemy, death, is vanquished. As the hymn by William Williams puts it:

Death of death, and hell's destruction,
Land me safe on Canaan's side.

He is the "death of death"; He is "hell's destruction"! He has conquered the last enemy. He offers us complete liberty, complete freedom. We can say with Charles Wesley, "Alive in him, my living head." He has conquered every enemy of the soul of man, and to all who believe in Him He offers a new life, saying, "If the Son therefore shall make you free, ye shall be free indeed" (John 8:36): free from the world and its enticements and attractions, free from lust, free from sin, free from all the things that get you down. This is what He offers to all who believe in Him.

So, then, let me sum it all up by pointing out some lessons that all this should teach us; they are the lessons pointed out by Stephen in his address. To reject the Gospel is to reject God. If you reject this message, you are not rejecting me—I am nobody, I am nothing. I am here today and gone tomorrow. You do not reject me, you do not reject man—this is not a human philosophy—you reject God. The children of Israel in their folly thought they were rejecting Moses. They caused Moses to flee, but this is what we are told: "This Moses whom they refused, saying, Who made thee a ruler and a judge? the same did God send to be a ruler." They were not rejecting Moses—they were rejecting God.

Do you realize that if you do not believe the Gospel you are pitting yourself—pigmy as you are—against the everlasting and eternal God? Your breath is in His hands, you will soon be dead, and after death comes the Judgment—you will stand before Him.

Second, our rejection of the Gospel and of God's plan makes no difference whatsoever to the plan, none at all. The Israelites rejected it in Moses, but it was still carried out. God sent him back, and he did the work. Peter put it to these clever members of the Sanhedrin in this way: "This is the stone which was set at nought of you builders, which is become the head of the corner" (Acts 4:11). They thought they were very clever on the day we call Good Friday because they had accomplished His death. Can you not imagine the meetings that night of the Pharisees and scribes and Sadducees and priests? Can you not see them congratulating themselves, drinking to one another's health? They had got rid of this agitator, this nuisance. They had finished Him. I can hear the jeering and the mocking and the laughter. Oh, the blind fools, fighting God! Their rejection made no difference. God raised Him from the dead!

There He is, the head of the corner, the hope of eternity, the Christ of

God. The fact that you reject Him makes no difference to God's plan and purpose. And whatever the modern world may do in its cleverness makes no difference at all. When God's appointed time shall come, He will send this same Jesus back into this world. The world will see Him "coming in the clouds of heaven with power and great glory" (Matt. 24:30). What will He come for? He will come for the final judgment—and nothing can stop it. Nothing can make Him His purpose forego. He will destroy all His enemies, and He will set up His glorious kingdom.

Jesus shall reign where'er the sun
Does his successive journeys run;
His kingdom stretch from shore to shore,
Till moons shall wax and wane no more.
Isaac Watts

He will come! And then shall be the end! Your rejection makes not the slightest difference.

But listen to my last point: If you do not belong to the people of God, if you persist in your rejection of this message concerning Jesus of Nazareth, the Son of God, and His miraculous life, His atoning, sacrificial death, and His glorious, wondrous resurrection—if you persist in rejecting Him, you will be included in the destruction of His enemies when He comes to judge the world in righteousness. Can you be guilty of such folly? Oh, my dear friend, why do you resist Him? Are you like those foolish Pharisees and scribes and Sadducees? Do you feel that it is insulting that you should have to believe that another dies for you? Do you want to save yourself? By your good life or by your philosophic understanding do you think you can encompass God? Because of your pride, you are rejecting the Gospel and bringing damnation upon yourself.

Oh, do not be foolish. Listen to the word that Moses was told by God to utter to the children of Israel: "Fear ye not, stand still, and see the salvation of the LORD" (Exod. 14:13). You can never save yourself, and the world can never save itself—there is no need to try. This is God's glorious message to every one of us.

You may be steeped in sin, you may have lost your willpower, you may be a slave to drugs, drink, or whatever—you may feel completely hopeless, and everybody may have given up on you—but this is my commission to you: "Fear ye not, stand still, and see the salvation of the LORD." Look at this blessed Son of God. See Him coming into the world; see Him fighting, conquering, mastering all your enemies; see Him in the final agony—defeating the last enemy, death! See Him rising, conquering all! You have nothing to do but just to look at Him, to believe in Him, and to surrender yourself to Him. "The LORD shall fight for you, and ye shall hold your peace" (Exod. 14:14). "By grace are ye saved through faith; and that not of yourselves: it is the gift of God" (Eph. 2:8). This message tells you that the Son of God has come into the world to save you. He has done it all. Look at Him, believe in Him, surrender your life to Him, rise up and follow Him, and He will lead you to liberty and ultimately to the Canaan of your desires, to the glory of God and everlasting bliss.

5

God Has Spoken

This is that Moses, which said unto the children of Israel, A prophet shall the Lord your God raise up unto you of your brethren, like unto me; him shall ye hear. This is he, that was in the church in the wilderness with the angel which spake to him in the mount Sina, and with our fathers: who received the lively oracles to give unto us.

—Acts 7:37-38

If we count the number of verses Stephen devoted to the different men referred to in his sermon, we see that his key argument involves the case of Moses, who was, of course, an outstanding man in the story of the children of Israel. Stephen had been reminding the members of the Sanhedrin of the essential elements of the story of Moses.

Now Stephen said about this man, "This is that Moses, which said unto the children of Israel, A prophet shall the Lord your God raise up unto you of your brethren, like unto me; him shall ye hear." Then he told them another thing about him: "This is he, that was in the church in the wilderness with the angel which spake to him in the mount Sina, and with our fathers: who received the lively oracles to give unto us."

Stephen, having stated the facts, was showing their significance and importance. And in doing so, he emphasized the two most important things about Moses: first, he was the man through whom God gave His law to the children of Israel; and, second, he was the man who clearly prophesied the coming of our Lord and Savior, Jesus Christ. So Stephen dealt with two fundamental matters—the law and the prophets—and he wanted to show the

Sanhedrin that in a very remarkable manner the law and the prophets were represented in this one man, Moses.

Stephen therefore said in effect to the members of the Sanhedrin, "You are perfectly right in revering the memory of Moses as you are doing. Though you do it in a way that is unintelligent and is indeed a denial of the real significance of Moses, nevertheless, in revering this man you are doing the right thing. Now let me tell you why . . ." And he then expounded the story of Moses in these two verses. What was it that made Moses the man he was? Or let me put another question: What was it that made the Jews, the children of Israel, the remarkable people that they were and still are? What is the secret of these people? What is the uniqueness that belongs to them?

Now this is a phenomenon, a fact that we must all consider. If you are merely interested in history, you must consider this. Look at this little nation, the Jews, living in a very little land, the land of Palestine. There they are, and looked at from the natural standpoint, they are quite insignificant and unimportant. They were surrounded by great dynasties, great empires, great nations—Egypt on the one side and Babylonia, Persia, and other great powerful dynasties and empires on the other. And yet we know from history—both the history that is recorded in the Old Testament and, equally, that which is recorded and substantiated by secular historians—that this little nation, this little people, oftentimes dominated the entire scene and became conquerors and were the key factor in the lives of other nations, indeed of the whole world. But going beyond that, we know that out of this people came the one who has dominated the whole of human history, out of this nation came the one who is the universal benefactor, the one whose cross "towers o'er the wrecks of time."

We are confronted, then, by the remarkable fact that this small, apparently unimportant nation became extremely important, and the question we have to consider is: What accounts for that? How did they ever come to be so important in human history? Why are we concerned about this Jesus of Nazareth? Why has He become such a key factor in all human thinking and human endeavor?

There is only one answer to the question as to how these people became so important, and it is given in our text. These people of Israel were "the church," or if you prefer, "the people of God": "This is he, that was in the church in the wilderness with the angel which spake to him in the mount Sina, and with our fathers."

Now the Greek word here translated "church" means "a people who are gathered out," "a special gathering," "a special assembly." It is a word that was first used in a secular context, but always with the connotation of a group of people who met together for some specific purpose. From there it developed into the word *church* as we normally use it at the present time. Now from the standpoint of the world and mere secular history, you cannot understand the Jewish people at all. There is only one way to understand them, and that is as they are described by Stephen—they were the people of God, the church of God, the assembly of God's people. That is the grand message of the whole of the Old Testament. The Jews are different from every other nation for the sole reason that they are a people who are in this particular relationship to God.

Then the question is: How did the Jews ever enter into this special relationship? How were they separated out? How did they become distinct in this way? And the only answer is that God had spoken to them. God had given them the truth. And it was because of this that they were the people they were; that was their secret. That is a teaching that is given very often in the Old Testament. As long as these people were true to that relationship with God, they were victorious. When they forgot it, as they sometimes did, and wanted to have kings and be like other nations, down they went. Then the moment they came back to God, their fortunes, as it were, were restored, and they went on from conquest to conquest and triumph to triumph.

So the whole secret of the Jewish people was that God had spoken to them. Go back to the beginning of Stephen's address to the Sanhedrin. He started with Abraham, and this is how he put it: "Men, brethren, and fathers, hearken; The God of glory appeared unto our father Abraham, when he was in Mesopotamia, before he dwelt in Charran, and said unto him, Get thee out . . ." "Said unto him"! This is the explanation of the case of Abraham. He was not a man who suddenly developed a kind of wanderlust. He did not say, "I would like to move. Why should I spend the rest of my life in the place where my fathers have always lived? I must develop a spirit of adventure." Nothing of the sort. There is only one reason why he ever came out: it was because God spoke to him and said to him, "Come out!" And so it was constantly—with Jacob and with Isaac and with Joseph, and now here again in the case of Moses.

Moses, I repeat, was a very special case. Having given the history, Stephen now brought it to a point and said in effect, "The thing that made Moses the unique man he was, the thing that makes you, as a nation, the unique people you are, is that God spoke to this man, and he spoke to you through this man." That is Stephen's whole point. "This is he," he says, "that was in the church in the wilderness with the angel which spake to him in the mount Sina, and [he was also] with our fathers: who received the lively [living] oracles to give unto us."

The apostle Paul makes exactly the same point. At the beginning of the third chapter of his epistle to the Romans, he puts this question: "What advantage then hath the Jew?" In the previous two chapters, Paul has been demonstrating that the Jews and the Gentiles are all guilty before God. He is out to show that salvation is by faith, and by faith alone; so he has to demonstrate that the Jew is as guilty as the Gentile. But then he raises a question that somebody may be asking: "What advantage then hath the Jew? or what profit is there of circumcision?" The question is: "Paul, are you not denying the whole of Jewish history? Are you saying that it is all unimportant? Is there no point at all in being a Jew?" And here is Paul's answer: "Much every way: chiefly, because that unto them were committed the oracles of God" (Rom. 3:2). The advantage that the Jews have, says Paul, is that to them, and to them alone, God has given His Word, this written Word, the Scriptures. What an advantage!

And again in the ninth chapter, when Paul comes to give an account, almost a catalog, of the advantages of the Jews, this is what he says: "For I could wish that myself were accursed from Christ for my brethren, my kinsmen according to the flesh" (v. 3).

What about them?

> *Who are Israelites; to whom pertaineth the adoption, and the glory, and the covenants, and the giving of the law, and the service of God, and the promises; whose are the fathers, and of whom as concerning the flesh Christ came, who is over all, God blessed for ever. Amen.*
>
> —*Rom. 9:4-5*

Now in those statements Paul is simply saying what Stephen was saying to the members of the Sanhedrin. Stephen said in effect, "I am talking about this Moses who received the living oracles from God and transmitted them to your fathers, and subsequently to us as a people. This is the key to the understanding of your own history, your own greatness, and your own uniqueness."

But like the apostle Paul, I can imagine a question being asked: "What on earth does all this have to do with us? When we're struggling with all our problems, don't you have anything better to put before us than some old history, some case that occurred in Jerusalem 1,900 years ago? What is the relevance, what is the point, of all this to us at this present time?"

I want to show you that this is the most important matter you could ever consider. I want to show you that this is more relevant to your position and to mine than anything else in the world at this moment. Why? Because here is the crucial factor that determines whether men and women go to heaven or hell, whether they will live lives of conquest and victory or of failure, defeat, and misery. The servant of God, Stephen, was here dealing with the fundamental, initial, crucial matter of our whole relationship to God.

Now most people who are in trouble about the Christian faith are in trouble because they start wrongly. The most important thing is to start correctly. Suppose you want to travel from London to Edinburgh. If you set off in a southwesterly direction, then no matter how great a genius you may be, you will not arrive in Edinburgh. There is nothing more important than the right start, the right approach. Of course, I have people who want to argue with me about miracles and about various other matters. But do not start there. The trouble is not over details. The real fundamental problem is over the whole approach to this question of truth, and that is where people go wrong. It is a basic initial error, and because they start wrongly, they are going to be wrong all the way through, all along the line and with regard to most of the details.

There are ultimately only two positions: we either submit to the Word of God or we do not. It is as simple as that. This is the great watershed that divides the human race. This is, in other words, the starting point of the Christian Gospel, the Christian message of salvation. Let me put this to you in the most modern terms. What is our great need today? I think we will all agree that it is the need for wisdom, the need for understanding. Look at our world—why is it as it is? Why have we had two world wars? Why are people living as they are? Why is there a mounting moral problem? Our prisons are crowded. Why? Why the strain of life? Why, with all our increased knowledge and education and culture, is there so much unhappiness? What is the matter with the world? What is the matter with humanity?

Here, surely, is the fundamental question. Many of the problems would be solved if the fundamental human problem were solved. The world is perplexed at this point. It does not know the answer; it does not understand. Men and women have a sense that there is something outside themselves, bigger and greater than they are.

> *There's a divinity that shapes our ends,*
> *Rough-hew them how we will.*
>
> *Hamlet*, Act 5, Scene 2

But no one can get further than that.

Now it is a great tragedy that in a world that is in as much trouble as our world is, in a world that is ready to listen to any theory or proposition, any newfangled idea, any new cult, and will rush after it, there is a persistent refusal to listen to God's answer. That is the point Stephen was making to the members of the Sanhedrin. They were rejecting God, the Son of God. They rejected Him in the crucifixion. They were fighting God; they were refusing His way. And the world is still doing it. That is why this message in Acts is so relevant. The world has not changed at all. Men and women today are repeating what was done by the members of the Sanhedrin and, 1,400 years before that, what was done to Moses, that great prophet of God, the great lawgiver.

It is so tragic that though the Bible is God's Word, humanity will not listen to it. The question is, why not? I answer this perfectly in terms of this ancient history. Here is this unique nation, the Jews, and they *are* a unique nation; through the Lord Jesus Christ, they became the benefactors of the whole world. He was born a Jew—"which was made of the seed of David according to the flesh" (Rom. 1:3). This is why the Jews are unique.

Look at the other nations—great nations, many of them—and yet they are not in the same class. Why not? Because they sought wisdom in other ways. I need not weary you with the list of these ways—it is still the same today. They tried witchcraft; they tried sorcery; they tried magic. They believed in animism, which means that they believed there were spirits in trees and in stones. They were polytheists and believed in a multiplicity of gods—a god in the moon, a god in the sun, a god in the stars, a god of war, a god of peace, a god of love. We are familiar with all this; you can read it in the Bible and in other places. These were their ways of trying to understand the human problem and predicament. Whenever they failed to understand, they said, "Well, let us try these other forces."

But the supreme effort, the most serious attempt that has ever been made by humanity to discover the cause of its own ills and a possible solution, was that which we know as Greek philosophy. That was the whole meaning of those great philosophers—Plato, Socrates, Aristotle, and so on. These men were grappling with the problem of life and living, the unseen. These were the questions that concerned them. But we must realize that their search was all based on human ability, human powers, human understanding and reason and logic. Having confidence in that, they set out upon this great quest, this great search. They indulged in what we call today research. The apostle Paul, when he visited Athens, reminded the people there that they were seeking for God "if haply they might feel after him" (Acts 17:27). They were really trying to find him. That was why they had erected an altar in Athens that was dedicated to "THE UNKNOWN GOD." They were trying by wisdom, human power, and capacity to arrive at the knowledge of this power that seemed to be controlling the world.

That was the way in which all the nations, apart from the Jews, had been trying to tackle the problem of life and living. That is what the world is doing at this present time. In exactly the same ways as these ancient nations, people are trusting to human understanding, human knowledge, and human wisdom. Many are trusting to what they call "the scientific method." It is a method of research and experimentation, a method of reason and of logic, but it is all based upon a fundamental confidence in innate human power and ability. People believe that they have it in themselves to encompass all truth, that they can arrive at the knowledge that is requisite for their deliverance—they only have to apply themselves to this and they will get there.

Now that is the most intelligent portion of the community. Others are turning to astrology, fortune-telling, spiritism, and all sorts of practices, but at its most intelligent level, humanity turns to the philosophers and the great people of today. It is no longer the preacher, no longer the politician even, whom they trust. The philosopher, and especially the scientist—these are the ones to be trusted, these are the ones who really know.

But what does all this lead to? That is the question we should ask every time we hear one of these so-called "great philosophers" speaking. Oh, yes, he is very clever with his words, he is very wonderful. But how is he living? What is his past history? Is he successful in his marriage? Is he faithful to his wife? Does he know how to live?

Further, ask, does he know how to die? Can he help us with what lies beyond? Those are the questions that matter, not the clever bandying of words—millions can do that. When the philosopher or scientist comes to the ultimate questions, what does he say then? You will find it is always the same—Paul has put it in one sentence: "The world by wisdom knew not God" (1 Cor. 1:21). It tried its best. The flowering period of Greek philosophy had ended before the Son of God ever came into this world. They had completely failed; those ancient nations were steeped in vice and sin and ignorance and darkness.

You need not take my word for this. You have descriptions of it in the New Testament, in the second half of Romans 1 and from Ephesians 4:17 to the end. Read your secular books; read about suicide among philosophers and the whole moral condition of the Greek and Roman world. It is a familiar story of failure and bankruptcy. And it is still the same today. Nineteen hundred years have passed since the time of Stephen, and we talk about our advances, our developments, and our gaining of knowledge, but is the world any better, is it any different essentially? No! People are falling into the same sins. The modern world is becoming increasingly like that described in the second half of Romans 1. We are reverting to that. And we are doing so because men and women are trusting their own understanding, their own power, their own knowledge and ability and research. They believe they can arrive at a knowledge of God and at a knowledge of the ultimate solution. But they cannot. They are failing as much today as they did in the first century, and as much as those other nations had failed throughout the centuries before our Lord ever came into this world.

It is inevitable that they should fail. The reason for this is elementary, and yet it is where people go so sadly astray. Men and women must of necessity fail, first, because of the greatness of God. God, by definition, is unknowable to human beings as they are because He is infinite, because He is absolute, because He is eternal, and because He is holy. Puny men and women think they can understand the everlasting and eternal God because they can split the atom, because they can send a man a certain distance into outer space. How monstrous, how ridiculous that is! If only people would stop to think before starting on their quest, they would realize that it is useless and condemned to failure. That is why the world in its own power is no nearer to the answer now than it has been throughout the centuries.

The second reason for their failure is the condition of human beings. Oh, how finite, how limited we are! How small we are! How small is our knowledge; how little we really know. We put the emphasis on what we have discovered, but what is really important is what we do not know. I can put that in a ridiculous form to you. We can cure many tremendous diseases, but we still have no cure for a cold! We boast of our great advances in knowledge, but we do not stop to consider our ignorance.

But not only is man finite, he is sinful, and how can sinful man know the holy God? The principle underlying this is one that we have discovered in human relationships. There must be something in you that is like another person if you are really to understand that person. You can be acquainted with someone, but that is not to know that person. To know someone there must be some affinity, some accord. And this is infinitely more true in our relationship to God. God is holy. But men and women are sinful; they are blind and ignorant. Not only that, they are antagonistic to God and at enmity with Him. They are "alienated and enemies" in their minds (Col. 1:21). This is why they cannot arrive at a knowledge of God and the ultimate solution to their problems.

The Greek philosophers had a great slogan; they said the secret of life was this: "Know thyself." But we never do know ourselves. We cannot. We always fool ourselves. And if we cannot know ourselves, how can we possibly know God? That is the explanation of the failure; that is why all the nations have failed. That is exactly what makes these little people called the Jews so unique. These people possessed the treasure—they had something that nobody else knew about. What was it? "The lively [living] oracles" (Acts 7:38), the oracles of God.

What does the word *oracle* mean? It means a word, a statement from God. If you are interested in ancient mythology, you will know that people used to consult the oracle at Delphi and other places. It was all wrong, of course; it was imagination, sometimes the work of the devil and his agents. But people believed that you could get a word from this wise person, the priestess of the god, the oracle of Delphi. And, says Paul, as Stephen says here, the secret of the Jews was that they had the living oracles, the oracles of God, and that is just another way of describing the Bible, the Old Testament and the New.

Let me put this as simply as I can. The factor that made the Jews the people they were was that God spoke to them, that they realized that and listened to Him. And this is the only hope for any of us. God has spoken! He has spoken about you; He has spoken about your world; He has spoken about the only way of deliverance, the only way of salvation. God has spoken! I am proclaiming to you the Word of God, not my own word.

Now this is the point at which I see people go wrong at the very beginning. They set out on a search for God, on a search for wisdom. But they never find it, and the tragedy is that they need not even have made the effort, for God has already spoken. We already have God's Word, God's revelation, as we call it. The message of the Bible is that God has taken hold of certain chosen men and has spoken to them. He has spoken to them and has given them a message, as He said to Moses on that mountain: "Go back; speak to them; tell them that I, the Lord God, have said this."

The essence of the Christian position is that God has spoken through men—through Abraham, through Joseph, through Moses, through the prophets, through John the Baptist. And above all, God has spoken in His Son. "God, who at sundry times and in divers manners spake in time past unto the fathers by the prophets, hath in these last days spoken unto us by his Son" (Heb. 1:1-2). That is it. The Son of God has come, bearing God's message to us. This is the Gospel. This is the message of the Bible.

Can we not see the difference? This is not man discovering—this is God revealing. This is not man arriving at the knowledge—this is God imparting the knowledge, transmitting it. All these men in the Bible are unanimous in saying that. Abraham reported how God had spoken to him in the land of the Chaldees; Joseph repeated what was said to him; Moses went down to the people and told them what God had said. When he went back to Egypt, he said to them in essence, "I am not a good speaker. I am nobody. So why am I here? My only reason for being here is that God has sent me to you."

You remember the story of God's call—how even when God did speak to him, Moses remonstrated and said, "When I come unto the children of Israel, and shall say unto them, The God of your fathers hath sent me unto you . . . they shall say to me, What is his name? . . . But, behold, they will not believe me, nor hearken unto my voice" (Exod. 3:13; 4:1). And God said in effect, "Tell them that I AM has spoken unto you. I AM has sent you. Say that you are a mouthpiece, that you are but a channel, a vehicle, that you do not have a brilliant idea of your own, but I have sent you."

And that is what Moses did. He said in effect, "God spoke to me at the bush, and He gave me a message, and I am here to tell you that message." And then later Moses came down from Mount Sinai, and he said, "This is what God has said to me." Moses did not invent the Ten Commandments. He would have laughed at the very suggestion. He never invented the commandments nor the moral law nor all the teaching about the construction of the tabernacle. No; he had a command: "Look that thou make them after their pattern, which was shewed thee in the mount" (Exod. 25:40).

And that is not only true of Moses. Read the prophets—they all said exactly the same thing. They said, "This is the message the Lord has given to me." They do not say, "You know, I have been doing research for years. I have been investigating the human situation. I have been looking at the problem of the children of Israel. Having considered the possibilities, I have come to this conclusion: listen to what I have found . . ." Never! "The word of the Lord came unto me." "Thus saith the Lord." They were humble, modest men; they did not claim anything for themselves. Indeed, when we read the prophecy of one of them, a man called Amos, we find that he is saying in essence, "'I was no prophet, neither was I a prophet's son.' I am a sort of cattle-drover—that is my job. I am familiar with sycamore trees and pods and things like that. I am quite good at looking after cattle. I do not belong to any school of prophets; I have had no training. I am a nobody. So why am I speaking to you? It is because God has spoken to me and has told me to speak to you; that is my only authority" (see Amos 7:14-15).

And then we come to the New Testament, and there we read, "In the fifteenth year of the reign of Tiberius Caesar . . . the word of God came unto John the son of Zacharias in the wilderness" (Luke 3:1-2). "Came" to him! It was not a result of his research or his study or some postgraduate work. No! God spoke to him. This is the essence of the message. It is revelation, not research. The apostle Paul says exactly the same thing: "A dispensation of the gospel is committed unto me" (1 Cor. 9:17). Similarly, in Ephesians 3:2 he says, "the dispensation of the grace of God which is given me." And then in his second letter to Timothy he gives perhaps the most comprehensive definition that we have: "All scripture"—*all* Scripture—"is given by inspiration of God, and is profitable for doctrine, for reproof, for correction, for instruction in righteousness: that the man of God may be perfect, thoroughly furnished unto all good works" (3:16-17).

The apostle Peter says exactly the same thing:

> *For we have not followed cunningly devised fables, when we made known unto you the power and coming of our Lord Jesus Christ, but were eyewitnesses of his majesty. For he received from God the Father honour and glory, when there came such a voice to him from the excellent glory, This is my beloved Son, in whom I am well pleased. And this voice which came from heaven we heard, when we were with him in the holy mount.*
>
> *—2 Pet. 1:16-18*

"That is why you should listen to what I am saying," said Peter in effect. "Do not listen to me—I am nobody, merely a fisherman. I am just Peter. But I heard the voice, and that is why I speak, and that is why you should listen to me. We heard this voice from heaven when we were with Him in the holy mount."

> *We have also a more sure word of prophecy; whereunto ye do well that ye take heed, as unto a light that shineth in a dark place, until the day dawn, and the day star arise in your hearts: knowing this first, that no prophecy of the scripture is of any private interpretation. (vv. 19-20)*

Peter means that no prophecy of the Scripture is the result of human ability, the result of human thought or cogitation. He continues: "For the prophecy came not in old time by the will of man: but holy men of God spake"—how?—"as they were moved"—borne along, carried along—"by the Holy Ghost" (v. 21).

That is the secret! Israel became what she was because of this fact. It is also the whole secret of Moses. God had spoken. These men had heard, and they transmitted the message, sometimes orally, sometimes in a written form. Here is our Bible; here is our message; here is our only authority.

How did God speak to these men? In many different ways. Sometimes it was by what are called theophanies—by appearing in the form of an angel. He spoke many times in that way to Abraham. And that was how He spoke to Moses in the burning bush. It was the same on Mount Sinai when God gave Moses His holy law, the Ten Commandments. Read again that nineteenth chapter of the book of Exodus—the mountain quaking with fire, the smoke and the burning, the holiness. If any man even touched the side of that mountain, he would drop dead. God descended, as it were, and spoke, and the people, not fully understanding, heard a voice.

But God's message did not always come in that dramatic form. Generally with the prophets it happened like this: suddenly the prophet was aware that God the Spirit had taken hold of him. As Peter says, "Holy men of God spake as they were moved by the Holy Ghost." They were suddenly aware of a power coming upon them, and an illumination, and God opened their minds and revealed truth to them. So they wrote it, and they were conscious of being guided in their very writing. That is why they knew that it was true, that it was infallible, that there was no error. God had taken hold of them and possessed them. What is called "the divine afflatus" had come upon them and possessed them and used them in this marvelous manner.

The inspiration of the Holy Spirit is the only explanation for the whole of the Old Testament and the New Testament. I can prove this quite simply. Look at the knowledge possessed by these men. For example, Moses wrote the first five books of the Bible. At the beginning he tells you about creation. How did he discover this? He was not a scientist; he did not have the equipment that we have at the present time. How did Moses write the account that he gives us of creation? There is only one answer, and it is the answer I have already given you. This is how it is put in Hebrews 11:3: "Through faith we understand that the worlds were framed by the word of God, so that things which are seen were not made of things which do appear." Moses did not sit down with his brilliant imagination and picture how the world came into being. He would not have ventured to do such a thing. Nor was he trying to act as a scientist. He was not capable. God revealed it. "Through faith"! That is the way Moses discovered the truth, and he has passed it on to us.

And likewise with the first five books of the Bible. Look at the knowledge Moses possessed; look at his understanding of the times; look at his wisdom; look at the brilliance, if I may use such a term, of the moral law, even from a medical standpoint. Look at the nature of the truth that it expounded, its glorious character, its purity, its holiness! Look at the life that the children of Israel were called upon to live—contrast that with the life of every other nation. Did they arrive at all this as the result of human reasoning? Of course not. God gave these commands.

And then there is the strongest proof of all—the verification of prophecy. We have already looked at Peter's words in 2 Peter 1. The fulfillment of prophecy is proof of God's speaking. Remember this: God speaks to men and women! That is why there is Christianity. That is why there is a church. It is because God has spoken. And we can prove that He has spoken by verified prophecy. Hundreds of years before the event, God told the Jews what was going to happen, and it happened, even down to the smallest detail.

Here is the great message—God has spoken. God has given "the living oracles." He gave the Ten Commandments, the moral law, to Moses on the mount. He said, "Go and tell them that this is the solution."

And he has spoken in an infinitely greater way in the Son of His love, our Lord and Savior, Jesus Christ. God's Son came into the world, and He has spoken to us. He has said everything we ever need to know. He has told us how to be right with God, how to have our sins forgiven. He has told us how we can have a new nature, a new start, a new life, become new persons. He has said it all. It is all here—everything the human race needs. If only people believed it today, the world would become Paradise.

What must we do, therefore? It is very interesting to see how perfect the Scripture is. You notice how it is put here: "This is that Moses . . . This is he, that was in the church in the wilderness with the angel which spake to him in the mount Sina, and with our fathers"—notice—"who received"—*received*—"the lively oracles to give unto us." All Moses did was to receive them. And it is my privilege to tell you that this is all that you must do: you simply have to receive God's word.

We are told that Moses said, "I exceedingly fear and quake" (Heb. 12:21).Why? Because of the manifestation of God. And this is the starting point for all of us: we must all be humbled. We will never receive until we are humbled. The Lord Jesus Christ put it like this: "Except ye be converted, and become as little children, ye shall not enter into the kingdom of heaven" (Matt. 18:3). "Little children"! If modern people—sophisticated, clever, scientific, learned—want to be delivered from the world and the flesh and the devil, if they want their lives to become successes instead of the miserable failures they are, they must become as little children. As our Lord put it to

Nicodemus, "Ye must be born again" (John 3:7). Nicodemus was asking clever questions, and that was the answer Jesus gave him.

This means we must admit that we know nothing—that we know nothing about God. Oh, we talk about God, and we express our opinions about Him. But what are they based on? Nothing. We can speculate, but that is not knowledge.

So if we want to be delivered, if we want to become the people of God, if want to become like Moses, if we want to become like all these great prophets, the saints of the centuries, this is the secret—we must become little children, admitting that we know nothing. A child does not know, and he knows he does not know—he admits it. He is ready to listen, to be guided. Give up trusting in worldly wisdom; give up boasting in science, in knowledge, in philosophy. They are all right in their realm, but when they try to deal with these questions, do not trust them. Philosophers and scientists do not know more than people knew hundreds of years ago. So give up trying to *find* truth because you will never find it. Give up trying to understand. Become as a little child. Submit yourself utterly, completely, absolutely to God.

This can all be seen clearly in the story of the man called Saul of Tarsus, who became the mighty apostle Paul. He tells us in Acts 26: "I verily thought with myself, that I ought to do many things contrary to the name of Jesus of Nazareth" (v. 9). He thought with himself! He criticized Jesus and condemned Him and was putting his tape measure over Him. That is the wrong attitude. But then Saul met the Lord on the road to Damascus, and lying helpless on his back, he looked up and said, "Lord, what wilt thou have me to do?" That is it!

Moses said, "I exceedingly fear and quake." Do you not realize the enormity of trying to understand God, of trying to pit your mind against the everlasting and eternal God? Humble yourself! Become as a little child. Look up into the face of Christ and say, "I don't know. I'm a miserable, wretched failure. I'm nothing—tell me." Listen to Him. Receive His oracle, His word, and He will tell you everything you need to know.

6

THE WORD OF GOD

This is that Moses, which said unto the children of Israel, A prophet shall the Lord your God raise up unto you of your brethren, like unto me; him shall ye hear. This is he, that was in the church in the wilderness with the angel which spake to him in the mount Sina, and with our fathers: who received the lively oracles to give unto us.

—Acts 7:37-38

Stephen had taken the Sanhedrin through the salient features of the history of Moses. He had reminded them that Moses brought the children of Israel out "after that he had shewed wonders and signs in the land of Egypt, and in the Red sea, and in the wilderness forty years" (v. 36). So there was the end, as it were, of the story of Moses, and Stephen now turned to the Sanhedrin and said, "This is that Moses, which said unto the children of Israel, A prophet shall the Lord your God raise up unto you of your brethren, like unto me." He was also, said Stephen, the same Moses "that was in the church in the wilderness with the angel which spake to him in the mount Sina, and with our fathers," and it was the same Moses "who received the lively oracles to give unto us."

This is most important because here Stephen was singling out, as it were, two main facts that made Moses the man he was. The first is that he was the great lawgiver, or at least the man through whom the law was given. Second, he was a prophet who foretold the coming of the Son of God. So, confined in this one person of Moses you have the law and the prophets. Now that is a summary of the whole of the Old Testament. That is what the Old

Testament is—"the law and the prophets." And here in this man Moses these two meet together.

But Stephen's point was this: What was it that made the Jews such a remarkable, unique people? Why did they stand out among all the nations of the world? It was not their size or their natural ability; they were a small agricultural people, an unimportant nation in many ways, and yet they stood out and were of great importance. So what made them the people they were?

And the answer is that they were unique because of these "lively [living] oracles," this word from God Himself that they had received. That is the whole secret of the amazing story of these people. And yet, as Stephen had to point out to the Sanhedrin, though they were the people of God, they were often in trouble, and that was always because they turned their backs on God or refused to listen to the word of God. The whole story of the children of Israel is that when they listened to this word, all was well with them, but when they did not, things went wrong.

The point that Stephen was anxious to establish with these members of the Sanhedrin was that in rejecting Jesus of Nazareth, the Son of God, they were rejecting the Word of God—and this is the most terrible thing that people can ever do. That is what Stephen brought home to them. The most important thing that anybody can ever do in this world is to listen to this Word.

Let me, then, put it to you in its modern form. Why is it that men and women, the vast majority of people today, are not Christians? That is the great question. Or let me put it like this: Why is the world as it is? Why is the world in trouble when here in the Bible, in the Word of God, we have all we need? Why is this? And the answer is that the world will not listen to God's Word; it dismisses it. At the present time men and women are still doing exactly as the members of the Sanhedrin were doing. And this is, I have suggested, because we go wrong at the very beginning, in our very approach to God's Word. And the cardinal error of which we are guilty is always that we do not realize the uniqueness of the Word. The Bible is the oracle of God; it is the Word of God Himself, God's revelation. And we have tried to demonstrate that the truth of this can be proved by the evidence of fulfilled prophecy. We concluded our last study by looking at what we must do, and we said that we must receive God's words. The secret of Moses is that he "received the living oracles," and you and I must also receive them.

What keeps people from doing this? What stops them from believing and receiving God's word? The first obstacle is that they do not realize that the Gospel is all a matter of revelation. But there are further things that they do not realize, and the one I want to concentrate on now is this word "lively"—"the lively oracles"—or, to give a better translation, "the living oracles." We must not forget that an oracle is a word spoken by God, and here Stephen was referring to the Word of God, the word of "the living and true God" (1 Thess. 1:9). He is saying that this Word is a living Word. I want to deal with this description of God's Word, the Bible, because it is of such vital importance, and I want to deal with it in particular as it is expounded for us in Hebrews 4:12-13:

> *The word of God is quick [that, again, means "living"], and powerful, and sharper than any two-edged sword, piercing even to the dividing asunder of soul and spirit, and of the joints and marrow, and is a discerner of the thoughts and intents of the heart. Neither is there any creature that is not manifest in his sight: but all things are naked and opened unto the eyes of him with whom we have to do.*

What a commentary upon Stephen's expression "lively oracles"!

This description of God's Word is not confined to the Epistle to the Hebrews. All the New Testament writers say the same thing. Listen to Peter:

> *Seeing ye have purified your souls in obeying the truth through the Spirit unto unfeigned love of the brethren, see that ye love one another with a pure heart fervently: being born again, not of corruptible seed, but of incorruptible, by the word of God, which liveth and abideth for ever. For all flesh is as grass, and all the glory of man as the flower of grass. The grass withereth, and the flower thereof falleth away: But the word of the Lord endureth for ever. And this is the word which by the gospel is preached unto you.*
>
> —*1 Pet. 1:22-25*

This is God speaking. It is "the word of God, which liveth and abideth for ever." It is the word of the Old Testament—the Law and the Prophets. It is the word of the Lord Jesus Christ. It is the word of the apostles. It is the word of the confessors and the martyrs and the great reformers—and, thank God, it is the word of the living God. That is what we are considering.

"Why should I listen to this?" asks someone. Let me tell you something about the general characteristics of the Word, or these words of God. We have already seen that the Bible is the Word of God. If we did not have anything else, that would be enough for us. Are you not rather tired of the words of men? Now I do not want to say a word against anybody—philosophers, politicians, or anyone else—but I am rather tired of their words. Is it not about time that the world, in its bankruptcy, its penury, its despair, its hopelessness, its failure, and its shame, began to listen to the words of God? But this is the trouble with the world today—it is not listening.

But what does Stephen mean when he says that this Word is alive? Why does he talk about "living oracles"? Why does the author of the Epistle to the Hebrews say that "the word of God is quick"—living, full of life? What does he mean? Well, what he is really saying—we must emphasize this—is that this Word is as true now as it has ever been. That is where it is eternally different from every philosophy. Philosophy is not alive. Why not? Because the philosophers are always dependent upon us, upon our abilities, upon our strength, upon our qualities and powers. Philosophies have nothing in themselves. We have to think them out; we have to write them and publish them. It is all *our* activity. All the time we are having to push these words and do something about them.

But the Word of God is altogether different—it is alive! It has life in itself. God's words come to us and speak to us. They are something apart from us. Their life is not in us and does not depend upon us. These words, I repeat, address us; they come to us; they awaken us. These are the characteristics of this great Word, the Bible, and they are all summed up in the word "alive" or "living." What a wonderful contrast this is with human words! Do you not feel, as you listen to men and as you read their words, that they are lifeless? They seem to die as they come from the speakers' lips. They have no power in them, no vigor.

There, then, is the first great contrast, but I want to stay with this first point because not only does this Word have, as its essential characteristic, that it is alive, but it is a Word that is *continually* alive—that is inherent in the word "quick" in Hebrews 4. And, again, that is where this Word of God, the Bible, is so different from all other words. We talk about "dead languages," do we not? Latin and Greek are "dead languages." But though Old Testament Hebrew is older than both Latin and Greek, it is not a dead language. This is a Word that never ages.

Again, let me contrast the teaching of the Bible with philosophy. Take the great teachings of the great philosophers of Greece who flourished before our Lord ever came into this world. We have their teachings, but they are now largely of antiquarian interest; they are dead, ancient philosophies. They are of interest only to students of the classics who try to show us that these philosophies are of contemporary relevance. But we know, as we read them, that they did not accomplish anything in their own day and generation, and they have never been able to do anything since then.

But the Word of God is in an entirely different category. It is a very old book, one of the oldest books in the world. And the amazing thing is that it is as alive today as it ever has been. "[Moses] received the living oracles," and this Word is as alive now as it was in the days of Moses. A part of this living quality that belongs to it is that it is always contemporary, it is always up-to-date.

Many people today say, "How astonishing that intelligent people still go to a place of worship on Sunday! How astonishing that any intelligent people in this enlightened, scientific age can possibly go on studying that old book! What on earth does it have to say to us in this modern era with all our teeming problems? It was all right at one time, it no doubt had something to say to its own generation, but what interest do *we* have in Moses?"

That is the very essence of the modern fallacy, and the answer is perfectly simple. This Word is not only alive and up-to-date and contemporary—it is the only word that *is* truly contemporary and up-to-date. Look at the problem of the world as it is at the present time. How do you face it? Well, first of all, you ask: What is the world? Where did it come from? Where has the cosmos come from? What are human beings? What is creation? You must face all that.

"Ah," you reply, "but science answers those questions."

Does it? Can you get unanimity among your scientists? Can you get anything beyond theories—contradictory theories at that? That is the best you will get from them. They do not *know*. You are asked to believe—if you listen to modern scientific opinion—that the world is probably the result of an accident. Two planets, some say, passed a bit too near to one another, and one knocked a bit off the other, hence the cosmos. But they do not tell us where the planets came from originally. They leave you with great questions quite unanswered.

I do not want to waste time with this, but consider the opinion of a man like Sir James Jeans. Having studied science all his life, he came to the conclusion that there must be a great mind behind the universe, and it is the mind, he said, of a great mathematician. In his view there was no other explanation. And that, of course, is the explanation of the Bible. "In the beginning God created . . ." So even when you look at it as broadly as that, the Bible has a great deal to say, and I think you will find, as the years pass, that the theories that have been so popular will disappear like their predecessors, and you will have to come back to the Bible in regard to the whole question of origins.

But come to a second more urgent and contemporary practical question: Whatever its origin, why is the world as it is? Why the trouble? Why the wars? Why the confusion? Why the unhappiness? Why the moral problems? These are the questions that concern the politicians and civil servants—juvenile delinquency, drugs, all that we read of in our papers and hear on the news so constantly that we almost despair. The great question is: What is the cause? And I suggest to you that the only modern answer is the answer that is given here in the Bible, and nowhere else. It is in the Old Testament—in the Law and the Prophets. "There is no peace, saith my God, to the wicked" (Isa. 57:21).

It does not matter how wealthy you are, says the Bible; it does not matter how sophisticated or how highly developed intellectually, politically, or in any other respect—if you are in the wrong relationship to God, you are not at peace. Our era towers over all others in knowledge and discovery and understanding, in wealth and in communication, but look at it! "The way of transgressors is hard" (Prov. 13:15). If you disobey the law of God given to Moses, the Ten Commandments, you will pay for it, you will suffer for it. It does not matter who you are, here is the only answer. This message is as contemporary today as it has ever been, and it is the only message that holds out any hope or way of salvation.

Do the politicians or the philosophers or any of our wise men have the answer? We know they do not; they are completely bankrupt. We are doing the wisest thing we can do when we listen to the word of the living God, this word that is alive. It speaks to the contemporary situation, to the modern man and woman, in a way that nothing else can.

But we can go further and say that this word will *always* be alive. It is the *everlasting* Gospel. Peter speaks of "the word of God, which liveth and abideth for ever" (1 Pet. 1:23). It has life in it—the life of God—and therefore it is eternal. It will never end, and it will never fail. Now you cannot say that about anything else; you cannot say that about human words. I am old enough to have seen how the words of men die. I remember a great orator in the First World War; people remember almost nothing today of what he said. They are already forgetting the words of Sir Winston Churchill—his words will soon be forgotten altogether. Twenty years or so ago we thought, "These words are indestructible, they will always last." But they will not. The words of men begin to die the moment they are uttered. Soon they cease to speak to us.

And have you not noticed that human words depend so much upon us? There are words that speak to us when we are children, but we ridicule them when we become adolescents, they say nothing to us when we are middle-aged, and they are useless when we are old and dying. Some words speak to us when we are healthy, others when we are ill. Some speak to us when everything is going well, but they do not speak to us when things go wrong and against us. There is only one word that goes on speaking and speaks always, whatever my state, whatever my condition, whatever my circumstances.

It woke our wondering childhood
To muse on things above;
It drew our harder manhood
With cords of mighty love.

Here is the only word that speaks in life and speaks in death. Wherever I am, whatever my condition and circumstances, here is a word that goes on speaking. It is a living word; it has the power of God, the life of God, as it were, in it.

Now that is the first aspect of this word "living," but it introduces the second, which is the element of power that I have just mentioned, and this is a most remarkable feature of this word. Because it is the Word of God, it is a word that does things, a word that produces effects. The Bible is always emphasizing this aspect of God's Word. It says: "He spake, and it was done" (Ps. 33:9). Or listen to Jeremiah: "Is not my word like as a fire? saith the LORD; and like a hammer that breaketh the rocks in pieces?" (Jer. 23:29). Here is a word with power. It is like a fire. It is like a hammer; it can break rocks. No human word can do that. Or take another passage: "The heathen raged, the kingdoms were moved: he uttered his voice, the earth melted" (Ps. 46:6). His voice, His word! When He speaks, the earth melts before Him. What a word!

This is why we should be listening to this word; it is because of this power. Look at it in a more general sense. I have already referred to creation. It is by God's word that everything has come into being. "In the beginning God created . . ." How did he create? We are told that he said, "Let there be light," and then there was light (Gen. 1:3). That is the power of the word of God.

And that is the kind of word that is in the Scriptures. Human words cannot do things like this. The word of God has produced the entire cosmos, and that cosmos is also upheld by the word of His power (Heb. 1:3). This is the same power that can punish the world. What happened at the Flood? God spoke; God commanded; God told the heavens to open, to send rain down, and it came down. This word! The power of God.

You find the same power in connection with the giving of the law.

Stephen was talking to the Sanhedrin about Moses up on the mount receiving "the lively oracles" from God, and in the nineteenth chapter of the book of Exodus we are given a description of that event: God spoke the law, and the mountain quaked; the smoke appeared, and there was thick darkness. The power of God was in the word of God as He was giving the law.

We have already heard about this power in Stephen's address. A man was living in Ur of the Chaldees, doing what his forefathers had always done before him, and God suddenly appeared to him and said, "Get thee out," and he went out. The word came to Joseph as well, and then later the same word came to Moses at the bush, speaking in the flame of fire. Moses felt the power, the command, and had to act. This is the characteristic of this word everywhere. It is a word that enables men to work miracles. You find this in the Old Testament. This is how it happens: when God gives a man His word, He gives him power. Here are the children of Israel, led by Moses, but they have no water. What happens? God says to Moses, "Speak ye unto the rock before their eyes; and it shall give forth his water" (Num. 20:8). Moses speaks, and the water comes out. This is the word of God. It is a powerful word; it is a mighty word. It is the word that enabled Elijah to work similar miracles, the word that can take a feeble man and so fill him with power that his word becomes a command.

But, of course, if you really want to see all this, you must look at the blessed Lord Himself as you find Him in the pages of the four Gospels. Have you ever followed Him, as it were? Have you joined the crowd and stood among them and listened to Him? Listen to the people after He has spoken—they are astonished. Matthew says, "For he taught them as one having authority, and not as the scribes" (Matt. 7:29). The officers sent to arrest Him said, "Never man spake like this man" (John 7:46). Have you felt the power in His words? Have you noticed the difference between His manner of speech, His word, and that of all teachers who have gone before or after Him? There is nothing tentative; there is no mere suggestion; He does not just put points of view to us. He speaks, and He speaks with authority!

Then have you noticed the word of command in His miracles? He works His miracles by speaking. There He is one day, very tired. Jesus and the disciples are crossing the sea, and He has gone to the rear of the boat. He is lying down and has fallen asleep. But a great storm arises, and the poor apostles are troubled and in despair. The billows are rolling, and the wind is howling, and they are afraid they are going to drown at any moment. So they awaken Him. "Master, carest thou not that we perish?" Then Mark says, "And he arose, and rebuked the wind, and said unto the sea, Peace, be still. And the wind ceased, and there was a great calm" (Mark 4:38-39).

Our Lord can command the lame to walk. He said to a man whose arm was withered, hanging helpless at his side, "Stretch forth thine hand." And the man stretched out his hand (Mark 3:1-5). The word put power into a paralyzed arm. But consider the most striking example of all: He had a great friend called Lazarus. Lazarus died, and our Lord eventually arrived when Lazarus had been in the tomb for four days. The two sisters were weeping and wailing, breaking their hearts, but He went to them, and there He stood, looking at the tomb. Then, writes John, "He cried with a loud voice, Lazarus, come forth. And he that was dead came forth" (John 11:43-44). Human beings cannot do things like this. This is God's word that we are considering.

But God's word was not confined to our blessed Lord—He was able to give it to the apostles. Look at Peter and John, going up to the temple one afternoon at the hour of prayer and confronted by the man born lame who sat every day on the pavement outside the Beautiful Gate of the temple. Nobody could do anything for him. Peter and John fastened their eyes upon him, and Peter said, "Silver and gold have I none; but such as I have, give I thee: In the name of Jesus Christ of Nazareth rise up and walk" (Acts 3:6), and he did so immediately. That is the great record that we have in this book, and Stephen and the others were on trial because of these very miracles.

But look at the power of God's word in the preaching. Look at the words of these men. Look at a man like Peter, a fisherman, a man who is described in Acts as "unlearned and ignorant" (Acts 4:13), yet who stood up in Jerusalem on the Day of Pentecost and expounded the Scriptures. You can read his words for yourself in the second chapter of Acts. You may say, "Is there anything remarkable about this?" Well, this is what I know—after Peter had been preaching for a while, those listening were "pricked in their heart" and began to shout out saying, "Men and brethren, what shall we do?" (Acts 2:37). That is the power of the word of God!

Likewise, the apostle Paul says to the Corinthians, "And I, brethren, when I came to you . . . I was with you in weakness, and in fear, and in much trembling. And my speech and my preaching was not with enticing words of man's wisdom, but in demonstration of the Spirit and of power"—why?—"that your faith should not stand in the wisdom of men, but in the power of God" (1 Cor. 2:1-5). Here is a word that can turn the world upside down and has changed the whole course of history. You cannot understand history apart from it.

But to come to the most vital and urgent matter of all for us, consider the power of this word when it deals with us from the standpoint of salvation. Look again at what we are told: "The word of God is quick, and powerful, and sharper than any two-edged sword, piercing even to the dividing asunder of soul and spirit, and of the joints and marrow, and is a discerner of the thoughts and intents of the heart" (Heb. 4:12).

It is a convicting word, a deep word, a penetrating word. Oh, the contrast this presents to the word of men! How superficial the latter are, how superficial the words of the politicians and the philosophers.

"Ah, but the psychologists," you may say, "have deep analysis."

But when you put their analysis by the side of this word, the psychologists' words are merely like ripples on the surface. Here is the only word—God's word—that can really convict and penetrate. Notice the terms used: "two-edged sword"—not merely one edge but two edges; it cuts twice, it cuts thoroughly. And it is "sharper." That means that God's Word is incisive; it is penetrating. It has a quality that enables it to lay bare all self-delusions, all sophistries, all pretenses and excuses. It is "piercing even to the dividing asunder of the soul and spirit, and of the joints and marrow." It gets down to every part and portion of life.

Nothing else does that. Some teachings affect you in one part of your experience, others in another, but here is a word that deals with every single part. It analyzes, it dissects, it opens our "soul and spirit . . . joints and marrow." There is nothing about us that it does not know. Moreover, we are told here that it is "a discerner of the thoughts and intents of the heart." The word "discerner" means that it has a judging quality, a discriminating quality. Like a judge on the bench, it can sift and analyze the evidence. The advocate puts his case very plausibly. He does not reveal certain facts; he brings others out and exaggerates them. Ah, but the judge sitting on the bench can discriminate, he can analyze; he puts the relative and due proportion to every statement that is made. That is the meaning of the word "discerner." And the Word does this with the very thoughts and intents of our hearts—our reflections, our imaginations, our ideas, our conceptions—and it does this at the depth of our being, in that which is called "the heart." And then, to sum it up, the writer says, "Neither is there any creature that is not manifest in his sight: but all things are naked and opened unto the eyes of him with whom we have to do" (Heb. 4:13).

What all this means is that here is the only word in the world that exposes the real problem of the human race. Nothing else does. You are familiar with all the other explanations. Some people say that what we lack is knowledge, education, or culture. Others say what we really need is more money, better living conditions, or better food. They all have their little remedies, but not one of them really faces the essential problem of the world and the human race. Here is the only word, I repeat, that penetrates right down to the depths and exposes them and reveals them. And it tells us that the problem of the world is that men and women are disobedient to God, not listening to the living oracles, but rather rebelling, raising themselves up against Him. That is the only answer.

So here, also, is the only word that tells us the full truth about ourselves. Politicians never do—they want our votes! The philosophers never tell us—they want us to believe that there is no such thing as sin, no such thing as evil, that these are merely negative qualities or the absence of qualities. None of them tells us that sin is active, that it is a power. They hate this truth and speak against it. Only in God's Word do we find the full truth about ourselves. We all like to have a good view of ourselves, but here is a word that tells me that I am so hopeless that nothing but a new birth can ever put me right. I cannot be improved. I must be made anew; I must be born again. I need a new heart, a new spirit within me. God's Word alone really gets down to the truth of who I am: here it is with its analysis, its discrimination, its penetrating quality, and here I am exposed—I am rotten. And here is a word that always exposes my attempts at hypocrisy and at rationalizing and all my attempts at pretense and show.

Do you not see this in the life of our blessed Lord Himself? Why did the Pharisees so hate Him? Why were they so malicious? Why were they so bitter? Why were they against Him? Why did they resent Him? There is only one answer: He exposed their hypocrisy. He spoke about the depths. They were the teachers; they were better than other people, they thought; they could hide, and they could manipulate. They said, "As long as you do not actually commit adultery, you are not guilty of adultery." But they committed adultery in their hearts. Jesus exposed the heart; He exposed the thoughts. He said, "From within, out of the heart of men, proceed evil thoughts, adulteries, fornications, murders" (Mark 7:21). It is not that which goes in, it is that which comes out that defiles you. "Your hearts are dark," He said. That is the cause of the trouble. And so they hated Him. They needed to be saved as much as the publican and sinner, but they would not have it.

Take the account in John 8 of our Lord and the woman caught in adultery. She was brought to Jesus by her accusers, but He stooped down and wrote on the sand, and they all slinked away. This is because this word of His is always quick and powerful, analytical, discerning, penetrating, leaving everything exposed, nothing hidden. And this is a word that confronts us with the two destinies that face us all. Here is a word that confronts us with a choice that we must make. Moses did that, did he not? He was given this living word on Mount Sinai, and he preached it to the people. And before he left them at the end of his life, when he knew he was going, he called the people together and said to them, "See, I have set before thee this day life and good, and death and evil" (Deut. 30:15).

That is what this word does, and it is the only word that does so. The word of men can address you on other things: Will interest rates go up or down? Should we have a certain type of education or not? Ah, they can speak to you about these things, and, of course, these things are important, temporarily. But not one of them—including the words of philosophers and poets—presents us with the ultimate question. It is God or man. It is "life and good" or it is "death and evil." It is Mount Ebal or Mount Gerizim. It is this way or that way. Your house is either on the rock or it is on the sand. There are only two ways—the narrow way or the broad way.

So here and here alone we are brought face to face with fundamental issues and the ultimate destiny of life. The fourth chapter of Hebrews refers to Joshua, who, when he came to die, put the same choice to the people. "Choose you this day," he said, "whom ye will serve" (Josh. 24:15). And that is why you and I should listen to this word, that is why Stephen pled with the Sanhedrin, and that is why the author of the Epistle to the Hebrews pled with his Hebrew Christian readers. Our eternal destiny is dependent upon our reaction to this word. That is the whole argument of the author of Hebrews. He says, "Think of your forefathers—they heard the word, but they died in the wilderness. They never entered the land of Canaan." Why not? "The word preached," he says, "did not profit them, not being mixed with faith in them that heard it" (Heb. 4:2).

But, lastly, this is the only word that is able to give us salvation. "I am not ashamed of the gospel of Christ," said Paul. Why? "For it is the power of God unto salvation to every one that believeth" (Rom. 1:16). This is a word that shows us what we are in all our ugliness and foulness and helplessness. But thank God, it does not leave us there. The Moses who received the law that condemns us was able to prophesy of the coming of the Savior, the deliverer. Here is the great message, and the writer of Hebrews leads up to it in chapter 4: "Seeing then that we have a great high priest, that is passed into the heavens, Jesus the Son of God, let us hold fast our profession" (v. 14). He is our glorious, mighty Savior. "There remaineth therefore a rest to the people of God" (Heb. 4:9).

Here is the only word in the world that can speak to us when we know we are lost, when we are condemned, when we are failures, when sin gets us down, when we are afraid of death, afraid of the Judgment, and afraid of eternity. Here is the only word that can speak to us comfort and peace and give us hope. What does it speak? It speaks a message of forgiveness. Here is a word that in the mouth of the Lord Himself could turn to the vilest kind of sinner and say, "Thy sins be forgiven thee" (Mark 2:9), and to the woman caught in the act of adultery, "Where are those thine accusers? . . . go, and sin no more" (John 8:10-11). It is a word of authority that assures us of forgiveness.

Men and women cried out to Peter on the Day of Pentecost, "Men and brethren, what shall we do?" Back comes the answer: "Repent, and be baptized every one of you in the name of Jesus Christ for the remission of sins, and ye shall receive the gift of the Holy Ghost" (Acts 2:37-38). Or as Paul later said, "Believe on the Lord Jesus Christ, and thou shalt be saved, and thy house" (Acts 16:31). Here is an answer, a powerful answer. It is not man suggesting that because God is love He is likely to forgive me; it is the Son of God saying, "I will forgive you, for I have died for your sins; I have borne your punishment. I have given My soul as an offering for your sins: believe on Me—come to Me."

But this word not only tells us of forgiveness— it tells us that we can have a new start, a new life; we can be "born again." Our Lord can bring into being something that was not there. He can give us a new start. He will fill us with His own power, and He will be with us and lead us all on the journey until we are safely in the glory. "Being born again, not of corruptible seed, but of incorruptible, by the word of God, which liveth and abideth for ever" (1 Pet. 1:23). It is a word that enables us to "come boldly unto the throne of grace, that we may obtain mercy, and find grace to help in time of need" (Heb. 4:16), and it is a word that opens out to us the prospect of glory in the presence of God and the holy angels. It promises "an inheritance, incorruptible, and undefiled, and that fadeth not away, reserved in heaven" (1 Pet. 1:4) for those who believe this Gospel.

But I also want to remind you of this: "Neither is there any creature that is not manifest in his sight: but all things are naked and opened unto the eyes of him with whom we have to do" (Heb. 4:13). There will be a final reckoning. There is one with whom we all have to do—the living God. "It is appointed unto men once to die, but after this the judgment" (Heb. 9:27). Do you know on what terms you will be judged? Listen to our Lord:

> *I am come a light into the world, that whosoever believeth on me should not abide in darkness. And if any man hear my words, and believe not, I judge him not; for I came not to judge the world, but*

to save the world. He that rejecteth me, and receiveth not my words, hath one that judgeth him: the word that I have spoken, the same shall judge him in the last day.

—John 12:46-48

I have to die, you have to die, and we all have to stand before God in the Judgment. He will remind us that He made human beings in His own image, that He made them perfect, that He has given us His law, that He has shown us the way of salvation, that He has even sent His Son into the world. Jesus Christ is the Word of God, He has come, and He has done everything that is necessary. We have heard the word, and if we arrive at that bar of eternal judgment and are lost, we will have no excuse at all to give.

The loving God has spoken to us. He has done everything; there is nothing more that He could do. Have you heard this living word? Do you know that your sins are forgiven? Do you feel there is new life in you? Are you aware that you have become a child of God? Are you beginning to look forward to the eternity that awaits you and all the people of God?

7

THE MESSAGE OF GOD

> *This is that Moses, which said unto the children of Israel, A prophet shall the Lord your God raise up unto you of your brethren, like unto me; him shall ye hear. This is he, that was in the church in the wilderness with the angel which spake to him in the mount Sina, and with our fathers: who received the lively oracles to give unto us.*
>
> —Acts 7:37-38

Stephen had been saying to the Sanhedrin that the key to understanding Moses and their own nation was to realize that they were unique because they had received the word of God, "the lively oracles." Furthermore, he was showing them that they were rejecting this self-same word. Humanity, in rejecting Christ today, is repeating the old error of the Sanhedrin. It is still true to say that what makes the difference to individuals or to nations is their relationship to this word. This is as true now as it has been throughout the centuries. What differentiates Christians from all others is that they have received this word and submitted themselves to it, while others have rejected it. What a tragedy the latter choice is!

Let me put this to you in another way. Would you like to live in this world as Moses did, or as Abraham had done before him, or as Joseph had done, or any of these great heroes and giants of the faith? What men they were! They were in this same old world that you and I are living in; they were subjected to the same stresses and trials. Do not let us be foolish enough to think that because they did not have jet airplanes there were no stresses. Of course there were. Life has always been difficult and trying, life has always been a fight, and these men were of like passions with ourselves; they had the same frailties, the same weaknesses—the world, the flesh, and the devil were there against them. And yet they stand out as giants, heroes, men who laughed at life and went through it and out of it triumphantly and gloriously. Do you want to be like that? Would you like to live as they lived? Would you like deliverance from your problems and from the things that get you down? Well, there is only one answer to that. You have to accept and submit to the word of God.

That is why we are examining this question: it is the key to the whole of Christianity. Christianity is God's word to human beings; it is God's revelation, the living, searching word of God. The whole of the Bible is the living oracles of God; it is the living Word of God—the whole of it. That is the fundamental truth. Moses "received" the living oracles. He did not go up onto the mountain to do research work or to spend time thinking with a towel around his head in order to work out a philosophy.

We have seen that God's Word searches us. It is "the dividing asunder of soul and spirit, and of the joints and marrow, and is a discerner of the thoughts and intents of the heart" (Heb. 4:12). We have also seen that it is a powerful word, a mighty word, the word of miracles. It is a word that confronts us with the only two great eternal possibilities: you are either for God or you are against him. That is the only distinction that matters in the world today.

But what is the message of this word? We have looked at the general characteristics, but what does it actually say to us? Stephen says that Moses, when he was up on the mount, "received the lively [living] oracles to give unto us." Stephen, of course, was particularly concerned about the law that God gave to Moses on the mount, but I believe that the phrase "lively oracles" includes everything that was given to Moses that enabled him to write the first five books of the Bible, the "books of Moses"—not only the Ten Commandments, but the whole revelation that was given to Moses.

Now the revelation on Mount Sinai was only one incident in the giving of this word of God. The prophets had the same word given to them. In a sense, they were nothing but expositors of the law that was given to Moses. They worked it out and applied it to their own time and generation, but it was all the same eternal word of God. We read that the word of God came to so-and-so, and later that it "came" to John the Baptist in the wilderness (Luke 3:2), and it came to the Son of God Himself, who said, "For I have not spoken of myself; but the Father which sent me, he gave me a commandment, what I should say, and what I should speak" (John 12:49).

Are the apostles just giving us the result of their own meditations and thoughts and reasoning? Not at all. It is revelation! "A dispensation of the gospel is committed unto me," says Paul (1 Cor. 9:17). "We preach not ourselves, but Christ Jesus the Lord" (2 Cor. 4:5). The given word! Paul says in essence, "We are nothing but heralds, guardians, custodians of the faith, stewards of this mysterious word of God."

So the whole Bible is the Word of God. We divide it into Old Testament and New, and there are many people, I find, and even some Christians, who are rather surprised that we still use the Old Testament. Indeed, there may be some who are surprised that I am repeating these words of Stephen, a man who died in the first century. But if you say that, you have missed the whole point. This Word is eternal. The word of God to Abraham is as applicable to us today as it was to Abraham. It is always the same word; it does not change. So you must take the whole Bible.

Is there any relationship between the Old and the New Testaments? There is, of course, because it is all the Word of God. The way to look at it is this: the Old Testament is a book that prophesies and prepares for and leads to the New Testament. They are different and yet the same. So the word that was given to Moses—and this is the whole point made by Stephen—was a word that was pointing to this Jesus whom the members of the Sanhedrin rejected. So Stephen was covering the whole of the Old Testament, and rightly so.

I want, then, to show you the message of the Old and New Testaments. What is this message of which you and I and all humanity stand in need? What is this word of God? What does it have to say to us? Here we are in our troubled modern world—we know all about that—and we need to listen to something that is unique and exceptional—the word of God. What is its content? Moses received it, delivered it, and passed it on to us. What is it about? Let me give you a summary. As a reminder, read again the Ten Commandments as they are recorded in the twentieth chapter of the book of Exodus. That is just a summary of this great word of God. What is it that men and women need to know? The vast majority of the people in this country do not ask the questions I am raising.

In various ways, we are all in trouble; we are unhappy in certain respects; we are aware of failure, weakness, shame, fear. We do not like the thought of death and wonder what happens beyond it. People do not listen to this word unless, somehow or another, they are conscious of some need.

Do we need to hear a political word? We certainly do not! We hear plenty of political speeches, and they do not solve our problems. Do we want a psychological word? Well, there has been any amount of that, but that is not the answer either, is it? All the other words that the world is offering do not help us either. Why not? Because they all make a fatal mistake: they start at the wrong point. They all start with us, as if we mattered first and foremost. And then they offer us some panacea, but it does not help us, it does not satisfy us. So they start in the wrong way.

So what is this word of God? What is the content? What is the message? Well, it starts with God! We cannot repeat this too frequently. The thing that differentiated the children of Israel from all the other nations was that they were the people of God, that God had spoken to them. He had not spoken to the other nations, but He had spoken to them. He had created them as a nation in order that He might speak to them, that He might give to them these living oracles. That is the point made by Paul at the beginning of the third chapter of his epistle to the Romans and at the beginning of the ninth chapter of the same epistle.

The other nations had what they called their gods. They made their idols out of wood or gold or silver or precious metals; they carved their gods. They built temples for them, and then they worshiped them. They had other gods, too—the sun, the moon, stars. Some people were spiritists, animists, believing in spirits in trees and stones and other natural objects.

That was the characteristic of the other nations, but their gods, as the Old Testament particularly points out, were dead—that was the whole difficulty with them. Look at the sublime sarcasm of some of the psalms. The psalmist asks the pagans to look at their gods, and he asks the children of Israel to look at the gods that they in their folly were turning to, having turned their backs upon the God of Israel. Look at your gods, says the psalmist: "They have mouths, but they speak not: eyes have they, but they see not: they have ears, but they hear not: noses have they, but they smell not: They have hands, but they handle not: feet have they, but they walk not" (Ps. 115:5-7). They are dead; there is nothing there. And Isaiah adds in essence, "You have made them. and they cannot even move themselves—you have to move them. Those are your gods, and you are mad enough to be worshiping dumb, dead, lifeless idols" (Isa. 46:6-7). But the children of Israel presented an amazing contrast.

Consider the world apart from God at its best and highest. Take the great Greek philosophers. Ah, they were learned men. They were seeking God. They were aware of the problem of life, and they had a feeling that there was someone beyond it all, but they could not find him—in Athens they had an altar with the inscription TO THE UNKNOWN GOD (Acts 17:23). They had nothing but their thoughts. They were brilliant thinkers—there is no need to detract from the greatness of the Greek philosophers in order to preach Christ. We only do that when people put their faith in Greek philosophy rather than in Christ, and then we show them what fools they are. Greek philosophy at its best is only human endeavor. Greek gods were dead and lifeless.

But the children of Israel knew about a living God, the God who had created the whole universe, the God of history, the God who acts, the God who intervenes in individual lives and in the lives of nations—not a dumb idol, not something inanimate, but the living God! Let me put this in one great picture—the story of a mountain called Carmel, where there was a great competition, a great contest. There was the representative of God, a prophet called Elijah, and opposing him were 850 false prophets—400 belonging to one section, 450 to another—850 against one man. They claimed that their gods were the real gods, and they had persuaded the foolish children of Israel to go after those gods and forsake the God of Israel.

But the great testing moment came. Who was right? Elijah, the servant of the living God, said they could easily test this. He said in effect, "Let us go onto this mountain. You build an altar, and I'll build an altar; then you kill an ox, and I'll kill an ox, and you cut yours into pieces, and I will cut up mine. Then we will get wood and sticks and so on, and you will pile them up together to make a fire, and I'll do the same; then we'll put the pieces of each ox on top of the wood. This will be the test: you pray to your gods to send down fire from heaven to consume your offering, and I will do the same for my offering. The God who answers by fire, let Him be accepted as the true God."

And they did that. The 850 had the first chance; Elijah gave them that opportunity. So they put everything in position and began to pray. But nothing happened. There they were, about midday, and Elijah came and laughed at them and said, "What's the matter? Why haven't your gods heard you?" Then he said in effect, with delightful sarcasm, "Perhaps he's asleep—you're not shouting loudly enough. Perhaps he's gone on a journey; perhaps he can't hear you. Look here, shout a little more. He must be there. Why doesn't he answer you?"

So they screeched and shouted and cut themselves with knives and lancets. But nothing happened. Why? Because there was nothing there! Just dead gods, idols, vacuity, emptiness.

And then Elijah turned to his altar and said, "Fill our barrels with water, and pour it on the burnt sacrifice and on the wood." They poured on so much that there was a kind of trench of water around the altar. And then quietly Elijah prayed to God, and said, "LORD God of Abraham, Isaac, and of Israel, let it be known this day that thou art God in Israel . . . hear me, O LORD, hear me." And God did hear him, and the fire fell and consumed the offering and licked up the water that was in the trench. "The God that answereth by fire, let him be God," Elijah had said, and God honored His servant. He manifested Himself (1 Kings 18:19-39)

We must start with God as we learn about Him in the Old Testament, this God who made a nation out of one man, who delivered His people from their enemies, the God of miracles. This is sheer, solid history. We cannot explain this except by one supposition: He is the living God, a God who can hear and answer prayer, a God who can do things for us, a God who can change our lives and give us a new nature and make new men or women of us and give us new strength and power.

But because He is the living God, He is also the only God, and He emphasizes that in the Ten Commandments. He says in essence, "Do not make any other gods. Do not bow down to any other gods. Do not put Me in the same category as your lies."

And this is what the modern world needs to know. The modern world is full of idolatry. People are worshiping false gods even today. They do not necessarily make them of wood and precious metals. But people worship themselves, they worship human ability, they worship the astronauts we send into outer space. They worship science, as if science were a god, as if it were a living being with understanding!

It is man who is being worshiped—man's thoughts projected and systematized. People ridicule the worship of God, just as those people in Elijah's time did under the influence of the 850 false prophets. The world today is worshiping false gods. But at the time of crisis and need, their gods are silent, and they cannot help them. That is why the world is crumbling visibly before us, morally and in every other respect. The gods of the modern man are useless, and they fail us just when we need them most of all. We must bow before the only God—the only true and living God!

And what of God's character? He is a holy God. He has said, "Be ye holy; for I am holy" (1 Pet. 1:16). "God is light, and in him is no darkness at all" (1 John 1:5). Oh, what a contrast with the gods of men! What a contrast with man himself! A God of righteousness, a God of justice, a God of truth, a God of holiness. We cannot understand God; we cannot define Him; all we know is that He has revealed these certain attributes of His, these truths about Himself. God is glorious, He is beyond description, but this is what He has been pleased to reveal to us concerning Himself.

God is the eternal opposite of what you and I know so well in this world. What do we know? We know selfishness and self-interest; we know lying, not truth; pretense and sham, not eternal rightness. We know ugliness instead of ineffable beauty and brightness and holiness. What do we know? Lust, passion, desire. These are inconceivable in the God who cannot lie, the God who is "of purer eyes than to behold evil, and canst not look on iniquity" (Hab. 1:13). What the world needs to know above everything else is that God *is* and that He is holy and that He is over this world. He has made it, He has brought it into being, He owns it, and He sustains it in His hand.

The other thing God has revealed about Himself is that He demands worship from us. "Thou shalt have no other gods before me. Thou shalt not make unto thee any graven image" (Exod. 20:3-4). This is what God is saying to the modern world, the world that is worshiping education and culture, philosophy and science and knowledge, and all our marvelous advances. He is saying to such a world, "You must not bow down to these things. These are the false gods that will destroy you and wreck your whole civilization. You must worship Me, and Me alone. 'I am the LORD: that is my name: and my glory will I not give to another'" (Isa. 42:8).

I am explaining to you why the world is as it is. God says, "I the LORD thy God am a jealous God" (Exod. 20:5). It makes no difference whether or not you and I believe these things—God *is*, and He will not suffer us to put any gods by His side. He will crush them! If you put a god beside God, He will smash it, as He smashed Dagon of old. And that is what He is doing in this modern world. Look at the foolish twentieth century. We made ourselves new gods. It began in the Victorian era with German philosophy masquerading in the form of what was called "higher criticism" of the Scripture: God being put on one side, revelation being thrown aside, and in its place, human understanding, the worship of scholarship, belief in man's capacity to make a new world.

Shame on our grandfathers who began worshiping politicians. Before the First World War politicians would address Christian assemblies as if they could show us the way! Since then we have read biographies and autobiographies of some of them, and we have seen that they were "gods" with feet of clay—indeed, they were never gods at all. But in our folly we worshiped these people and believed this was the way to bring in the New Jerusalem. Rubbish! Nonsense!

And we can see how God has ridiculed such folly. In two world wars he smashed our gods before our eyes and made them look ridiculous. He is still doing it, and as long as humanity in its folly goes on making its gods and bowing down to them, He will smash them. Do what you like with your civilization, organize it to perfection, it will never work. It cannot. God will not tolerate it. He is a jealous God, and a man or a nation or a world that bows down to any other god will be humbled, punished, ridiculed. He is the eternal Judge, and He has made it perfectly clear that He is "a jealous God, visiting the iniquity of the fathers upon the children unto the third and fourth generation of them that hate him" (Exod. 20:5). If you have any insight into the force and meaning of history, you will see that this has been happening through the centuries.

It is terrible to try to defy this living God; if you do, you will suffer for it. Nations have suffered for this, as have individuals. This is what God said in those "lively [living] oracles" that He gave to Moses to deliver to the children of Israel. This is the essence of His law—it is about God Himself.

But it does not stop with God. He also tells us about human beings, and it is astonishing to see how much we need to be told about ourselves. This is where modern men and women show their unutterable folly. They are like the members of the Sanhedrin—they do not understand man. These Jewish leaders were glorying in Abraham, Joseph, and Moses, the temple, the prophets, the word of God. They said, "We have the law!" They were glorying in the fact that they alone had the law, but the whole time they had misunderstood it completely.

And that is what modern men and women are doing with regard to themselves. They put themselves on a pedestal and worship themselves. Modern men and women are worshiping man! But the whole tragedy is that they do not even know what man is. They do not know the nature of man. And they will never know that until they accept God's word. This is the only word that tells us the truth about man as well as about God. Many theories convey the modern ideas of man, and the proponents of these theories often disagree tremendously among themselves. There is the purely biological view—we need not waste time with that. Those who put forward this view say that man is just the result of his ductless glands, and they actually say—I am not inventing this—that you can easily explain Shakespeare, Beethoven, and Napoleon entirely in such terms!

Then there is the view of man as an economic unit. Man is just the result of the interplay of economic forces, the result of supply and demand—the whole of history and everything else is explained in that way, we are told. I read a book by a man who tried to explain Puritanism in those terms!

And there are various other views of man, but they are all wrong. Is man just an animal? This is the great question, is it not? This is what will decide so many other things. Is man simply an animal? Of course, an animal that is more highly developed than the others. We have not yet arrived at perfection, but we are moving forward from where we are to something even better. Is man really nothing but a body? He has a brain, of course, as part of his body, and it is highly developed, especially the cerebrum, and therefore he is able to do things that certain other animals cannot; but essentially he is an animal. That is what some claim.

So here is a most vital question. Are you concerned about your failures? Are you troubled by the modern-day turning to drugs and all the multiplying problems in every realm of life? The question is: Why do people do that? Why all the wars? Now the first way to answer these questions is not to sign a resolution to end all bombings or all war, as if this is the message of Christianity, as if this is the word of God! No! We have the only solution because we have the only understanding of the problem, and it is an understanding of the nature of man.

What, then, is the nature of man? The Word of God reveals that man is not just an animal but a creature made in the image and likeness of God. Man is the lord of creation, not a part of it, not just the most highly developed section of it. He is distinct; he is unique; he is God's representative, given the great privilege of naming the animals. That is man—he has something of God about him, a dignity, a greatness. He has a mind, he has understanding, he has a soul and a spirit, he is meant for communion with God, the eternal, the unseen, the spiritual, and the everlasting—that is man! That is how he was made; that is how he was meant to be. God looked upon His creation of man and saw that it was good.

If only the whole world knew that! If only the whole world believed it! What a transformation, what a difference it would make! Why are people living as they do? It is because they hold the view of themselves that they do. If I am just an animal, then I should behave like an animal. If people think we are all animals in the farmyard, it is not surprising if they behave like animals in the farmyard, and it is not surprising that we have widespread infidelity and divorce and adultery and all the other practices that are prohibited in the Ten Commandments. If that is what man is, then why are we surprised that he behaves in that way?

So because of the problems of man, we have to pass laws and multiply our prisons. Poor man, he is only doing what they say is the truth about him. That is the world's view. But the world needs to listen to the Word of God, which says that man is made in the image and likeness of God and is responsible to God. God has set him in this world and is going to judge him and hold him responsible. That is what this modern world needs to know.

I am not an expert in politics—no preacher is. Though some religious leaders have great titles in the Christian church, they know no more than I do. They talk and give their opinions about these matters, but that is not the word of God—that is their opinion. The Gospel is the word of God, and if the Christian church does not preach it, who will? I know nothing apart from what I see in Scripture. I know nothing about myself or about man but what I find there, and what I see there is that we will never understand man until we look at him in the context of God.

The Word of God, then, reveals to us, first, the truth about God, second, the truth about the nature of man, and, third, how we should live. God has not left us in ignorance. I know that the popular modern idea is, "Do as much good as you can, and don't do certain things, and you will be all right." Moral ethical teaching. What is religion? "Morality touched with emotion," Matthew Arnold said, as if the Bible had never been put before him, as if God had never spoken. Not so. The life you and I are called upon to live is not a life that any human being has stated or defined; it is not just morality and ethics and decency and goodness and kindness and benevolence and protesting against obvious evil. That is not it. Men like Bertrand Russell can do that, and they believe that what they are doing is right. But it is a shame and a disgrace to see men and women who claim to be Christians following in Bertrand Russell's train and regarding him as their leader—a man who has already written a book to tell us why he is *not* a Christian. The man is blind—*anyone* who rejects the Word of God is blind. Such a person just fumbles and stumbles through life, eventually going out in final hopelessness and despair and failure.

If you want to know how to live, you must come to the Word of God, the Bible. How are men and women to live in this world? The Lord Jesus Christ summed it up for us: "Thou shalt love the Lord thy God with all thy heart, and with all thy soul, and with all thy mind, and with all thy strength: this is the first commandment. And the second is like, namely this, Thou shalt love thy neighbour as thyself" (Mark 12:30-31). It is all there; we must start with God. If we want to help men and women, we must not start with them. Start with God; if we want to help our fellow human beings, we must get ourselves right first. If we have a wrong view of ourselves and a wrong view of others, how can we possibly help them? We cannot. That is what the world has been trying to do, and it is a dismal failure. We must love the Lord our God with the whole of our being and then love our neighbors as ourselves. People are trying to banish war without mentioning God; they are looking only at their neighbors. They foolishly imagine that they can fulfill the second commandment while they take no interest in the first. It just cannot be done.

I prophesied for many years before the second world war that the League of Nations would be a complete failure, and it was. I say the same about the United Nations. Men and women will never solve this problem. Never! We must start with God, and until people are humbled before God, they will fight one another and clutch at one another's throats because they set themselves up as gods, and gods are jealous.

Are we worshiping God? Are we living to His glory and to His praise? He has made us in order that we might do that. That is why He gave us being and existence. Not for ourselves. We belong to God who made us and who has endowed us with the faculties we possess. We have not created them—we have simply inherited them. God means for us to display His glory through the very gifts He has given us. Because people do not do that, they are in trouble. That is why the world is as it is. We are jealous of another person or they are jealous of us. And then we want more, and they want more. Fighting! "From whence come wars and fightings among you? come they not hence, even of your lusts that war in your members?" (James 4:1).

So we must start with God, with the first table of the law, the worship of God, honoring him in all our ways. And then, because He knows us so well, there are the negative injunctions. If the world needs to hear something more than anything else, it is this: "Thou shalt not kill. Thou shalt not commit adultery" (Exod. 20:13-14). What a difference it would make if everybody observed that! Law after law tries to deal with this question, with the church setting up commissions to find a way out of the problem. Oh, the tragedy of it all!

> *Thou shalt not kill.*
> *Thou shalt not commit adultery.*
> *Thou shalt not steal.*
> *Thou shalt not bear false witness against thy neighbour.*
> *Thou shalt not covet thy neighbour's house, thou shalt not covet thy neighbour's wife, nor his manservant, nor his maidservant, nor his ox, nor his ass, nor any thing that is thy neighbour's.*
>
> —*Exod. 20:13-17*

If only the whole world lived like that, most of the problems would be banished; they would vanish into thin air. "The powers that be are ordained of God" (Rom. 13:1). Why? Because of our sin and our failure to live in the way that God has commanded us to live and to conduct ourselves in this life.

This is the content, the message, of the Word of God. And this is a word that condemns every single one of us. Have we lived to the glory of God or to our own glory? Have we kept the Ten Commandments positively and negatively? We need not read books on philosophy—it is all here. All we need to do is obey those commands. But we cannot, can we? Of course not. And the Word of God tells us that. The law was not given in order that we might save ourselves by keeping it. It was to show us that we *cannot* keep it. This is a word that condemns us and tells us that we are lost.

God's Word goes further; it tells us that we can do nothing about our salvation. But, thank God, it does not leave us in failure, misery, and condemnation. "This is that Moses, which said unto the children of Israel, A prophet shall the Lord your God raise up unto you of your brethren, like unto me; him shall ye hear." "When the fulness of the time was come, God sent forth his Son, made of a woman, made under the law, to redeem them that were under the law" (Gal. 4:4-5).

We are all condemned by this Word of God. But listen to the other side: "Believe on the Lord Jesus Christ, and thou shalt be saved" (Acts 16:31). God is not only holiness and justice and righteousness and truth—He is a God of love. "God so loved the world"—this world that has been exposed under His law—"that he gave his only begotten Son, that whosoever believeth in him should not perish, but have everlasting life" (John 3:16). And this is His word to you now. Through the cross behold the crown. As you are, conscious of failure, misery, guilt, condemnation, look up unto and believe on the Lord Jesus Christ. Believe this word that tells you that when God's Son died on the cross, He laid your sins upon Him and punished them there and is offering you free pardon. You can be delivered immediately, now, without doing anything—simply believe.

Only believe, and thou shalt see,
That Christ is all in all to thee.
John S. B. Monsell

Do not be like the blind, foolish members of the Sanhedrin addressed by Stephen. Turn to the only one who can save you in time and in eternity—Jesus of Nazareth, the Son of God.

8

The Purpose of the Law

This is that Moses, which said unto the children of Israel, A prophet shall the Lord your God raise up unto you of your brethren, like unto me; him shall ye hear. This is he, that was in the church in the wilderness with the angel which spake to him in the mount Sina, and with our fathers: who received the lively oracles to give unto us.

—Acts 7:37-38

We have seen that Stephen was on trial before the Sanhedrin—the Jewish law court—because he was a Christian, active in the life and work of the church. The Sanhedrin regarded his preaching as blasphemous. They believed he had been preaching against Moses, against the temple, and against the law, which were more precious to them than anything else, and they felt that such a man was not fit to live.

If you look at Stephen's reply from the standpoint of a defense, it was brilliant. A good advocate always addresses the judge and jury, and that is what Stephen was doing. He met the Sanhedrin on their own ground. He took them through their own history in order to show that they had completely misunderstood it. They were condemned by the very historical facts of which they were so proud. Stephen showed them that the real reason they were rejecting Jesus of Nazareth was that they had never understood Moses, never understood the law, and never understood the real meaning of the temple. The essence of the tragedy was that they were rejecting the very Savior who had been prophesied by Moses, the law, and the temple. There is no tragedy that is in any way comparable to this.

All this is brought to a focus in verses 37-38—the verses we will now consider further. I am calling your attention to these verses, I repeat, because the terrible modern tragedy is that the world today is still rejecting this message. There is therefore nothing more important than that we should understand this word delivered by God to Moses. And now I particularly want to consider with you again that last statement about Moses, namely, that he "received the lively [or living] oracles to give unto us." We saw in our last study that Moses did not go onto Mount Sinai to enter into a sort of retreat in order that he might have time to do research work, to think in peace and quiet and evolve his theory, and then come down and give his teaching to the people. That is the exact opposite of what happened. God gave revelation; Moses received it. That is what differentiates this Gospel from everything else in the world; everything else is the product of human ability and understanding. This is of God and from God. It is God's word.

I am no better than anybody else. I have no message of my own. I am as fallible as all other men. My only authority is that I am simply passing on "the lively oracles" received by Moses. I am simply a mouthpiece. The business of the preacher is to expound, to open the word of the living God. He has no other right or business whatsoever.

So I am not preaching human understanding, I am not preaching modern philosophy, I am not preaching modern politics or sociology. I am simply holding before you the word of God that is recorded in the Bible—the word that God has used throughout the centuries. We have looked at its great characteristics. It is a living word; it is a powerful word; it is a penetrating word; it is a convicting word; it is a word that searches us and examines us. That is why it annoys so many people. No preacher has ever annoyed congregations as much as the Lord Jesus Christ did. We read that the Jews "murmured" at Him because of what He said (John 6:41). Sometimes after He had preached, they took up stones to throw at Him (John 8:59; 10:31), and in the end they killed Him; they crucified the Son of God.

But modern men and women think Jesus talked about pacifism and peace and love, and they all think that they like Him. But take it from me, if they heard Jesus preaching, they would hate Him. The very people who praise Him would be the very first to hate Him. They would think of Him exactly as those members of the Sanhedrin did, those people who were misunderstanding Moses and the law and the temple.

This, then, is the word that we are considering. What is its message? The message of the law received by Moses is primarily about God: it starts with Him. Then it comes to men and women and tells them the truth about themselves, about their own essential greatness as made in the image and likeness of God. This word also tells men and women how they should live. We have seen that there is no need to argue about this, as God has told us in the Ten Commandments.

That, then, is a kind of introduction to this word of God, this word of the law, but what we must now concentrate on is the penetrating character of this word. What does it reveal to us? What does it really tell us about ourselves? We have seen already that we cannot keep God's law, that none of us has done so, but that is not the whole truth about us. Are we ready to hear the truth about ourselves? Are we ready to come under the X-ray of God, for that is what His word is. It is unvarnished truth and searches "even to the dividing asunder of soul and spirit, and of the joints and marrow" (Heb. 4:12). Nothing is hidden; everything in the recesses is brought out and exposed.

This word tells us about what I may describe as the depths of sin. Here is what the modern world needs to know. It is not surprising that the world is as it is. It is like that because it does not know the cause of its troubles. That is where our poor statesmen—how else can I describe them?—are so missing the mark. They think they are dealing with the real problem, but they are not. Of course, various issues have their place. You must have politics and economics, but what is so ludicrous is that anybody should imagine that this is the ultimate way of dealing with the problem of humanity. It is not. It deals totally with symptoms and manifestations. The fundamental problems are only dealt with in this book, the Word of God, and literally nowhere else. The Bible reveals what I am calling the depths of sin, and the word of God, the law, was given especially to Moses in order to bring that out. Why did God call Moses onto that mount and give him this word, this law? It was in order that the human problem might be revealed as it is—that is the first point we must notice about the giving of the law.

Let me put it to you like this. Men and women have always known there is something wrong. Indeed, they have always known that they are wrong and that they are guilty. There is not a living being who has not, at some time or another, suffered remorse. That means that they are aware that they have done something wrong; they are unhappy about it and say, "I'll never do that again."

But what produces remorse? There is a simple answer. From the beginning there has been in every one of us what is called the conscience, a sense of right and of wrong. In other words, before we do certain things, something tells us, "Don't do that—it's wrong." But we ignore that prompting and do that thing, and then we suffer, we are punished. Our conscience speaks to us, and it keeps hammering away at us. We try to fight it, we try to dismiss it psychologically, but it does not matter—it is there, and it goes on speaking. This is innate in every human being; everybody has a sense of right and wrong. That is what makes us all responsible. Even the law of the land recognizes that and holds us responsible for our actions.

The apostle Paul puts this very plainly in the epistle to the Romans where he says:

> *For as many as have sinned without law shall also perish without law: and as many as have sinned in the law shall be judged by the law. . . . For when the Gentiles, which have not the law [this law that was given by God to Moses on the top of Mount Sinai] do by nature the things contained in the law, these, having not the law, are a law unto themselves: which shew the work of the law written in their hearts, their conscience also bearing witness, and their thoughts the mean while accusing or else excusing one another.*
>
> —*Rom. 2:12, 14-15*

Now that, Paul says, is true of everybody. The Jews have been given the law through Moses, but everybody else, even those who did not have the law, have, in a sense, received all that is stated in the law, in principle, "written in their hearts," as their consciences prove. And then Paul says we accuse one another and excuse ourselves—"accusing or else excusing one another." On what grounds do we do that? It is because we have this conscience, this sense of right and wrong. When someone says, "You've done wrong—you shouldn't do that," I explain it away, I excuse myself. But I know I am wrong. And my conscience tells me I am a hypocrite.

Now I repeat that this sense of right and wrong is in every single one of us. Why, then, was the law ever given? The law was given through Moses in order that the truth about which our hearts tell us might be revealed to us, opened up to us, made so plain to us that we cannot get away from it. That was the whole object and function of the giving of the law. I could give you many quotations to establish what I have just been saying; they are chiefly written by the apostle Paul. He says, "The law . . . was added because of transgressions" (Gal. 3:19). "Moreover the law entered, that the offence might abound" (Rom. 5:20)—that it might be seen more and more clearly. And then Paul puts it like this in Romans 7:13: ". . . that sin by the commandment might become exceeding sinful." The law was sent in order that sin might appear as sin. We are all so clever, we manipulate our conscience, we explain things away. But then the word of God comes and says, "Wait a minute, listen to this," and it convicts us, and we cannot wriggle out of it. It is there, and it speaks; it explains the wrongdoing. We have nothing to say; we just hold up our hands. The X-ray has revealed "the exceeding sinful[ness]" of sin. "By the law is the knowledge of sin" (Rom. 3:20).

Let me divide that last statement up a little so you can see what Paul means. In Romans 7:7 Paul gives the example of coveting: "What shall we say then? Is the law sin? God forbid. Nay, I had not known sin, but by the law: for I had not known lust, except the law had said, Thou shalt not covet." We are all so clever, are we not? We tend to think of ourselves only in terms of actions, and we tend to say, "I've never been drunk. I've never committed adultery. I've never done this or that." And therefore we think we are perfectly all right and do not need Christ or the Gospel.

But wait a minute, says the law. It is not quite as simple as that. Have you ever coveted? Have you ever lusted? "You know," says Paul in effect, "there was a time when I used to judge like that—and I thought I was almost perfect. But the law suddenly said to me, 'Thou shalt not covet! Thou shalt not covet thy neighbour's wife, nor his manservant, nor his maidservant, nor his ox, nor his ass, nor any thing that is thy neighbour's.' And you know," says Paul, "the moment I realized that, I died, I was finished. I had been standing on my feet, a wonderful man, but the law says you must not covet! The law says that a desire is as damnable as a deed, that it is as reprehensible to covet as it is to commit an evil action."

That is the kind of message that the law brings home to us. We can manage our conscience all right—we've never done this or that—and on we go happily. But suddenly the law comes and says, "But let me examine your mind, your heart, your thought, your imagination."

Our Lord made this even more clear. He turned to people and said, "For out of the heart proceed evil thoughts, murders, adulteries . . ." (Matt. 15:19). We think we are innocent, we think we are pure, we are blaming the age in which we live; we blame the films and the billboards and the novels and other books, and we say, "I'd be all right if only I were left alone."

"You are not all right," says our Lord. "You are a liar." "That which cometh out of the man, that defileth the man" (Mark 7:20). People sinned before there were movie theaters or television; people sinned before they could read. Where does sin come from? It comes from the heart. Coveting! A man looking at another man's wife, or a wife looking at another woman's husband. Coveting! Desire! This is what God's Word alone reveals to us, and it brings us under condemnation.

Further, as the Word reveals our sin, it shows us the depth of our sin. It reveals our heart to us, and again, nothing else does this. I often quote Psalm 51. Poor David! That poor king of Israel! He was a man of strong passions, and he suddenly saw another man's wife and was attracted; he lusted, desired, coveted! And he was so lustful that he not only committed adultery with the woman, but he killed her husband so he could have her. And he was quite happy; everything was all right; he had his desire. But God sent His word to him through the prophet Nathan and convicted him and brought his sin home to him.

Then David wrote the fifty-first psalm and admitted it all. "Create in me," he said, "a clean heart, O God; and renew a right spirit within me" (v. 10). The trouble is not so much temptation but that within me that responds to it. "I am vile, I am foul; wash me!" But David did not see that until the word of God came to him. That is what the word of God does. That is what the law of Moses does. "Thou shalt not covet." David came to see that. This law, when it comes to us, makes us see that we are rotten in our hearts and that what we really need is to be born again.

But there is something else—it is all in the seventh chapter of the epistle to the Romans: nothing on earth enables us to see these things but the Word of God. Look at what Romans 7 tells us about the power of sin. Modern men and women do not like the term *sin*. "Nonsense!" they say. "Sin? There's no such thing. I'm not as good as I ought to be, I'm not a hundred percent perfect, but I'm not bad. I'm not evil. I'm not really sinful. If I want to stop doing a certain thing, I can."

Men have told me that hundreds of times about giving up drinking or some other habit, but it is very much easier to *talk* about it than to *do* it, is it not? How easy it is to talk, but oh, the power of sin! And it is only in the Bible that we read about that power. Listen to Paul: "For we know that the law is spiritual: but I am carnal, sold under sin. For that which I do I allow not"—I know that what I am doing is wrong, I do not allow it, and yet I do it—"for what I would, that do I not; but what I hate, that do I" (Rom. 7:14-15).

That is the simple truth about you, as it is true of me, by nature. Nothing but this word tells us that, does it? Psychology does not tell us that, and politicians most certainly do not! You do not get votes by telling people the truth, especially about themselves. Nobody tells us the truth but this word of God, and this is what it tells us: "What I hate, that do I" (Rom. 7:15). Here is our trouble. "For I know that in me (that is, in my flesh,) dwelleth no good thing: for to will is present with me; but how to perform that which is good I find not" (Rom. 7:18).

Why not? What is the matter? Why cannot we all do what we know to be right? We read books on idealism, on philosophy and humanism, and we are told, "This is the way to live, and if only we all did this, our problems would be solved." Our clever leaders can solve the whole problem of war. "It's quite simple," they say. "You only need to know this and that. War is folly, so just stop waging war." Then why, in the name of conscience, is the world still going on with these things? That is the question. There is only one answer—it is the power of sin.

> *Now if I do that I would not, it is no more I that do it, but sin that dwelleth in me. I find then a law, that, when I would do good, evil is present with me. For I delight in the law of God after the inward man: but I see another law in my members, warring against the law of my mind, and bringing me into captivity to the law of sin which is in my members. O wretched man that I am!*
>
> *—Rom. 7:20-24*

Is not that the truth about all of us? Of course it is! But where else did we learn that? Nobody else has ever told us that; nobody ever will. The law was given through Moses in order to show that there is "another law in my members," that there is a power in you and me greater than ourselves, that even though we know what is right, we cannot do it because we are captives, slaves to sin and lust and passion. Here alone are we given that information.

And not only are we slaves to sin, but Paul shows sin's perverting power. This is the most terrible thing about sin in us: it will twist anything. Sin is so powerful that it will even twist the law of God. That is Paul's whole argument in Romans 7. In verse 7 he asks this question: "What shall we say then? Is the law sin?" Why does he raise that question? Why does he go on to say, "Wherefore the law is holy, and the commandment holy, and just, and good. Was then what which is good made death unto me?" (vv. 12-13). What is all this about?

This, in effect, is what Paul is saying: "When I really saw the true character of the law"—he had thought he knew what God had said to Moses, but when he was convicted by the Spirit he understood it for the first time—"I discovered that the very law that God gave to me through Moses made me worse instead of better." Listen to the fifth verse: "For when we were in the flesh, the motions of sins, which were by the law"—aggravated by the law, energized by the law—"did work in our members to bring forth fruit unto death."

Put in very simple terms, that argument means this: if you tell the natural man or woman not to do a thing, at that moment you create within them a desire to do it. You have seen that in babies and children, have you not? You tell them not to do something, and they want to do it immediately. The moment your back is turned, they do it. That is the whole of human nature. So the very law of God becomes an enemy to us.

Now I could very easily spend much time showing you the practical relevance of this principle to the moral problem confronting every other country in the world. Politicians think it is enough to tell people, "Don't do that because it is bad; do this because it is good." But that is no help. In a sense you make them worse by telling them not to do things. You are reminding them of these things—you are introducing them. Indeed, people will read books on the evil effects of certain practices in order to get a kick. A man says, "I think this book will help me with the sex problem because it shows me the possible dangers and evils," and he tries to persuade himself that is why he is reading it. But that is not his reason at all. He is reading it because he knows it will stimulate him, and he will be worse at the end than he was at the beginning.

I remember a minister telling me that a book he once read called *The Mastery of Sex* did him more harm than anything he had ever read in the whole of his life! You will never master sex by reading about it. Sin twists the law, even the law of God, which is so good. "I found that the law was against me," said Paul in effect. "It was doing me harm rather than delivering me." Why? Not because there was anything wrong with the law, but because of the nature of the sin that was in him. "But sin, that it might appear sin, [was] working death in me by that which is good; that sin by the commandment might become exceeding sinful" (v. 13). What a terrible thing this is.

Now can you not see that it is only this message that tells us things like this? Is not this the truth that the world needs to know above everything else? There is a recent illustration from the world—the world even at its best, at its academic best—of how blind it is to the nature of the problem. The city of Cambridge has decided to introduce as soon as possible the use of natural gas rather than manufactured gas. Why? Because of the number of suicides among poor students, who put themselves to death by gassing themselves! What do the authorities do about this terrible, tragic problem? They introduce natural gas instead of manufactured gas! That is a perfect illustration of how the world without the word of God misses the whole problem. They change the gas instead of changing the nature of the poor unfortunate students. The question is: Why does anybody want to commit suicide? What is it that has brought a poor, tragic student to such a condition that he can no longer face life? That is the problem! But people do not see that.

If it were not so tragic, this would be the joke of the centuries. But it is so typical of human beings without the word of God. They do not realize their problem; they do not realize the nature of sin, the depth of sin, the power of sin, and nothing will ever bring them to that realization until they come face to face with the living word, the living oracle of God as given through Moses and the prophets, and perfectly through the Lord Jesus Christ, the Son of God. That is what this word teaches us.

In the second place, the law was given to reveal to us our utter and complete helplessness. That was the tragedy of those members of the Sanhedrin. Why had they rejected Christ? It was because they thought that they were satisfying God by their own efforts. There was no other reason. That was the trouble with the Pharisee. He thought he was satisfying God, he thought he was keeping the law, but he had completely misunderstood it.

To know about the law is of no value in and of itself. The object of the law is that we should keep it. Listen to Paul in Romans 2: "For not the hearers of the law are just before God, but the doers of the law shall be justified" (v. 13). The foolish Jews say, "We are all right—we are the people of God."

"But," you ask, "how do you know you are all right?"

"Well," they say, "we have the law. God has given it to us and not to the Gentiles. It is taught in our synagogues every Sabbath: we are the hearers of the law."

They think that because they are listening to the law, they are all right. But Paul says that to be interested in morality and ethics is not of the slightest value. The question we will have to answer at the bar of God's judgment is not, "What did you think?" but "What did you do?" That is one fallacy.

Here is another. It is no use saying, "I'm all right because I've kept 99 percent of the law." That will not help you at all. The law of God must be kept in its entirety. You can be convicted for having failed on the 1 percent you did not keep. This is stated clearly by James in the second chapter of his epistle: "For whosoever shall keep the whole law, and yet offend in one point, he is guilty of all. For he that said, Do not commit adultery, said also, Do not kill. Now if thou commit no adultery, yet if thou kill, thou art become a transgressor of the law" (vv. 10-11). Imagine that you are charged in a court of law—let us take an example at random—with having stolen somebody's property. So you are asked by the magistrate, "Have you anything you would like to say for yourself?" You say, "Yes. I've never committed adultery. I've never been drunk. I've never exceeded the speed limit." And on you go with a great list of what you have not done. That does not help you. You are guilty of the offense you are being charged with. You do not pick and choose in the law; you must keep it all, and if you do not, then you are guilty.

Next, it is important to understand that the spirit of the law is more important than the letter. The failure to understand this principle was another tragic blunder on the part of the Pharisees and those members of the Sanhedrin. They thought that as long as you kept the letter of the law, as they understood it, all was well. But why did God ever give the Ten Commandments? Why did he ever say, "Thou shalt not kill, thou shalt not commit adultery," and so on? What is the point of it all? Our Lord gave the answer in the Sermon on the Mount: the spirit of the law is much more important than the letter, and what God wants is that we should love him preeminently and love our neighbor as ourselves.

Our Lord was asked one day, "Which is the first and the greatest commandment?" These Jewish leaders knew that there were 613 points in the law; they were arguing and wrangling about them, some saying, "This is the most important," and others saying, "No, that one is." So they came to our Lord and asked Him. He said, "Thou shalt love the Lord thy God with all thy heart, and with all thy soul, and with all thy mind, and with all thy strength: this is the first commandment. And the second is like, namely this, Thou shalt love thy neighbour as thyself" (Mark 12:30-31).

This is what matters. Why are you not to kill? Why must you not steal or commit adultery or covet? Because you are meant to love your neighbor as yourself. You can go around the world and say, "I've never struck my neighbor. I've never spat on him. I've never done this and that to my neighbor." And you think you are a paragon of all the virtues. But the law of God comes to you and says, "Look here, my friend, the question is: do you love your neighbor as yourself? What have you thought about your neighbor?" And it is the same with your attitude toward God. That is where the Pharisees were unmasked and exposed, and that is where the members of the Sanhedrin showed they had never understood the true nature of the law. They were interested in the letter: "We have never done this; we have never done that."

"Listen," says Christ in effect, "you say you have never committed adultery. All right, let me ask you a question: Have you ever looked upon a woman to lust after her? If you have, you have already committed adultery in your heart. It is the same with killing. You say, 'I have never committed murder.' Have you ever said of your brother, 'You fool!'? If you have, you have already committed murder in your heart" (see Matt. 5:21-28).

That is what the Word of God tells us; this is the meaning of the law. It exposes the real nature of sin. When men and women think that they are perfect and that they can satisfy God, the law speaks, and they are condemned. They are guilty and powerless; they are vile and filthy.

Nothing but the word of God, nothing but the law of God, can ever bring this knowledge to us; and it does so always and invariably. This is why the law was given by God to Moses on Mount Sinai—so that which is there in embryo in the heart might be made explicit, and so we might all realize that we need to be delivered from the guilt of sin, from the power of sin, and from the pollution and the filth of sin. That is the trouble; that is the need. That is what Stephen is saying to the members of the Sanhedrin. He said in essence, "You say that I am blaspheming by speaking against the law. It is because you have never understood the law. I am telling you the real meaning of the law. That is what Jesus whom you have crucified did. You hated Him because when He expounded the law, He convicted you; that is why you rejected Him and crucified Him."

That is Stephen's message, and it is the message to modern men and women who say they do not need Christ and who talk about their learning and morality when their world is in chaos and their hearts are rotten and vile. No human effort can ever deliver them. The law shows us our complete helplessness.

But the law not only shows us that we can do nothing about our guilt or ever deliver ourselves from the power and the pollution of sin—it also shows us that we can never satisfy God and stand before Him. You say, "But surely God is a God of love, and if I say that I'm sorry, God will forgive me." But the law that God gave to Moses on Mount Sinai gives the lie to that argument, and I can prove that quite simply.

What did God tell Moses on that mount? He gave him the Ten Commandments, but He did not stop at that—He also gave him very detailed instructions about building a tent, called a tabernacle, and He told him to build it according to certain specifications. God gave Moses certain measurements and told him what material to use and how much to use. He told Moses to build an altar, and then He gave him a great list of rules and regulations. They were about sacrificing various animals, including a lamb every morning and every evening, then taking the blood and presenting it as an offering. There were rules about all the burnt offerings and sacrifices and meal offerings and peace offerings. Have you ever read the books of Exodus,

Leviticus, and Numbers? They are part of the Word of God, part of the word that Moses received from God on Mount Sinai, and when God told Moses to go down, He said, "See that thou make all things according to the pattern shewed to thee in the mount" (Heb. 8:5).

So many people say today, "I'm not interested in the Old Testament. I can't be bothered to read those books you have mentioned and all about this shedding of blood, the offerings and sacrifices—all that has nothing to do with me." But it has *everything* to do with you. What is the Word saying? It is saying that God demands satisfaction and that He will have it. He is the Judge. *He* decides, not us. Modern people say, "Say you're sorry and all will be well. We'll all go to heaven." You will not! That is what you say, but you have no authority at all. Do you want to know what God says? Well, here it is—God's word. He gave it to Moses, and Moses gave it to the people. But the members of the Sanhedrin completely misunderstood it. They said, "This man Stephen and these Christians are blaspheming against the temple." They did not know the meaning of the temple. They thought it was just a place where you went through certain rituals and ceremonies, and then you walked out all right. You earned your salvation.

What a travesty of the word of God! No; the whole object of the temple and the tabernacle and their ceremonies and all the burnt offerings and sacrifices and all that you read in the Old Testament was to teach one lesson only—that God is to be propitiated, that God demands satisfaction. "Without shedding of blood is no remission [of sins]" (Heb. 9:22). God wants a perfect offering from us. But we cannot give it.

"But," you say, "my good works, surely, are going to count?"

No; that is the cardinal error. God has said, "All our righteousness are as filthy rags" (Isa. 64:6).

Not only the Jews at the time of the Old Testament, but even a man like the apostle Paul before his conversion fell into the error of thinking one can be saved by keeping the law. That is what he tells us in that bit of autobiography in the third chapter of the epistle to the Philippians. He says that if any man ever had a right to have confidence in the flesh, he had more. Why? Well, he was "circumcised the eighth day, of the stock of Israel, of the tribe of Benjamin, an Hebrew of the Hebrews; as touching the law, a Pharisee; concerning zeal, persecuting the church; touching the righteousness which is in the law, blameless" (vv. 5-6).

And Paul really believed that. He was a highly intelligent man, but he had so misunderstood the law of God that he thought he was literally blameless. Because he had never actually murdered a man, he was not guilty of murder;

because he had never actually committed adultery, he was not an adulterer; and so on with all the commandments. But suddenly he saw the spirit of the law, and he realized he was a terrible sinner. So having boasted of all his marvelous righteousness, he now said:

> *But what things were gain to me, those I counted loss for Christ. Yea doubtless, and I count all things but loss for the excellency of the knowledge of Christ Jesus my Lord: for whom I have suffered the loss of all things, and do count them but dung, that I may win Christ, and be found in him, not having mine own righteousness, which is of the law, but that which is through the faith of Christ, the righteousness which is of God by faith.*
>
> —*vv.* 7-9

And there is the whole thing. The word that God gave to Moses is a word that tells us that nothing we can ever offer to God is of the slightest value. We can tell Him about all the good works we have done, and He will dismiss them all because He knows our mind, He knows our heart, He knows our imagination, He knows the foulness and the darkness that is there; it is all "filthy rags," it is dung, it is loss and refuse. We can take to Him all our money, and we can say that we have given a fortune to this cause and a great deal of money to another, but it is valueless; nothing we can do is of any value. God demands a perfect sacrifice; He demands a life. And that was the teaching He had given the children of Israel by means of the burnt offerings and sacrifices. He said, "Take a lamb, put your hands on its head, and metaphorically transfer your sins to the animal. Kill the animal, take the life, and present the life in the blood to Me."

But God made it perfectly clear that this was only temporary, this was only prophetic. He said in effect, "This is only a way of covering over your sins for the time being; this is not going to save you. It is pointing forward to something that I am going to do that will save you." In telling them to offer a lamb morning and evening, God was saying, "A day is coming when I am going to provide the Lamb; a day is coming when I Myself will provide the perfect sacrifice, and He will be big enough and great enough and pure enough to take your sins. The blood of bulls and of goats and the ashes of a heifer can never cleanse the soul. It is not enough: it is only a prophecy, it is an adumbration, it is a type pointing to the Lamb that I am going to produce."

That is just another way of saying what Paul wrote in these words: "Wherefore the law was our schoolmaster to bring us unto Christ" (Gal.

3:24). God never gave the law to the children of Israel in order that they might save themselves by keeping it. He knew they could not keep it. Their consciences were already condemning them, and to define the sin makes it still more difficult, "that sin by the commandment might become exceeding sinful" (Rom. 7:13).

Have you seen the exceeding sinfulness of sin in yourself? Have you realized how you stand in God's sight at this moment, as you are by nature? Do you know you are guilty? Do you know you have a vile nature that you can never put right? Do you know that you need someone outside yourself to put you right with God? Has this word of God acted as your "schoolmaster" to teach you to say:

Not the labour of my hands
Can fulfil thy Law's demands;
Could my zeal no respite know,
Could my tears forever flow,
All for sin could not atone;
Thou must save, and thou alone.
Augustus M. Toplady

If it has, you are blessed of God, you are reconciled to Him, you have nothing to fear from the law, and heaven's gate is open wide for you.

9

Prophet, Priest, and King

This is that Moses, which said unto the children of Israel, A prophet shall the Lord your God raise up unto you of your brethren, like unto me; him shall ye hear. This is he, that was in the church in the wilderness with the angel which spake to him in the mount Sina, and with our fathers: who received the lively oracles to give unto us.

—Acts 7:37-38

The essence of the tragedy of the Sanhedrin and all the Jewish people was, as we have seen, that they put Moses and the law and the temple over against the Lord Jesus Christ. So Stephen was trying to show them that if they only understood this word, these "lively oracles," they would have an entirely different view of these subjects, and, above all, of the Lord Jesus Christ. The reason why the Jews were outstanding among all the nations of history was that God had spoken to them, that He had given them revelation and made them its guardians and custodians, entrusted with the responsibility of passing it on.

And the same is true of the Christian church. I am not interested in the church as an institution. I am interested in her because it is to her that this word has been given, the word that was preached by the first apostles, men like Stephen and others. So the one thing that matters is that we understand this word and that we not be blind to its true meaning, as the members of the Sanhedrin were.

Now this word of God is all in the book that we call the Bible, which is divided into two sections—the Old and the New Testaments. We have so far been considering the message of the Old Testament, the word that was given to Moses on the mount—called the law—and the teaching of the prophets. As we have seen, it tells us about God, it tells us about man, and it tells us about man's guilt before God because he does not live as God in the law has taught us to live.

This word also tells us that God commanded that certain sacrifices be offered to him, and it tells us that he gave instructions to Moses to build a tabernacle. God told Moses how to furnish it, what animals to kill, and how to present the blood and all the offerings and sacrifices. It is all there, and the prophets expounded it and showed its inner meaning.

And, finally, we have seen that the whole of the Old Testament pointed forward to a coming one who would one day deliver us from all the sin and guilt from which the law, with all it had to offer, could not save us. The Old Testament shows us the final inadequacy and indeed the futility of trusting to morality, trusting to a good life, trusting to good deeds and good works. It goes even further. The Old Testament shows us the final futility of trusting even in religion, as the members of the Sanhedrin were doing. Religion is inadequate; it cannot save.

Do you see the relevance of all this today? Many people still reject and refuse the Lord Jesus Christ as their personal Savior and Redeemer because they are trusting in their good lives. They say, "I've never done this or that. I'm doing a lot of good. I'm a religious person, a church member." That is exactly the fallacy of the members of the Sanhedrin with their reliance upon good works and upon an external religion with its forms and ceremonies. So the whole purpose of the Old Testament message is to show us the final futility of all that. That is its message.

What, then, is the message of the New Testament? It is that God has fulfilled His promise, that God has done what He had promised to do, and that He has done it in Jesus of Nazareth, His only begotten, dearly beloved Son. That was the message of the apostles, and it was Stephen's message. It tells us that Jesus Christ is the only Savior and that our full salvation is altogether and entirely in Him. This had been made quite plain and clear before Stephen was ever arrested. Peter and John had been arrested for preaching the same message, and Peter had had the boldness to say face to face with the members of the Sanhedrin, "This is the stone which was set at nought of you builders, which is become the head of the corner. Neither is there salvation in any other: for there is none other name under heaven given among men, whereby we must be saved" (Acts 4:11-12). This is the crux of the whole position, and the message of the Christian faith is still that Jesus Christ is God's way of salvation, and there is no other.

Now in verse 37 this is put before us in a very interesting way: "This is that Moses," says Stephen, "which said unto the children of Israel, A prophet shall the Lord your God raise up unto you of your brethren, like unto me; him shall ye hear." Stephen was saying that Moses—the Moses whose name they revered—had prophesied the coming of the Messiah, and Jesus is that

Messiah. The people had been looking forward to His coming, and yet these miserable members of the Sanhedrin had crucified Him and wanted to put to death the people who preached Him. They were blind to the coming of the Messiah who they claimed to be expecting.

And this is still the difficulty with the world. It is still rejecting its only Savior. So I am trying, feebly, to do now with you what Stephen did before the members of the Sanhedrin. I am asking you to join with me in considering Him, this prophet that the Lord your God "shall . . . raise up unto you of your brethren, like unto me." Let us look at Him as Moses described Him and as Stephen here repeated it. What do we find?

Well, as you look at the Lord Jesus Christ, the first thing you must note about Him is that He is "like unto [Moses]." There is a comparison here—Moses made it himself. He says in effect, "I am not the Savior, but God will raise Him up out of, or from, the midst of your brethren, and He will be like me." So in certain respects He resembles Moses.

What are these respects? First, as Moses tells us, God shall "raise [him] up." God had raised up Moses, as we have seen. You remember how Stephen put it: "When the time of the promise drew nigh" (v. 17; cf. v. 20), Moses was born. At the exact time that he was needed, God raised him. His birth was a miracle. And when you turn to Jesus of Nazareth, this is what you find: "When the fulness of the time was come, God sent forth his Son, made of a woman, made under the law, to redeem them that were under the law" (Gal. 4:4-5). It was God who sent Him into the world. "God so loved the world, that he gave his only begotten Son" (John 3:16). This is a part of God's great plan. The time was the exact time that God had predetermined before the foundation of the world.

Then, also, Moses was a man: "of your brethren, like unto me." Moses was a Jew. Jesus of Nazareth also was a Jew—"made of the seed of David according to the flesh" (Rom. 1:3). That is why you have the genealogical tables at the beginning of the Gospels of Matthew and Luke. He was truly a man—". . . the man Christ Jesus" (1 Tim. 2:5)—and you can trace his Jewish ancestry as truly as you can that of Moses.

What else? Well, Christ is like Moses in another respect. He is one who stands between God and man. That was the outstanding thing about Moses, as I have already reminded you. God called him up onto the mount to learn, and there he represented the children of Israel. He was standing on that mountaintop, as it were, between God and man. He was a kind of middleman, a mediator; he received the "lively oracles" to give to us. And exactly as Moses had done, so does Jesus of Nazareth. He stands between God and humanity today; He stands there uniquely, and He stands alone.

Then, too, Moses was a great teacher. He was taught of God, and he taught the people. He received the living oracles, and he delivered the message. So did the Lord Jesus Christ. Look at Him in the pages of the four Gospels. At the age of thirty He began to teach and to preach, and the crowds followed Him. He preached the Sermon on the Mount. He taught them, so that people said, "Never man spake like this man" (John 7:46), and we read in Matthew 7:29, "He taught them as one having authority, and not as the scribes."

Furthermore, Moses, as I reminded you, was the great guide and leader. When he first appeared in that role, the Israelites were annoyed with him. They asked him who he thought he was that he should set himself over them. They said, "Who made thee a prince and a judge over us?" (Exod. 2:14). But that was one of the great features in the life of Moses, the chosen leader, the guide who led the people from bondage and captivity, through the wilderness, to the land flowing with milk and honey, to the Canaan of their desire. And you and I, too, are walking through the wilderness. The world is a wilderness; it is a difficult place:

Guide me, O thou great Jehovah,
Pilgrim through this barren land.
I am weak, but thou art mighty;
Hold me with thy powerful hand.
William Williams

We need a leader; we need a guide; we need someone who can deliver us from our enemies, as Moses led the children of Israel through that weary pilgrimage of theirs. And Moses prophesied that God would one day raise up another "like unto me," one who will lead us in this spiritual pilgrimage in which we find ourselves.

All this, then, establishes the fact that Jesus of Nazareth was truly man, but we must ask a profound and important question: Why did He have to be truly man? Why the incarnation? Why the God-man? Why was that babe of Bethlehem ever born? It was essential, but why? The answer is this: He is to be our representative. Just as when Moses stood on that mount he was representing the nation, so our Savior is our representative. We are all sinners—the law has established that. We are face to face with God, and we need someone who can represent us before Him. And the person who represents us, who stands in our place, must be like us. The author of the Epistle to the Hebrews puts it like this: "Forasmuch then as the children are partakers of flesh and blood, he also himself likewise took part of the same" (2:14). He was not representing angels or animals or gods. We are human beings, and therefore our representative had to be a man.

There is another argument: Why do we face so many troubles in the world, including the last enemy, death? Where did death come from? The apostle Paul answers the question in the great fifteenth chapter of 1 Corinthians. He says, "Since by man came death, by man came also the resurrection of the dead" (v. 21). It is man who brought death into the universe. Man was not made to die. It is man's rebellion against God, it is man's sin, that has introduced death and all miseries, all the war and bloodshed and unhappiness and heartache—man has produced it all. So "since by man came death"—and all the accompanying problems—by man also must come the deliverance.

But, finally, there is another argument as to why He had to be a man—it was in order that He might represent us sympathetically. Now this is a great mystery, that one who is God but not man could not save us. We need one who understands us and who can sympathize with us. Our Savior had to be a man. The great message of that mighty Epistle to the Hebrews is that He knows our frailties and our weaknesses.

> *For we have not an high priest which cannot be touched with the feeling of our infirmities; but was in all points tempted like as we are, yet without sin. . . . For every high priest taken from among men is ordained for men in things pertaining to God, that he may offer both gifts and sacrifices for sins: who can have compassion on the ignorant, and on them that are out of the way; for that he himself also is compassed with infirmity.*
>
> —*Heb. 4:15; 5:1-2*

We are infirm, we are ignorant, and we are subject to temptation; and we need one who knows that, who can sympathize with us. Listen again to the great argument of the Epistle to the Hebrews. "For in that he himself hath suffered being tempted, he is able to succour them that are tempted" (2:18).

Though not the only ones, those are the main reasons why our deliverer had to be a man. He had to be born of a woman, for all of us are; He had to be born "under the law," for we are all under the law. That is the great proclamation of the Christian Gospel: "God sent forth his Son, made of a woman, made under the law" (Gal. 4:4). This is the first point. Jesus of Nazareth was a man as Moses was. He was truly a human being, just as we are. He lived the life of a human being here in this world of time, exactly as you and I are doing.

But notice that Moses says, "*like unto* me"—similar yet different. This is the point, and this is the message of the whole of the Old Testament. He must be a man, but if He is to save us, He must be more than a man, and this is the essence of the Christian proclamation. Man could not save us. I can prove that to you. The first man was perfect, and he was placed in a perfect environment. But he fell, and if God had created another perfect man, he would likewise have fallen. The one who is to save us must be man, but He must be more than man. So Moses says, "like unto me." "He must be more than I am. He will be like me in certain respects, but He must be above and beyond. He must come 'of your brethren,' He must be a Jew, but He must be more than that."

Our proclamation is that Jesus of Nazareth is God, the eternal Son. But He is *God* and *man*. Why is this essential? Why was it not sufficient for Him to be a man? Let us look at some of the answers. Moses was a very good man, but he was only a man; and as we are reminded in Hebrews 3:5, he was only a servant. He was a good servant, he was "faithful in all his house, as a servant," but he was no more than that. Not only that, he was a fallible servant, a servant who failed and sinned. Moses never entered the Promised Land. He took the children of Israel so far but no farther. He had already transgressed God's commandments. He was a man, yes, and a man like all of us. He failed, he sinned, and he disobeyed; and so he was incapable of leading the people finally into the Promised Land.

Not only that, Moses had only partial knowledge. He knew what God had revealed to him, but he knew no more. And he was sometimes forgetful even of that. So there was this limit to Moses.

Another aspect that is equally clear is that Moses was limited in the matter of his office. He was the lawgiver, he was the teacher and the guide, but that was not enough. We needed a priest also, and a priesthood, and a high priest to go once a year into the Holiest of All in the temple to represent the people. Moses could not do that; that work was given to his brother Aaron. Moses' capacity was limited, and he could only occupy one office. That is why he says, "one like unto me"—"He will be the things that I am, but He will be more, because you need more."

And then, as is argued in that great ninth chapter of the Epistle to the Hebrews, there is the fact that the whole of the teaching of Moses, and all that he introduced, was only a temporary expedient. Now we must be absolutely clear about this. These were the things that the members of the Sanhedrin gloried in, and they were rejecting Christ. But look at what they were holding on to! Take the law. Part of their whole trouble was that they did not realize that the law could not save anybody. The law can only tell us what to do; it cannot give us the power that enables us to carry out what it says. So the apostle Paul writes to the Romans, "What the law could not do, in that it was weak through the flesh . . ." (8:3). Moses stood before the people and said in effect, "Keep these commandments, and you will save yourselves." The law leaves it to us: "Thou shalt not kill. Thou shalt not commit adultery. Thou shalt not steal. Thou shalt not bear false witness. Thou shalt not covet." "Thou shalt love the Lord thy God with all thy heart, and soul, and mind, and strength, and thy neighbour as thyself." That is all right, but can you do it? The law says, "Do this, and thou shalt live." But no one can do it. So the law, as we have seen, leaves us condemned and hopeless and helpless and tells us that we need to be delivered.

And then these Jewish leaders gloried in the temple. They said that the conclusion to be drawn from Stephen's words was that ultimately we will not need the temple, we will not need all the priests and all the ceremonies and rituals and ornate buildings—this will all be unnecessary because we will go directly to God through Jesus. They were fighting for their law and their temple.

People today are fighting in the same sort of way. Some are turning back to the temple, so to speak, back to the ceremonies and the rituals and the priests. Why do people do this? They do it because they have not understood that all that is temporary; it is all but a shadow, not the substance. I invite you to read for yourselves the ninth chapter of the Epistle to the Hebrews. You will see that there the writer is saying that the temple is only a type; it is only a prophecy; it is only some kind of suggestion, a shadow, a pattern of things to come. It is an earthly tabernacle that simply gives us a kind of visual picture of a heavenly tabernacle. It is not meant to be permanent.

And then the writer says in effect, "Look at all that is done in your temple. You offer the blood of bulls and of goats, you have the ashes of a heifer, with water sprinkling all that is unclean, but what does that do? Is that going to emancipate anyone? Is it going to purchase forgiveness? Can the blood of bulls and goats reconcile us to God?" No; these are only pictures and types. All that happens in the temple, all the ceremonies, are "patterns of things in the heavens" (Heb. 9:23), simply temporary coverings of our sins until the perfect sacrifice has arrived and is offered.

And that is exactly what Stephen was saying to the members of the Sanhedrin, and indeed Moses had said it all himself. Moses had said in effect, "I am simply a road sign. God is going to raise up somebody who will be like me but will be infinitely bigger and greater." He was prophesying the coming of Jesus of Nazareth, the Son of God. This blessed person is the fullness and the completeness of everything that is hinted at and prophesied in the Old Testament. He has come; the Prophet like unto Moses has arrived, and He, in and of Himself, is everything that we can desire. He combines in Himself the satisfaction of all our needs. He is the fulfillment of all the promises of God. As Paul puts it: "For all the promises of God in him are yea, and in him Amen" (2 Cor. 1:20). This was the very fact that the poor members of the Sanhedrin were incapable of grasping. Here was the answer, and they refused Him. They were blinded by their mere traditions, which had overlain the real meaning of the things of which they were so proud.

Jesus of Nazareth—why should we believe in Him? Why should anybody believe in Him? Why should the members of the Sanhedrin have believed in Him? The answer is that He is in Himself Prophet, Priest, and King. Moses was a prophet and a teacher, but it was only a partial teaching. "God, who at sundry times and in divers manners spake in time past unto the fathers by the prophets . . ." (Heb. 1:1). One prophet was given this message; another prophet was given that. Moses was given a bit, another was given another bit, but it was all parts and portions. There was no completeness. The fullness is found in one person and in one alone, and that is Jesus Christ of Nazareth: "In whom are hid all the treasures of wisdom and knowledge" (Col. 2:3).

Now this is why Moses says in effect, "He will be like me, but only in certain respects. He will be altogether different and bigger. He will teach you all things; He will have all knowledge." Why? Here is the answer: "In the beginning was the Word, and the Word was with God, and the Word was God. The same was in the beginning with God" (John 1:1-2). Here is one who has looked eternally into the face of God. He speaks with authority. "No man hath seen God at any time; the only begotten Son, which is in the bosom of the Father, he hath declared him" (John 1:18). Here is one who comes from God and tells us about God. He knows. Not in bits and parts and portions—He knows God absolutely and perfectly. He was constantly saying this; listen to his words to Nicodemus:

> *Verily, verilly I say unto thee, We speak that we do know, and testify that we have seen; and ye receive not our witness. If I have told you earthly things, and ye believe not, how shall ye believe, if I tell you of heavenly things? And no man hath ascended up to heaven, but he that came down from heaven, even the Son of man which is in heaven.*
>
> *—John 3:11-13*

Do we want to know about God? There is only one who can do this for us. It is Jesus of Nazareth. He is God the Son. He has come out of the eternal bosom; He is co-equal and co-eternal with God. He says, "I am the light of the world" (John 9:5). He has all knowledge, and no one else does. He does not hesitate to stand before men and say, "He that hath seen me hath seen the Father" (John 14:9). Do you want to know about God? Do you want to know about man? Do you want to know about life? About death? About eternity? Listen to Him. Here is the only one who knows. Here is *the* prophet, *the* teacher, "*the* light of the world."

But He is not only the teacher. Moses was only a teacher and lawgiver, but here is one who is also the priest. Aaron was the high priest, not Moses; one man is not big enough or comprehensive enough. You have to have a number of men and divide the functions. But here is one who combines them all in Himself—Jesus, the Son of God, our great High Priest.

Do you realize what this means? What is our need? What is our problem? It is for someone who can stand in the very presence of God on our behalf—for we are all under God, we cannot escape Him. "It is he that hath made us, and not we ourselves" (Ps. 100:3), and we all have to die and stand before God. "It is appointed unto men once to die, but after this the judgment" (Heb. 9:27). So you and I will have to stand before Him, and what we need is someone who can do so for us and represent us and obtain our pardon.

Now this does not mean going into an earthly tabernacle or into a cathedral; it means going into that which is not the pattern but is the heavenly tabernacle, the heavenly place itself, and not merely into the representation of the presence of God, the *shekinah* glory (as it was in the old tabernacle), but into the very presence of God Himself. That is the need of men and women. Can you not see why this message is essential? No man can save us, no system can save us; we are concerned with facing the living God, and we need someone who can stand and represent us there.

There is only one who can do this—it is this Jesus whom the apostles preached. Why? Because He is God as well as man. He has come from God. He knows God. He is the Son of God. So He can stand before God. No human being can. God Himself has said, "There shall no man see me, and live" (Exod. 33:20). But there is one who can, the one who is perfect God and perfect man, all in one person.

What else must we say? Well, there is that law that was given through Moses, and we must keep that law. "The soul that sinneth, it shall die" (Ezek. 18:4). God did not give His law to play with us; He meant it to be carried out. So here is the law, but we cannot keep it. Moses could not. Nobody could. We must, therefore, be represented by someone who can. Here is one who is without sin, "[who] was in all points tempted like as we are, yet without sin" (Heb. 4:15). No one could charge Him with anything. He was never disobedient to His Father's will, to His Father's law. He gave perfect obedience to the law of God.

But what about our sins? The law demands, it exacts from us, it prescribes punishment. The law must be satisfied; not only its positive, but its negative demands must be satisfied, and the law has said, "without shedding of blood is no remission [of sins]" (Heb. 9:22). No man can help us because every man has sinned. The temporary arrangement was to transfer the sins to a bull or to a goat, then to kill the animal and take the blood; but that was only temporary. The punishment must be taken by man because man has sinned. We need a perfect offering, a perfect sacrifice, and there is only one—the one who entered into that holy place and offered not the blood of bulls and of goats but His own blood. He offered it as the High Priest, but He was also the sacrifice. He is everything. It is all in Him. He is "the Lamb of God, which taketh away the sin of the world" (John 1:29).

And He has offered this sacrifice once and forever. In Old Testament times, a high priest had to go into the Holiest of All once each year. Every year he had to do it afresh. The sin was only covered for a year, then another offering was needed. The priests were also offering sacrifices day by day. But we read in Hebrews 7:27, "who needeth not daily, as those high priests, to offer up sacrifice, first for his own sins, and then for the people's: for this he did once, when he offered up himself." Yet today there are people who, in a travesty of the Scriptures and in their wresting of the meaning of the texts, would say that at the Communion table Christ is offered again. Oh, what a lie! He has done it once and forever. One offering forever.

But, above all—and what a comforting thought it is—we need someone who is always there to represent us with God. No man can; the old Levitical priesthood could not. Priests became old and died; you had to appoint fresh priests, and then you had to make a new high priest. There was always this change. But here is one who lives forever because He is God. So we read in Hebrews: "Wherefore he is able also to save them to the uttermost"—to the end, to eternity—"that come unto God by him, seeing he ever liveth to make intercession for them" (7:25). He is not only the perfect prophet, He is the perfect High Priest, and He alone makes intercession for us and covers our every need.

And, finally, He is the King. We need a leader, do we not? We need someone to tell us how to live. We need someone to help us conquer our enemies. Who are we to fight a pharaoh? Who are we to part the Red Sea? Who are we to go through the wilderness? Who are we to cross the Jordan? Here is the problem. We need a leader, we need a ruler, a king, someone with authority who really can deal with our problems and our situation. And here He is, the same one. "Like unto Moses," but, oh, how much bigger! Moses was a very great servant, but, I repeat, only a servant. We need a master. Moses was a man who looked after the house. We need someone who owns the house, someone to whom it belongs. And this is the marvelous thing that we are told about this babe of Bethlehem, this Jesus of Nazareth, this Son of God. Do you know that the whole universe was made for Him? That is why God made it.

Now this is not my theory—this is what the apostle Paul teaches us quite plainly. He puts it like this: "For by him were all things created, that are in heaven, and that are in earth, visible and invisible, whether they be thrones, or dominions, or principalities, or powers: all things were created by him, and for him" (Col. 1:16).

This is why He is the Savior. This universe belongs to Him, everything in it—all the mountains and the valleys and the rivers and the seas and all the people and everything that is in the whole of creation. He owns it; He is the Master of the house. He is the Lord of the universe—God the Father gave it as a gift to His Son. That is why the Son is interested in it. And that is why He came into it to save it.

And having come into this earth, He conquered our every enemy—every one of them. He conquered sin, He conquered evil, He conquered temptation, as we have seen. He conquered the devil—the devil himself, who tempted him in the wilderness for forty days and who came back many other times, especially in the Garden of Gethsemane and when Christ was on the cross. The Son conquered him; He routed him. He has conquered death, the enemy we are all so afraid of—death, the last enemy. He has conquered hell and the grave. He has risen from the dead; He has ascended into heaven; He "sitteth on the right hand of God" in the glory everlasting (Col. 3:1). And just before He ascended into heaven He said, "All power is given unto me in heaven and in earth" (Matt. 28:18).

Read again these magnificent words at the beginning of Hebrews:

> *God, who at sundry times and in divers manners spake in time past unto the fathers by the prophets, hath in these last days spoken unto us by his Son, whom he hath appointed heir of all things, by whom also he made the worlds; who being the brightness of his glory, and the express image of his person, and upholding all things by the word of his power, when he had by himself purged our sins, sat down on the right hand of the Majesty on high.*
>
> —*1:1-3*

And there He is, "expecting [waiting] till his enemies be made his footstool" (Heb. 10:13).

Christian people, do not be discouraged. All other people, tremble. Everything is in His hands. He is permitting certain things for the time being, but He is the ruler of the nations. Because of what He did:

> *Wherefore God also hath highly exalted him, and given him a name which is above every name: that at the name of Jesus every knee should bow, of things in heaven, and things in earth, and things under the earth; and that every tongue should confess that Jesus Christ is Lord, to the glory of God the Father.*
>
> —*Phil. 2:9-11*

Without a doubt, He is coming again to rid the universe of evil and sin and hell; to perfect His own possession—"new heavens and a new earth, wherein dwelleth righteousness" (2 Pet. 3:13)—and He will reign over it all, the King eternal, invisible, immortal, "Lord of lords, and King of kings" (Rev. 17:14). The world is His inheritance, and He came into it to save it, to punish all His enemies, and to restore the fallen cosmos to its former and its pristine perfection.

Now He has already done this. That is what Stephen was saying to the members of the Sanhedrin. Why was he preaching? Why did the apostles preach? Because Jesus has risen! The apostles did not believe in Him properly until they saw Him risen from the dead. This is not a theory; this is not some fantasy that has been concocted. No! He rose from the dead; He appeared to chosen witnesses; in their very sight He ascended from Mount Olivet into heaven. He has done it; He has given the evidence.

The change in the apostles themselves is evidence that He lives, that He reigns, that He is the King over all. But the members of the Sanhedrin were blinded, and they could not see it. They said, "This is blasphemy!" They were holding on to Moses, they were holding on to the law, they were holding on to the temple, and they were rejecting all that these things point to, the fulfillment of all the promises, the full, the complete, the entire Savior, and the perfect salvation that He offers.

Are we like the members of the Sanhedrin? Are we just trusting the "fact" that we are better than somebody else? Are we just trusting to the fact that we have never been drunk or have not committed adultery or murder? Are we just trusting the fact that we are religious and are trying to be good and pious? Moses and the Old Testament tell us that is not enough. There is only one who can save, this one raised up of God to do so, God's only begotten Son. "God so loved the world, that he gave his only begotten Son, that whosoever believeth in him should not perish, but have everlasting life" (John 3:16). Have we seen Him? Have we recognized Him? He is Prophet, Priest, King. He is eternal, immortal, invisible! Have we fallen at His feet and given ourselves to Him as willing sacrifices? He will receive us. If we have never done so before, let us do so now.

10

THE WORK OF THE HOLY SPIRIT

This is that Moses, which said unto the children of Israel, A prophet shall the Lord your God raise up unto you of your brethren, like unto me; him shall ye hear. This is he, that was in the church in the wilderness with the angel which spake to him in the mount Sina, and with our fathers: who received the lively oracles to give unto us.

—Acts 7:37-38

In his great defense before the Sanhedrin, as we have been seeing, Stephen was really saying, in summary, Abraham was the man he was because he heard the word of God and recognized it. He was a pagan living among pagans in Ur of the Chaldees when suddenly the word of God came to him, and as the writer to the Hebrews says, "[He] obeyed; and he went out, not knowing whither he went" (11:8).

The same was true of Joseph. His whole story is really to be understood in that one way—here was a man who was sensitive to the word of God. And when Stephen came to the case of Moses, it was still the same. This is what made Moses such an outstanding man. He turned his back on all his glittering prospects because he recognized the word of God, and he was always sensitive to this word. Furthermore, Moses had been in the unique position of being called by God up to the top of the mount to receive the word of God for the whole Jewish nation.

So Stephen was really telling the members of the Sanhedrin, "All that you boast in is the result of hearing the word of the Lord. It is the word of the Lord that has made your nation, as it has made all your great men." Stephen's object was to show the Sanhedrin that their whole trouble at that moment was that they were insensitive to the word of God, that they were failing to hear it. That is why they regarded the preaching of the Christian message as a contradiction of the word spoken through Moses. Stephen wanted to show them that the Christian message is the same word, that it is a continuous word, and that any person or nation that is insensitive to the word of God ultimately fails. On the other hand, the secret of success in this world is to hear and to recognize and to give obedience to the living, lively, powerful word of God. That is what Stephen was doing, and I, in my feeble manner, am trying to do the same thing because it seems to me that the situation today is very similar to that described in Acts. Our world is as it is because it does not know the word of God, or to put it positively, the only hope for the world is that it should hear this word.

What is this word? This is the message that runs through the whole of the Bible. We call it the word of God, and it is. It is one great word, subdivided into particular words for special occasions. And its great message and theme from beginning to end is that God is interested and concerned and that He has a plan for the salvation of humanity and for the restoration of the whole universe to its original condition of perfection.

The Bible tells us there are three Persons in the Godhead, and so far we have been considering God the Father—God the Creator, the God who gave the law to Moses on Mount Sinai. He is the one who planned this amazing salvation before the foundation of the world. We have seen that salvation was the Father's idea and that the Son came to put it into operation. We have seen how the Son was prophesied and predicted in the Old Testament in types and shadows and adumbrations and how, "when the fulness of the time was come," He appeared and did His work. He was a man "like unto [Moses]," but more than a man—God the Son.

Now that is the point at which we have arrived, but it does not stop there. The message tells us that God the Holy Spirit is involved in this great plan of salvation. What is His part? Well, a simple way of looking at it is to see that the Father planned the salvation, the Son came to do the work that was absolutely essential to its being carried out, and the Holy Spirit applies it to us. He mediates it to us and puts it into execution in our lives. He works in our minds and in our hearts, and He brings the knowledge and the power of this great salvation to us.

Now this is the very truth that Stephen, in a different way, was putting before the members of the Sanhedrin. Why was he there? Why was he charged with blasphemy? Why had all the apostles already been arrested more than once and put on trial? The Sanhedrin were puzzled. They did not understand this new phenomenon, for after all, these apostles and others were ordinary men. In the opinion of the Sanhedrin, they were "unlearned and ignorant men" (Acts 4:13).

They were not a collection of philosophers from Greece; they were not Romans, experts in legislation. They were ordinary fishermen. They were men who had not passed through any theological training; they had no background; they had no culture. They had nothing except this: they had "been with Jesus" (Acts 4:13).

It is further known that something amazing and extraordinary had happened to these men on the Day of Pentecost. From that moment on, they had been transfigured. Before that they had obviously been very ignorant men. They had been given some remarkable powers, but when their Lord and Master, their leader, was crucified, they had lost all hope and had nearly given up. Some of them, like Thomas, had disappeared and only came back later. They had been in utter confusion. But suddenly they were all changed; on that Day of Pentecost an amazing power had come upon them. They were able to speak with power and authority and understanding; they were able to speak in other languages, and they were able to work miracles. "What is this?" That was the problem confronting the Sanhedrin. To them it was blasphemy, something that must be stopped; it was surely harmful to the people. So they arrested the apostles, and now they had arrested this man Stephen and were putting him on trial.

And Stephen, in his reply, was really saying to them: "You know what happened to Jesus of Nazareth. He lived among you for three years; you heard Him preaching, and you saw His miracles. You know, too, what happened on the Day of Pentecost and what has happened since, and though you have seen and have known these things, you still regard it as blasphemy. You say that it is against all that was taught to us by Moses and by the temple and its ceremonies. Oh, you are blind! You cannot see that all this is nothing but the fulfillment of what was prophesied."

That is what Stephen was saying. Everything that had taken place was the fulfillment of what Moses had anticipated. But here is the important question: What was it that enabled Moses to say, "A Prophet shall the Lord your God raise up unto you of your brethren, like unto me"? Here is a direct statement made by Moses. Moses, let us never forget, lived 1,400 years before the birth of Jesus of Nazareth in Bethlehem; yet he prophesied the coming of the Lord Jesus Christ, what He was going to say and what He was going to do. And remember, that includes His teaching about His sending the Holy Spirit upon the church on the Day of Pentecost. Moses anticipated that this one would be the messenger of salvation. What had enabled Moses to do that? There is only one answer. It was the result of the operation of the Holy Spirit upon him.

And this is not only true of Moses, it is true of all the other prophets. This is a most important matter, it is not something academic, and I am going to show you its practical relevance to every one of us. Both Moses and these other prophets, whose works are recorded in the Old Testament, prophesied in various ways not only the coming of the Lord Jesus Christ but also the fact that He would be the one who would send, and baptize with, the Holy Spirit. How did they do this? They gave details; they told us where He would be born and how He would die.

Now this is sheer fact—you can read it all for yourselves. These prophecies were made eight centuries, and sometimes more, before the birth of Christ. Indeed, David did so ten centuries before—Peter quoted him in his sermon on the Day of Pentecost, along with the prophet Joel and others. And because of this, the whole Jewish nation was not only looking forward to the coming of the Messiah, it was looking forward also to what it called "the promise of the Father" (Acts 1:4). Now this "promise of the Father" was the descent of the Holy Spirit, the coming of this divine power upon men and women, as a result of which, said Joel, "Your sons and your daughters shall prophesy, your old men shall dream dreams, your young men shall see visions" (Joel 2:28). It would be a mighty transforming power that would change everything.

So how was it that the men in the Old Testament were able to prophesy in this way? There is only one answer to the question, the answer given by Peter in his second epistle. He was writing, just before his death, to the church and the Christian people with whom he was familiar, and he knew that for various reasons they were rather dejected.:

> *For we have not followed cunningly devised fables, when we made known unto you the power and coming of our Lord Jesus Christ, but were eyewitnesses of his majesty. For he received from God the Father honour and glory, when there came such a voice to him from the excellent glory, This is my beloved Son, in whom I am well pleased. And this voice which came from heaven we heard, when we were with him in the holy mount.*
>
> *—1:16-18*

"I am going to die, but hold on to this," says Peter. "We are witnesses. James and John and I were with him on the holy mount of transfiguration, and we heard the voice."

But, Peter says, not only that:

> *We have also a more sure word of prophecy [a word of prophecy substantiated, proved]; whereunto ye do well that ye take heed, as unto a light that shineth in a dark place, until the day dawn, and the*

> *day star arise in your hearts: Knowing this first, that no prophecy of the scripture is of any private interpretation.*
>
> —*vv.* 19-20

A prophecy such as you have in the Old Testament is not the result of some farsighted man, some unusually intelligent being who can see a little bit further than somebody else—that is not the explanation. It is not something produced from the mind of man—it is not some "second sight"—that is impossible. There is only one answer: "For the prophecy came not in old time by the will of man: but holy men of God spake as they were moved by the Holy Ghost"—as they were influenced, controlled, carried along, borne along by the Holy Spirit of God (v. 21).

Now this is of the first significance for us all. It means that the Holy Spirit alone, the third Person in the blessed Holy Trinity, could make known this truth to men so many centuries ahead of time. He made it known to Moses; He made it known to the great succession of prophets. They could not have imagined this. They all said that it was "given" to them. They said, "the burden of the Lord," "the message of the Lord." They would go into some almost ecstatic condition, the imparting of truth would come upon them, and they would have clarity of understanding. The truth would be opened before them, and they would be controlled in their recording of it.

This is important in that here is an absolute proof of the reality of the spiritual realm. It proves the reality of God, the reality of the unseen realm, and the truth and reliability of the Bible. It is "a more sure word of prophecy." And so, as we live in this world and say, "What can we do? Is there anything beyond human beings?" I say, listen to this word of God. Here is a word that in the days of the prophets spoke of something that would happen centuries later. This was because of the revelation of God. There is no other explanation. That is a part of the significance of this Day of Pentecost. The Holy Spirit had been acting upon men even before the birth of the Son of God.

But these things, and this Day of Pentecost in particular, had been anticipated not only in the words of Moses and the prophets, but also in the very teaching of the law. If you go back and read the books of Exodus and Leviticus and parts of Numbers, you will find that great instructions are given there, not only about burnt offerings and sacrifices, but also about certain feasts to be held, and among them is the feast that is called "the feast of weeks," later called the feast of Pentecost. In the second chapter of Acts you will find that at that time in Jerusalem there were "devout men, out of every nation under heaven" (Acts 2:5). We are told:

> *Now when this was noised abroad, the multitude came together, and were confounded, because that every man heard them speak in his own language. And they were all amazed and marvelled, saying one to another, Behold, are not all these which speak Galileans? And how hear we every man in our own tongue, wherein we were born?*
> —*Acts 2:6-8*

These visitors were "Parthians, and Medes, and Elamites, and the dwellers in Mesopotamia, and in Judaea" and so on (see vv. 9-11). What were they doing in Jerusalem? They had gone up for this great feast of Pentecost. That celebration had been given to them through Moses, and the Jews had observed it regularly ever since.

There were a number of feasts—you can read about them for yourselves. But what is interesting for us is this: there was a feast when the Jews celebrated the Passover, in which they remembered the escape from Egypt and how, through the painting of lambs' blood on the doorposts and lintels of their houses, the angel of death had passed over them. The Passover is the feast in connection with what we now call Easter. Then seven weeks after the Passover, they were to observe this feast of weeks or Pentecost. During the Passover, they were to offer sheaves to God, but now they were to offer two baked loaves (Lev. 23:10, 15, 17).

What is the meaning of the feast of Pentecost—this feast that brought these people to Jerusalem on this momentous occasion when the Holy Spirit came down upon the church and these astounding things began to happen? Well, the whole object of that feast was to prophesy the coming of the Holy Spirit. The exact timing is, again, most amazing and extraordinary. About 1,400 years earlier they were told in this pictorial manner that on the seventh sabbath after the rising of the Messiah, the Holy Spirit would come down, and that very thing happened.

So the coming of the Holy Spirit was prophesied by the very feasts and rituals and ceremonies of the temple. Another interesting way this was done was in the use of oil. Oil in the Old Testament generally represents the Holy Spirit. So we have in the Old Testament a prophecy not only of the coming of the Son of God, but of the sending of the Holy Spirit.

Then when you start to read the New Testament, what do you find? John the Baptist! Here is the first preacher, a strange man who dressed in an odd manner. He did not live in the towns but in the wilderness, and when he began to speak, people rushed out to listen to him. He was an extraordinary man, and they said, "This must be the Messiah. Here is the one we have been expecting. This is the Prophet." But John said:

> *I indeed baptize you with water; but one mightier than I cometh, the latchet of whose shoes I am not worthy to unloose: he shall baptize you with the Holy Ghost and with fire: whose fan is in his hand, and he will throughly purge his floor, and will gather the wheat into his garner; but the chaff he will burn with fire unquenchable.*
>
> *—Luke 3:16-17*

So John prophesied the coming of Pentecost. And our Lord did exactly the same thing. He said that this was going to happen and that they would see wonders and signs and miracles (see, for example, Mark 16:17-18).

Now the significance of this for you and for me can be put like this: Here is one called Jesus of Nazareth. He is only a carpenter. He has not been trained in the schools, but He makes extraordinary claims. He looks at people and says, "I am the light of the world" (John 8:12). He tells them He is going to die and rise again. He says that after He has gone He is going to send the Holy Spirit (John 16:7). He has committed Himself to these specific things. Yet people today do not pay attention to all this. But, my dear friends, these are the things that really matter.

Our Lord committed Himself specifically to sending the Holy Spirit upon His people. He was filled with the Spirit—"God giveth not the Spirit by measure unto him" (John 3:34)—and in this fullness of the Spirit He prophesied that He would send forth the Spirit. "Tarry ye," he said, "in the city of Jerusalem, until ye be endued with power from on high" (Luke 24:49). You are going to receive it, and then, and then only, "ye shall be witnesses unto me both in Jerusalem, and in all Judaea, and in Samaria, and unto the uttermost part of the earth" (Acts 1:8).

Then the Day of Pentecost came. What is its meaning? What is its significance? This is absolutely vital. It attests our Lord's person; it shows us that He is who He claimed to be. It establishes finally the fact that Jesus of Nazareth is the Son of God, the fulfillment of every word that had been given through the Holy Spirit to Moses and all the prophets. It is evidence of the authority of the whole of the Word of God, the Scriptures. That is the significance of this particular day. One of the great works of the Spirit is to give absolute proof that God is fulfilling His plan and His promise to save humanity through a series of saving actions—and this is the last of those great actions.

But the Spirit also has another function to serve, and this is equally important for us. It is the work that He does in us and upon us in a direct manner. Our Lord Himself, in promising the Spirit, had said, "And when he is come, he will reprove"—convince—"the world of sin, and of righteousness, and of judgment" (John 16:8)—and He does that. He began to do so immediately.

How does He do this work? Look again at the record in Acts 2, and you will see the whole thing, as it were, in a nutshell. "He will convince the world of sin, and of righteousness, and of judgment." Moses had seen all this; he knew that the law could do this. But he also knew that the law can be a dead letter: "The letter killeth, but the spirit giveth life" (2 Cor. 3:6). So Moses knew that the real work of conviction would be done when the Holy Spirit came in his fullness. Notice that on the Day of Pentecost, when Peter preached a sermon that seemed to be an exposition of Scripture and an explanation of certain old prophecies, extraordinary things happened. As he was preaching, suddenly the people were "pricked in their heart," and they cried out, saying, "Men and brethren, what shall we do?" (Acts 2:37).

This is the work of the Holy Spirit. This is the Holy Spirit convicting of sin and of righteousness and of judgment to come. What does He do? First, He convinces us all of our ignorance. Look at this crowd at Jerusalem that was listening to Peter. You know the sort of crowd it was. It was the same crowd that a few weeks before had been shouting out at the top of its voice, "Away with Him, crucify Him." The fickle crowd followed Jesus one day and proclaimed Him, then listened to their leaders, the Pharisees and Sadducees and scribes, and turned around and said, "Give us Barabbas. Away with Him, crucify Him." Now they were confronted by the phenomenon of these extraordinary, simple men who were speaking with power and authority and in strange languages—what was this? So they went out of curiosity to listen to what this strange preacher had to say.

But as they listened, they suddenly became convicted of their ignorance. This is what the Holy Spirit does, and He is still doing it. He opens our eyes to the realization that we have lived in utter unawareness of the fact that we possess a soul. How often do men and women think about their souls? Oh, I know they think about their pleasures, they think about work, they think about their birth, marriage, death, money, bank balance, gambling. They think about politics, and they get excited and will march and make their protest. But do they even realize that they have souls? So the Holy Spirit brings this word to us. It always comes as light and as teaching, and it enables us to see for the first time that we have a soul within us, that we are not money-making or pleasure machines. We are living souls.

We have been unaware of God. We have been so interested in ourselves and other people that we have not thought about Him. We may even have spoken like the "fool": "The fool hath said in his heart, There is no God" (Ps. 14:1). But now we are awakened to our appalling ignorance because prophecy proves that there must be a God, and this is demonstrated in other ways too. The Spirit has awakened us to our own ignorance about God.

Then we find that we have been entirely unaware of the whole object and purpose of life in this world. We used to think that we came into it as the result of some blind evolutionary process, that some impersonal force has produced us, and that we are here to have as good a time as we can, and then we die and that is the end of it. But now the Spirit awakens us to the realization that that is not life and that man is not an animal. We realize the truth of Henry Wadsworth Longfellow's words:

> *Dust thou art, to dust returnest,*
> *Was not spoken of the soul.*

The Spirit awakens us to the realization that we are immortal and that there stretches before us immortality, an everlasting condition.

Are we aware of this? Have these things been active in our consciousness? The Spirit of God alone brings these truths to us, just as He convicted those people in Jerusalem on the Day of Pentecost, that thoughtless mob, listening out of curiosity, in utter ignorance of God's plan. People today get so excited about elections, local and general; they get excited about politicians but never give a thought to God's plan for this world in its appalling mess and misery and shame and sorrow and degradation. Here is the ignorance: not knowing about God's plan of salvation and dismissing it even when they hear it; not knowing about the person of the Lord. Blindness! But then, "Men and brethren, what shall we do?" they say. They are convicted of their ignorance.

But the Holy Spirit does not stop there. He convicts us also of our utter inability to save ourselves, and this is much more serious. Men and women are proud of themselves, proud of their understanding, proud of their knowledge and learning. But the Holy Spirit shows them that all they are proud of is useless and valueless. With all their supposed genius and ability, they can never find out the things that really matter. "Canst thou by searching find out God?" asks Job's friend Zophar (Job 11:7). There is only one answer: we cannot. Paul says to the clever Corinthians who were so proud of their philosophers, "The world by wisdom knew not God" (1 Cor. 1:21). But people persist in thinking they can find God, and only when the Spirit has convicted them of the fact that they never can, that it is impossible, do they change.

Furthermore, the Spirit convicts us of something even worse than that: even when we are confronted by truth incarnate, we cannot recognize it. This is devastating. This is where the Spirit of God really shows us ourselves as we are. Not only can we not find God by searching, but we are so fallen that when God stands before us, we do not recognize Him. Paul says:

> *But we speak the wisdom of God in a mystery, even the hidden wisdom, which God ordained before the world unto our glory: which none of the princes of this world knew: for had they known it, they would not have crucified the Lord of glory.*
>
> —*1 Cor. 2:7-8*

Now that is simple fact. The world is so lost, it is so helpless and so vain, that when God incarnate stood before it, it did not recognize Him but said, "Away with Him." The members of the Sanhedrin were blind in this sense. That is what Stephen was saying to them. "Moses," he said in effect, "the man you revere, prophesied the coming of this one. You have seen Him, you have heard Him, you have seen His miracles, but you have not recognized Him. Why? Because you are blind." The Spirit alone can open our eyes so that we see our terrible danger. But listen to Paul again: "But the natural man receiveth not the things of the Spirit of God: for they are foolishness unto him: neither can he know them, because they are spiritually discerned" (1 Cor. 2:14).

This is terrible. "Listen," said Stephen in effect to the members of the Sanhedrin, "you know what happened on the Day of Pentecost. These things have happened before your eyes, and yet you do not believe them. Why not? Because you are spiritually dead." This is the whole tragedy of our modern world. We are trusting in cleverness, ability, knowledge, as if these can find God! The Spirit alone can bring conviction.

But, thank God, the Spirit does not stop His work at the negative action of conviction of sin. It is He who brings us the revelation of a great and glorious salvation. Our Lord had said, when promising the Spirit, "He shall glorify me" (John 16:14). And on the Day of Pentecost, when Peter was filled with the Spirit, he spoke about Christ, this blessed person, the one whom they had rejected. He told the people in essence, "He is the Son of God, the one whom David looked forward to." Peter quoted David's words in Psalm 16: "Thou wilt not leave my soul in hell, neither wilt thou suffer thine Holy One to see corruption. . . . The Lord said unto my Lord, Sit thou on my right hand" (Acts 2:27, 34). That could not have been spoken about David himself, said Peter in his sermon, because David's sepulchre was still there, and his bones were there. The Spirit enabled David to look forward to Christ.

And the Spirit still does that. It is the business and the work of the Holy Spirit to unfold to us that "God was in Christ, reconciling the world unto himself"

(2 Cor. 5:19). Men and women do not see this for themselves. They are convicted first, and then the Spirit shows them that God has provided a Lamb. "Behold the Lamb of God, which taketh away the sin of the world," said John the Baptist (John 1:29). Our Lord said, "the Son of man came not to be ministered unto, but to minister, and to give his life a ransom for many" (Matt. 20:28). Peter adds, "who his own self bare our sins in his own body on the tree, that we, being dead to sins, should live unto righteousness: by whose stripes ye were healed" (1 Pet. 2:24). The Spirit alone can enable us to see this; this is His work. It is foolishness to everybody else, but the Spirit can give us this understanding.

And that, again, is what Paul is constantly saying in that second chapter of his first epistle to the Corinthians:

> *Which none of the princes of this world knew: for had they known it, they would not have crucified the Lord of glory. But as it is written, Eye hath not seen, nor ear heard, neither have entered into the heart of man, the things which God hath prepared for them that love him. But God hath revealed them unto us by his Spirit: for the Spirit searcheth all things, yea, the deep things of God. . . . Now we have received, not the spirit of the world, but the Spirit which is of God; that we might know the things that are freely given to us of God.*
>
> *—1 Cor. 2:8-10, 12*

And at Pentecost the apostle preached, and the people "were pricked in their heart" and cried out, "Men and brethren, what shall we do?" And Peter answered them, "Repent, and be baptized every one of you in the name of Jesus Christ for the remission of sins, and ye shall receive the gift of the Holy Ghost" (Acts 2:37-38). Then we are told, "Then they that gladly received his word were baptized: and the same day there were added unto them about three thousand souls" (v. 41).

This is the work of the Holy Spirit. He pricks the heart. He reveals to us our ignorance and our sinfulness. He makes us see that the problem for us is not what men may be doing in South Africa or what is happening in Vietnam or various political, social questions. I am not saying these matters are not important, but they are not our primary problem. Our primary problem is: What am I? What is man? How am I going to die? For whatever I do, I must die. "And if man die, shall he live again?" (Job 14:14). What happens after death?

Those are the questions that only the Word of God can answer, and the Spirit brings it home to us. And when He does, our hearts are pricked, and we say, "Where are we? What have we been doing? We have not thought of these things. I have a soul, but what's going to happen? I'm lost. I'm a sinner. I don't know God. I can't get rid of my sins. I can't find God, and yet I need Him. What can I do?" "Men and brethren, what shall we do?"

Then the Spirit reveals the blessed fact that "God so loved the world, that he gave his only begotten Son, that whosoever believeth in him should not perish, but have everlasting life" (John 3:16). He was "delivered by the determinate counsel and foreknowledge of God" (Acts 2:23). That is the wonderful, amazing message! I do not understand it, I do not deserve it, but God has done it. He sent His only Son into the world and has put my sins on Him and has punished Him for me and offers me free pardon and forgiveness—that is the message.

What does all this mean to us? It was blasphemy to the members of the Sanhedrin. The astounding things—all that happened in Jesus of Nazareth (His coming, His living, His doing good, His miracles, His sacrificial death, His burial, His resurrection, His appearances, His ascension, the descent of the Holy Spirit, the change in these apostles, the miracles that they had been working, the miracle of the lame man at the Beautiful Gate of the temple)—were to them nothing but blasphemy. What was the matter with them? They were blinded by tradition, blinded by position!

Is that our condition too? Is this all foolishness to us? Is this some old story, some fairy tale, something unworthy of a modern, sophisticated, scientific man or woman? I want to remind you that the fact of Pentecost is a condemnation of our whole position. Moses had prophesied it. He could only have done so through the operation of the Spirit of God upon him. And it was the same with all the other prophets. Can we not see the facts? The Day of Pentecost was a historical event, a fact. There would be no church but for that. These men had been cast down; they had been mourning. Suddenly they were transfigured; they spoke with authority and power and worked miracles. And the church went on. Why? The Holy Spirit.

Have these things touched us? Have they shaken us? Have they revealed to us our ignorance about our soul and our eternal destiny, our ignorance of these mighty events and their significance? If so, the question is, what are we going to do about that ignorance? Do we resent it? Do we resist it? Are we battling for all we are worth with our mind and everything else we have against it? Oh, may we learn the lesson of these foolish members of the Sanhedrin, blinded by prejudice to the facts, and beware lest we be blinded by the same kind of prejudice and resist the Holy Spirit, even as they did and even as the children of Israel had so frequently done in their long story. God forbid that any one of us should resist the Holy Spirit of God and go to perdition.

11

LISTEN TO HIM

This is that Moses, which said unto the children of Israel, A Prophet shall the Lord your God raise up unto you of your brethren, like unto me; him shall ye hear.

—Acts 7:37

I want to call attention in particular to those last four words in the Authorized Version: "Him shall ye hear." In some of the other versions you will not find these words, because in some of the old manuscripts they were not present. But I call attention to them because Moses, we are reminded here, made a statement that is to be found in Deuteronomy 18:15. If you look that up, you will find that Moses quite definitely did make this statement about listening to this prophet who was to come. Furthermore, we have already had an account, in Acts 3, of Peter quoting this same statement: "For Moses truly said unto the fathers, A prophet shall the Lord your God raise up unto you of your brethren, like unto me; him shall ye hear in all things whatsoever he shall say unto you" (v. 22). This is a bit of elaboration by Peter of what Moses actually said. But Moses did say that God would raise up a prophet from among the people themselves; He would be like Moses in certain respects, and they were to listen to Him.

Now Stephen quoted these words, and you see the object that he had in his mind. He had been arrested and was on trial because he was preaching that Jesus of Nazareth is the Son of God and the Savior of the world. This was the message of all these early preachers, the apostles and others. But the members of the Sanhedrin did not believe it. So Stephen was saying, "Can you not see that by not believing in Jesus of Nazareth you are rejecting the teaching of Moses? He foretold this person, and he has urged you to listen to Him; but you refuse to do that. So you are denying the teaching of the man whose memory you revere so much, while I, on the other hand, and these other Christians, are obeying Moses. We are doing the very thing that he told us to do."

Here we are at the very heart and center of the Christian message. The purpose of Christian preaching is to call men and women to listen to the Lord Jesus Christ. This was the crux of the position in which Stephen found himself: Should you, or should you not, listen to this Jesus? That is the big question. It was the question for the Sanhedrin, and it is still the question for all of us.

I imagine that some may be asking, "Why should we listen to Him?" Many in the world are saying that. They are not listening to this Jesus. They regard Christianity as an irrelevance, antiquated, something that does not speak to modern men and women and their condition. After all, He lived nearly 2,000 years ago; is it right that we should be looking back? Why should we listen to this person, this Jesus, who was preached by Stephen and by the apostles? I want to answer that question.

First of all, we should listen because of our condition, because of our need. This is always a very good way of starting. You say, "Why do you preach Jesus? Why do you ask me to listen to Him?" Before we consider anything let's look at ourselves—what is our condition? And the moment we face that question, I think you will have to agree that our condition is primarily one of ignorance. Here we are, in this world as we all know it to be, with troubles, problems, unhappiness, tensions everywhere. What is the matter? We must start there.

But people do not do that. Normally they start with certain queries that they happen to have about statements that are made in the Bible, and they ask their tricky catch questions. But that is never the way to approach the Christian message. You and I must start with ourselves. And if you think that we are authorities, then I have nothing to say to you. Again, if you are perfectly satisfied with yourself and your own life and with the world as it is, then I have nothing to say to you. I could say certain things about you, but I have nothing to say directly to you—nothing at all. This message has nothing to say to people who say, "All is well," people who are fully satisfied and who think they are capable of managing their own lives. Our Lord Himself said, "They that are whole need not a physician; but they that are sick. I came not to call the righteous, but sinners to repentance" (Luke 5:31-32). We suffer from ignorance, especially about the most important things of all. And the tragedy of the modern man and woman is that they do not realize that. They talk and boast about what they know in a scientific sense, but they do not stop to think of what they do not know in a much more important sense.

This is what I mean. I know about scientific advances, and I am as proud of them as anybody else. Thank God for all the discoveries of science and the advances in medicine and all these things about which modern people are so proud—I agree, they are marvelous. But what I want to know is this: What is man? Certain diseases from which I suffer can be cured all right, but I am still here after you have cured my diseases. And what am I? That is what I want to know. What is the purpose and object of life, and how should I live?

Then there is the ultimate problem of death. I know modern people do not like thinking about it, but that is where they are foolish, that is where they show there is something wrong with them. They are afraid to face the facts. Death is an absolute reality. We talk about wars and so on, and it is right that we should do so and prepare for them. There may be a third world war, or there may not be. But death is not a possibility—it is a *certainty*. Nobody can avoid it; it must be faced. And when you come to that, you find that you know nothing about it. What lies beyond death? You hear of people dying, but what then? What happens to them? "If a man die, shall he live again?" (Job 14:14). At these points there is terrible ignorance. We just do not know; and this is why I say that we should be prepared to listen to this person, Jesus Christ.

Why do people behave as they do? Why is anybody unhappy? Why is there tension among the nations? Why is there fighting? Why is there war? Look at war objectively, and you must agree it is sheer madness, and yet the nations are fighting and have always fought. What is the cause of all this?

Now again I think you will agree that when we face these questions, we find that men and women are in a state of appalling ignorance. We must consider all these things; we must face them all. We must fully grant that there has been a 100 percent advance in scientific knowledge, but we must also face the fact that with regard to these other questions there has been no advance, no change, no increase in knowledge whatsoever. The world is proving that at this very moment.

And then in addition to our ignorance we are aware of our failure. Are we able to live even as we think we ought to live? Are we able to keep our own resolves and resolutions? Are we not all aware of defeat and unhappiness, shame and remorse, a kind of frustration? Anyone who thinks at all is aware of this. You find it in the biographies and autobiographies; you find it in all great literature, all great drama. The greatest drama is always tragedy. The greatest men and women have always observed that life is tragic. There is some sort of contradiction in life and in human beings that is baffling and confusing. And yet we all have a feeling that we were not meant to be like this; we have a feeling that things ought to be better, that things could be better, that things must be better. This is the whole story of civilization. The whole time we are aware of a final kind of frustration that in spite of advances in some respects, there is retrogression in others. Anybody who is prepared to face this present time and this present moment with honest eyes must admit that we are in a state of terrible confusion.

How do you explain man with the brilliance of his achievements on the one hand and his dismal, abject failure on the other? Why is it that man, who can show such genius in handling matters that are outside himself, is such a miserable failure in handling himself and the things that are inside himself? Why is it that man, who can invent all kinds of gadgets, cannot somehow produce happiness? What is the meaning of this essential contradiction that seems to be part and parcel of human nature? There is the essence of the modern problem.

> *There's a divinity that shapes our ends,*
> *Rough-hew them how we will.*
> *Hamlet*, Act V, Scene II

Humanity has felt this all along. You find it even in the great flowering period of Greek philosophy. That is demonstrated by what the apostle Paul discovered when he paid his first visit to Athens and found the place cluttered with many temples. Among them he found this exceptional altar: "TO THE UNKNOWN GOD" (Acts 17:23). Innate in human nature is this feeling that outside us, above us, surrounding us are powers and forces bigger and greater than ourselves and that we are being manipulated. All men and women who have thought have struggled with this feeling. They have fought against it, they have tried to get rid of it, but still the problem remains. And the result of it all is that humanity is in a condition of desperate need. So I would argue that this need is a very good reason for being ready to listen to this person, Jesus Christ.

A second reason for listening is that no one else can help us. On one occasion, when a great crowd went after our Lord, He began to say some very plain things to them. He put the truth to them almost in a blunt manner, and there were some people who could not take it—some people are always ready to be entertained, but when you come down to realities and brass tacks, they do not like it. And we are told, "From that time many of his disciples went back, and walked no more with him" (John 6:66). Our Lord saw the crowd leaving Him, and He turned to the twelve apostles and said, "Will ye also go away?" But Peter, in a moment of inspiration, looked at him and said, "Lord, to whom shall we go?" He said in essence, "We are not leaving. There is nobody else! We have already tried others, we have listened to them, and we know what they have to say—they cannot help us. 'To whom shall we go? thou hast the words of eternal life'" (John 6:67-68).

When we face these great ultimate questions and problems, we just have to come to the conclusion that the world cannot help us; it has nothing to say about these matters.

"But," you say, "what about philosophy?"

Philosophy will not help you. It can speculate, but that is all; the philosophers do not know the answers. Now certain statements seem to me to be basic in this whole matter, and if people only started with these, it would save them a lot of trouble and keep them from wasting breath and energy. Here is the fundamental postulate: "The world by wisdom knew not God" (1 Cor. 1:21). This means that philosophy cannot help us. It has done great things; its analysis has been wonderful; thank God for it, it is all very interesting and enlightening. But when you come to the ultimate questions, the philosophers are as ignorant as the rest of us.

And that is not only true of philosophy—it is true of religions. Take the great religions of the world, as people like to call them—not one of them can really help us at this point. The best that any of them can offer is to say that somehow or another we will in the end get rid of ourselves and be lost in some "Absolute" and be absorbed in some "Eternal." That is all they can offer, and they cannot even prove that—it is only theory. Some of these religions say we must come back many times into the world, that we go through many reincarnations. These religions are serious. They have been studied for centuries. But they are all pessimistic and hopeless and cannot answer our questions. Again, there are excellent teachings in many of them, and they have ethical systems and so on that are very good, but when you come to these fundamental matters, they cannot help us.

So why am I a Christian? Why do I believe in Christ? Why did I ever listen to Him? Why did I ever give my life to Him? The answer is that everybody else had failed me. The whole world had failed me, and I had failed myself. Our Lord Himself said that only people who are conscious of failure go to Him. They have realized their need; they have realized that nothing and no one else can help them or give them any assistance at all.

You may, however, still ask, "But why listen to *Him*? Who is He?"

I do not object to those questions. They are perfectly fair and good questions to ask, and I have some wonderful answers.

Why, then, listen to this Jesus of Nazareth? Let me put it like this. Why do you listen to anybody? Why do you read the writings of certain authors? The answer is that somebody has recommended them to you or you have seen their books advertised. All right, this is very good; so let us apply that same principle, and I have certain recommendations to give you.

My first answer is that the whole of the Old Testament encourages me to listen to this person. It recommends Him; it is preparing for Him. Indeed, the Old Testament is a massive advertising campaign for Jesus of Nazareth, the Son of God. It is the preliminary advertising—I am speaking in modern parlance—that is how we do things now, is it not? Before some important event, we have months and months of preliminary buildup. Similarly, the Old Testament is a buildup for Jesus Christ, and some great experts are speaking.

We take the advice of the experts, do we not? We listen to a man whose judgment we respect and value and who has proved in his own life that he is a man worthy of being listened to. So I listen to Jesus Christ because the patriarchs tell me to do so. I do not think a bigger personality has ever trod the face of this earth than a man called Abraham. He was called "the Friend of God" (Jas. 2:23). He was a great gentleman. He was a big man, made on a massive scale in every respect. Read his story. What I am told about him is this: "Abraham rejoiced to see my day: and he saw it, and was glad" (John 8:56). That man was enabled to live as he did and to triumph as he did 2,000 years before the birth of Jesus because he knew that Jesus was coming. He lived by faith. Abraham had his eye set on this: he knew that Jesus was going to appear. And he recommends me to listen to Him.

And the other patriarchs do exactly the same. If you read their stories, you will find that Abraham passed on a secret to Isaac, and Isaac passed it on to Jacob—it was passed on from father to son. What was it? It was this hope that animated the Israelite people, these Hebrews who had come out of Abraham and his ancestor Eber. It was the promise that God was going to send a deliverer. This was the secret that lifted them up and set them apart from everybody else; they were all saying, "Wait! He is coming! Listen to Him. He will have the answer."

So I am listening to their recommendation. And in the passage we are studying, of course, I am reminded of Moses. After the great patriarchs in the book of Genesis, you come to the book of Exodus, and suddenly there arises this towering figure of Moses, Moses the lawgiver, the man of God. Here again is a man who not only teaches the law but also, as we have seen, points forward: "A prophet shall the Lord your God raise up unto you of your brethren, like unto me; him shall ye hear." And I have shown how everything in the law of Moses, everything in the ceremonial ritual of the temple, all pointed to Christ's coming. So in different ways Moses was saying, "Him shall ye hear." Moses was only temporary; the great teacher was yet to come.

Read, too, the prophets of the Old Testament. The people were in trouble; indeed, the world has always been in trouble. Since the fall it has always been a place of unhappiness and misery. There is nothing new about the state of the world today. It has always been like this. There has been drunkenness and infidelity, divorce, separation, broken homes, theft, robbery—all these things. They are all described in the Old Testament. Humanity was trying to solve the problem; they were listening to the teachers, but still the problem continued. Was there any help? Isaiah's answer is this—and it is the great message of the Old Testament: "Comfort ye, comfort ye my people, saith your God." On what grounds? What comfort is there? Well, the comfort, says Isaiah in that great fortieth chapter of his prophecy, is that a great one is coming: "Prepare ye the way of the LORD, make straight in the desert a highway for our God. Every valley shall be exalted, and every mountain and hill shall be made low" (Isa. 40:1, 3-4). Make a way for the Deliverer, a highway for the Lord, the Messiah. He is coming, and "all flesh shall see it together" (Isa. 40:5).

That is a summary of the message of every single one of the prophets. They dealt with temporary problems, I know, but they were all pointing forward, and I listen to this blessed Person because the prophets are all recommending me to do so. They were great men. Read them, these men of understanding and ability. Some of them were tremendous poets. But they all say, "Do not stop with me. I do not understand fully. All I know is this—I have a message. There is one to come. He is the one to listen to. Wait for Him!"

And then I come to the last of the prophets—John the Baptist—this extraordinary man, preaching in the wilderness. There had been 400 years of silence, and things were hopeless for the Jewish people. Suddenly a voice appeared, as it were, and a man spoke, a strange man, and the people listening to him said, "This must be the Christ." And John said, "One mightier than I cometh, the latchet of whose shoes I am not worthy to unloose" (Luke 3:16). He said he was "the voice of one crying in the wilderness, Prepare ye the way of the Lord" (Luke 3:4). He also proclaimed, "I am not the Christ, but . . . I am sent before him" (John 4:28). He was saying, "He is coming after me, but though He comes after me, He will be preferred before me." "He must increase, but I must decrease" (John 3:30). So as I listen to John the Baptist, I hear him telling me, "Him shall ye hear! Listen to Him! It is what *He* says that will matter."

What a recommendation! The whole of the Old Testament! But not only that, I have listened to this Jesus because He is recommended by the apostles. Why is there such a thing as the Christian church? How did it all begin? Well, we are given the account in these early chapters of the book of Acts. The church is not a human institution; nor is she a society like the Royal Society or any one of the societies started by a group of scientists or philosophers or thinkers. Men have started many a society and institution, and they are valuable and very good; but the Christian church never began like that. No human being ever had an idea of starting the Christian church.

So how did the church ever come into being? If you read the story, you will see why I listen to this Jesus. I look at men like Peter or like this man Stephen. I look at John and all the other apostles. What were they? They were just ordinary men. They were fishermen, men who worked with their hands, not scholars or philosophers, and yet I find them standing up and speaking in a manner that confounded the great religious authorities. I find them working miracles and becoming a phenomenon. I find everybody listening to them, and I find them facing even the Sanhedrin, who were baffled by what they were doing. What is this?

To me there is only one answer: it was not the men themselves, and they said so. When Peter and John had worked the miracle on the lame man at the Beautiful Gate of the temple, the people came crowding around them, praising them and ready to revere them. But Peter said, "Why look ye so earnestly on us, as though by our own power or holiness we had made this man to walk?" (Acts 3:12). "We have not done it! It is this Jesus, the one you crucified—He did this miracle."

And a miracle had not only been done to the lame man, but also in the lives of the apostles. You cannot understand these apostles apart from this Jesus. He had changed them; He had made them what they were. He had come to Peter, who had been such a coward that in order to save his own skin he had denied his greatest friend and benefactor, and Jesus had turned him into a blazing prophet, a man filled with courage, ready to defy the Sanhedrin and the whole world. I am ready to listen to one who could do a thing like that to Simon Peter. These apostles recommend Him to me. The change in their lives, they said, was all due to Him. They were the men responsible for the Gospels. They said, "We were with Him, we saw Him, we heard what He said, we watched His actions—that is why we are preaching Him."

I also listen to Jesus because of the recommendation of the apostles, the foundation stones of the Christian church. And then I add the testimony and recommendation of the great martyrs of the early centuries, some outstanding, others quite unknown men and women. They were all animated by the same spirit, all ready to die for this Jesus, all saying that they had had such an experience of Him, such a transformation of their lives, that they would sooner suffer death than deny Him. Death was nothing to them any longer. It was Jesus who was important. He was everything to them. "Listen to Him," they say. I hear their message coming out of the catacombs outside Rome, and I hear them in other parts of the world.

I hear the confessors and the martyrs in this country [England]. All of them throughout the centuries are saying to me, "Listen to Him." I read the history of our own land, and I see that some of the greatest people who have ever lived have been these Christian people. They have been our country's benefactors. Where did hospitals come from? They came from the Christian church, from Christian men and women. Laws to help the poor came from the same source, and so did the educational system.

I have to say these things because people are ignorant of them. You should not thank any political party for hospitals or for education or for relief for the poor. Christian people gave us all these things, because of what Jesus had done for them. He had so transformed them that He had given them a compassion, a love for others, a desire to help others, and they are all encouraging me to listen to Him. That is their testimony. These are the external recommendations that urge me to listen to Him.

But I have a yet stronger reason for listening to Him, and that is His own invitation to me. I look at Him in the Gospels, and I hear Him calling. "Come unto me," he says. "Learn of me" (Matt. 11:28-29). We must face this. We are confronted here by facts, by history, by a remarkable phenomenon. Look at the authority that was claimed by this Jesus. This was what Stephen was really saying. Why did Stephen preach Him? Why did he commend Him to the members of the Sanhedrin? Why did he say that they were making a tragic mistake in rejecting Him, as they had all done when they crucified Him a few months earlier? Why should He be listened to? Why does Moses tell us to listen to Him? Why do they all tell us to do so?

It is because He claims a unique authority. He says, "Ye have heard that it was said by them of old time . . . But I say unto you . . ." (Matt. 5:27-28). Look at this person. He is walking along the shore, and some fishermen are mending their nets, cleaning out their boat, working with their father. He looks at them and says, "Follow me." He expects them to leave everything at once—their father, the boat, and their occupation—"Follow me!" (Matt. 4:19). And they followed Him.

Now this is a fact. This is why Christianity came into being. Who is this person? Listen to Him. He stands up and says, "I am the light of the world" (John 8:12). He seems to be a carpenter, an ordinary man, as it were, but He stands up and says, in a world of trouble such as this, in a world of darkness, a world of ignorance, a world of failure, "I am the light of the world: he that followeth me shall not walk in darkness, but shall have the light of life." Is not this what we need? Listen to Him again: "I am the way, the truth, and the life: no man cometh unto the Father, but by me" (John 14:6). He says, "Follow Me, and I will lead you to truth, I will lead you to peace, I will lead you to happiness. Listen to Me."

This person says that He has power even to forgive sins. He did not hesitate to say this. "Thy sins be forgiven thee," He said to the paralyzed man (Mark 2:5). The Pharisees brought Him a woman caught in the act of adultery, and they said, "Now, then, we will test Him and see what He does." And what He did was show them that they were equally guilty in their hearts and in their imaginations, and they slinked out, ashamed of themselves. And then He said to the woman, "Neither do I condemn thee: go, and sin no more" (John 8:11).

So here is the question: Who is this who makes these claims? What are His grounds for standing up and saying in a world of darkness and ignorance and failure, "I am the light of the world"—what right has He to say this? It is perfectly right to ask these questions, and here are the answers to them. The grounds on which He speaks are that He knows that He is the fulfillment of all the prophecies of the Old Testament. Read again the story about John the Baptist at the beginning of Matthew 11. Poor John the Baptist; he had prophesied that our Lord was coming and had told people to go after Him. He was standing one day with two of his followers when Jesus Christ passed by, and John said to them, "Behold the Lamb of God, which taketh away the sin of the world" (John 1:29). And yet look at poor John later. He was languishing in a dank and dark prison. He had lost his health; he was unhappy; he was very ill. And he began to be filled with doubts. So he sent two of his followers to this Jesus to say, "Art thou he that should come?" (Matt. 11:3). In other words, "Are you the one we have been expecting, the one whom all of us as prophets have foretold, or have we been wrong after all, and must we start looking for somebody else?"

And this is the reply our Lord sent back to John: "Go and shew John again those things which ye do hear and see." What were they? "The blind receive their sight, and the lame walk, the lepers are cleansed, and the deaf hear, the dead are raised up, and the poor have the gospel preached to them" (Matt. 11:4-5). Why did He say this? There is only one answer. The prophets had prophesied that when the great deliverer did come, that was the sort of thing He would do. So our Lord said in effect, "Go back and tell John that those are the very things you have seen Me doing; ask him to work it out from there." And our Lord added, "And blessed is he, whosoever shall not be offended in me." He is the fulfillment of all the prophecies. He did not hesitate to say, "Abraham rejoiced to see my day" (John 8:56). There is no question about this.

But our Lord went further; this is why you should listen to Him. He once spoke to a very learned Jewish teacher called Nicodemus. This man was arguing with Him because, although he was a teacher, he could not understand what our Lord was saying. And we read:

> *Jesus . . . said unto him, Art thou a master of Israel, and knowest not these things? Verily, verily, I say unto thee [listen to this!], We speak that we do know, and testify that we have seen; and ye receive not our witness. If I have told you earthly things, and ye believe not, how shall ye believe, if I tell you of heavenly things? And no man hath ascended up to heaven, but he that came down from heaven, even the Son of man which is in heaven.*
>
> —*John 3:11-13*

Why listen to Him? I will tell you why I listen to Him. I cannot save myself, and no human being can save me. I cannot get any light from anyone anywhere in the past or the present. I want to know about myself; I want to know about life; I want to know about death; I want to know about God. I am tired of speculation. I can speculate and theorize as well as anybody else. But I want authority. I want someone who can say, "I know," and here is the only one who can do so. Confucius, Buddha, Muhammad and all the rest—not one of them has said this; they do not know. But here is one who says that He has come from heaven, that He has come from God. He has looked into the face of God. He is speaking as a direct, immediate witness.

Our Lord went further: He said, "I and my Father are one" (John 10:30). Listen to Him: "I am come . . ." (John 10:10). "The Son of man is come . . ." (Luke 19:10). He was not born in the natural, ordinary way. He was born of a virgin; He never had an earthly father. There is a mystery, a miracle, a marvel about His very birth. That is why He kept on saying, "I am come." He did not say, "I was born." He was a visitor into this world. He said, "Ye are from beneath; I am from above" (John 8:23). As has often been pointed out before, either our Lord was speaking the truth, or else He was a stark lunatic! There is no alternative. He was either speaking the words of soberness and truth, or else He was mad. But look at this evidence, take it all together. Look at all this testimony and all this record.

In addition, here are further reasons for listening to Him—look at what He says, yes, but look also at what He does. I have already reminded you of His answer to John the Baptist: "The blind see, the lame walk, the lepers are cleansed, the deaf hear, the dead are raised" (Luke 7:22). Do you think there would ever have been Christianity and the Christian church if these things were not true? The idea that you can have Christianity without the miraculous element is sheer nonsense. Consider the miracles attested to Him. In his Gospel, John always calls them "signs," and we read in the fourteenth chapter how our Lord turned to the hesitating disciple, Philip (remember, there is nothing new about your doubts and your hesitations and your skepticism and your denial—He was rejected in his own day nearly 2,000 years ago), and He said, "Though ye believe not me, believe the works" (John 10:38)—"believe me for the very works' sake." He says in effect, "Why don't you face the facts? Let them speak to you. If you do not accept My words and teaching and testimony, listen to the evidence of the facts. They are speaking to you, and they are proclaiming who I am." The people said of Him, "John did no miracle: but all things John spake of this man were true" (John 10:41).

And add to that our Lord's perfect life. No one could point a finger at Him. No one could charge Him with any misdemeanors or any wrong. He gave perfect obedience to God's holy law. He was tempted by the devil—"in all points tempted like as we are, yet without sin" (Heb. 4:15).

Are we ready to listen to this one? Here is a man who has been in this world like you and me. He was tempted—all the insinuation and the innuendo of sin hurled itself against Him. Everything that gets us down was hurled against Him! But He never fell—never. He conquered the devil at the height of the enemy's temptation. The devil produced all his reserves, but our Lord defeated him utterly and absolutely. Are we ready to listen to someone who could walk through this world without being soiled and tarnished and polluted? I am ready to listen to Him. This is the kind of person I am anxious to meet. I want to hear what He has to tell me! I want to be like that! That is why I listen to Him.

Then I hear His teaching—His perfect teaching. I have already referred to His teaching about God—He speaks as one who knows Him. "No man hath seen God at any time; the only begotten Son, which is in the bosom of the Father, he hath declared him" (John 1:18). I know nothing about God ultimately apart from what Christ has told me. And then I read His Sermon on the Mount, with all the grandeur of its ethical teaching. We talk about our advances and developments. Tell me, how much has the world advanced in the matter of ethical, moral teaching since the Sermon on the Mount was preached? The world has had nearly 2,000 years to improve on the Sermon on the Mount, but has it done it? No; people are still having to go back to Him; they are still quoting Him. He still stands in His utter, absolute uniqueness as the supreme prophet and teacher of all time and of the whole universe.

Then look at Him as He faced His own death: He knew what was happening, and He faced it steadfastly. He could have escaped or avoided it, but "He stedfastly set his face to go to Jerusalem" (Luke 9:51). I see Him in a garden sweating drops of blood. Why? Because He was asked to take upon Him the sins of humanity. He knew what it would mean to Him; He knew the suffering before Him—to be separated from God. He said, "Abba, Father, all things are possible unto thee; take away this cup from me: nevertheless not what I will, but what thou wilt" (Mark 14:36). And He died upon the cross! Oh, I beseech you, look at Him dying there, and listen to Him!

They took down His body and laid it in a tomb. I will tell you why I listen to Him—He came out of that tomb! If He had not come out of that grave, Christianity would never have been Christianity. But he came out! "He burst asunder the bands of death, he arose triumphant o'er the grave." Nobody had ever done this before. He was the first to rise from the dead. This was not like certain people whom He raised Himself: they died subsequently. But He rose never to die again! He has conquered death and the grave.

This is a sheer fact, and that is why I listen to Him. Here is one who has conquered the last enemy, even death and the grave. The apostles were witnesses of this. They saw Him crucified; they saw Him die; they saw His body being buried; they saw Him afterward. He appeared to them in rooms; they could touch Him; He ate with them; He spoke to them; and He ascended into heaven in their presence. If these things are not so, I repeat, there would never have been a Christian church. I see these things, and I say, "Who is this?" He is unique. I am ready to listen to Him.

And then, finally, His sending of the Holy Spirit is the ultimate proof of who He is and what He is. He said He was going to do this, and He did it on the Day of Pentecost, as we have seen.

So let me sum it all up. Why did He do all this? Take this unique person, this one prophesied throughout the centuries; at last He came. He came in that extraordinary way as a babe in Bethlehem, in utter helplessness, born in poverty. He worked with His hands for all those years, and then He preached for just three years. He died and was buried, but then came the resurrection and the ascension. What is it all about? Why did He do this? And the astounding answer is that He did it for us—for you and for me. He did it because of our ignorance, because of our failure, because of our utter helplessness; that is why I am ready to listen to Him. He is one who came to deliver us; He underwent all this so that you and I could have the very thing we need above everything else.

Oh, I plead with you, I beseech you, look at Him, look at this person who has such power that He can raise the dead. But, oh, look at His compassion, look at His sympathy, look at His pity. "Then drew near unto him all the publicans and sinners for to hear him" (Luke 15:1). The people who were the outcasts of society drew near to Him, and they had a wonderful reception. Those clever, self-righteous, religious Pharisees said, "Behold a man gluttonous, and a winebibber, a friend of publicans and sinners" (Matt. 11:19). They jeered at Him and said, "He's ready to receive harlots. He'll take anybody, the refuse of society." But what a wonderful thing that such a person should be ready to receive publicans and sinners! He had pity on them. Mark tells us that when He saw the crowds, "[He] was moved with compassion toward them, because they were as sheep not having a shepherd" (Mark 6:34), and He had come to deliver them. In all His glory and His might and His authority He humbled Himself in order that He might deliver us. That is why we must listen to Him. Those are His claims.

But, lastly, there is another reason, towering above them all. I have told you I listen to Him because Moses said long ago, "Him shall ye hear." But I hear somebody else saying that. I read the account given of what happened to Jesus and to James and Peter and John when they went up to the top of a certain mountain. There He was transfigured before them, and His raiment began to shine, and His face began to glisten. He was transformed! Something of the glory everlasting appeared through His whole being, even affecting His clothing. Then this is what we read: "Behold, a bright cloud overshadowed them: and behold a voice out of the cloud, which said, This is my beloved Son, in whom I am well pleased; hear ye him" (Matt. 17:5). Who was speaking? God was speaking from heaven. The apostle Peter, as an old man, said in his last letters, "We have not followed cunningly devised fables, when we made known unto you the power and coming of our Lord Jesus Christ, but were eyewitnesses of his majesty." And Peter added, "This voice which came from heaven we heard, when we were with him in the holy mount" (2 Pet. 1:16, 18).

Why listen to this Jesus? He is not only recommended by patriarchs and prophets and kings and apostles and martyrs and confessors and reformers—God Himself is recommending Him. "Here is my beloved Son: hear Him." "Listen to Him." And the Holy Spirit, the third Person in the blessed holy Trinity, came on the Day of Pentecost, and He has been saying the same thing ever since. He has been working in us, and He has been saying to us, "Listen to Him"—"Listen to Jesus." This is the Holy Spirit's work: He was sent to glorify Jesus. God the Father recommends Him and invites us to come. What more can we desire?

Art thou weary, art thou languid,
Art thou sore distressed?
"Come to me," saith One, "and coming,
Be at rest."

If I ask him to receive me,
Will he say me nay?
Not till earth and not till heaven
Pass away.

Finding, following, keeping, struggling,
Is he sure to bless?
Saints, apostles, prophets, martyrs,
Answer, Yes.

John Mason Neale

Have you heard Him?

"Saints, apostles, prophets, martyrs," and even God Himself are all crying unto you, "Hear Him." Have you heard the mighty chorus? Is He sure to bless those who come to Him?

Saints, apostles, prophets, martyrs,
Answer, Yes.

Listen to them. Listen to Him. Believe in Him, and you will find that He is the Son of God, the Savior of your soul, the one who will do for you infinitely more than all you need and desire. Moses was right: "Him shall ye hear."

12

Listen to the Gospel

This is that Moses, which said unto the children of Israel, A prophet shall the Lord your God raise up unto you of your brethren, like unto me; him shall ye hear. This is he, that was in the church in the wilderness with the angel which spake to him in the mount Sina, and with our fathers: who received the lively oracles to give unto us.

—Acts 7:37-38

We are continuing with our consideration of the phrase: "Him shall ye hear." We have seen that Moses tells us to listen to Him. The prophets say, "Wait for Him." John the Baptist says, "I am not the Christ . . . He is coming . . . Listen to Him." The apostles tell us, "Listen to Him." "We are but ambassadors," they say; "it is not our message."

The message of the preacher is not his own message, and a man getting into a pulpit and voicing his own thoughts and opinions is a travesty of Christian preaching. I am only an ambassador, and God help the nation when the ambassador speaks for himself instead of for his country and for his government. An ambassador does not voice his own opinions but speaks on behalf of his homeland the message that has been given to him to give to the other nation. So the apostles call upon us to listen to Christ, and the saints of the centuries do the same.

But, above all, our Lord Himself invites us to come to Him and to learn of Him, and we have been considering something of His right and authority for calling upon us to do this very thing. We ended the previous study on this note: God Himself tells us to hear Christ. From heaven God said, "This is my beloved Son, in whom I am well pleased; hear ye him" (Matt. 17:5).

Now we must go on and consider why anybody should listen to the Gospel. That is a question many are asking in this modern world. They say, "The world has developed and advanced; why should I listen to such an old message?" So let me give you some further reasons. We should listen to our Lord because of what He Himself tells us, because of His teaching. We have looked at His person, we have looked at His authority, we have looked at His right to speak to us at all, but now listen to what He has to say—to the content of His message.

I shall only give you a broad summary of what this content is—this, I think, is what we need to hear. People lose themselves in details; they are lost in the application of the Gospel. They argue about particular problems and crises in various parts of the world, such as the Middle East, and say, "I wonder whether Christianity has a solving word about that?" My answer is, no, not directly. But I can tell you one thing about the Middle East and about the Far East that no politician is likely to tell you—I can tell you why it is all happening. They cannot. They think it is merely a question of politics. But it is not. It is a question of sin. All war is the result of sin. There would be no international tension if there were no sin.

So I can tell you the fundamental cause, but I do not have a solving word. I do not presume to tell the President of the United States or the Prime Minister of Great Britain or anybody else how to solve these particular problems. Who am I to do that? Who is any preacher to do that? Even an archbishop knows no more than I do. That is not our function. But we can tell men and women how they can deal with themselves and their own personal problems. We can tell the whole world how this can be done—and that is the message that is committed to us. And we therefore say to people, "Listen to Him."

What, then, does our Lord say? If you listen to His teaching—I am, let me remind you, only giving you a summary—you will find that the first great thing is this: He will expound to you the law that was given through Moses. That is where these members of the Sanhedrin were so completely wrong. They thought that Jesus Christ was against the law of Moses. The truth is, He, and He alone, can interpret that law. Even Moses did not understand it. Moses was a great man and a great teacher, but he never understood the law fully because he was only a man. If you really want an exposition of the real character of the law of God as given through Moses, listen to the Lord Jesus Christ. And, of course, He expounds the law especially in the great sermon that is called the Sermon on the Mount.

So what does Jesus Christ teach us? First, He, and He alone, can really tell us the truth about God. People think they can always express an opinion about what God is like and what God ought to be like, but they do not know, they do not understand. Only this blessed person can tell us the truth about the character of God, and He calls God, "holy Father" (John 17:11). Modern men and women who are not Christians are not interested in religion. Why? "God is love," they say, and that is all they know. That is the universal solution. No need for theology, no need for any of this at all. Do what you like. God is love, so all is well. That is the popular theory. But when you listen to this blessed person, He teaches us to pray, "Our Father which art in heaven, hallowed by thy name" (Matt. 6:9). And when He prays Himself, even though, as we have seen, He is the Son of God, He does not say, "Dear Father"—He says, "Holy Father." This is His teaching. He alone can tell us something of the truth about God.

And then listen to what He tells us about ourselves. The popular idea is that we do not need Christianity, we do not need all this teaching about the cross and the death of Christ and the atonement. "That's theology," they say, "and we don't want it; it's all nonsense. All that's really necessary is this: live a good life. If you do as much good as you can, you'll be all right. That's all God asks of you." That is why people are no longer interested in the Christian message. They say theology is something that this legalist Paul came and foisted upon the delightfully simple Gospel that just tells you, "Be a good person, and all will be well."

But that is not true. Listen to what our Lord says in the Sermon on the Mount about the scribes and Pharisees. Remember, these were good and religious men. When a Pharisee said, "I fast twice in the week, I give tithes of all that I possess" (Luke 18:12), that was not a lie—he was speaking the truth. The Pharisees lived very good lives; they were moral men. But this is what our Lord said about them: "Except your righteousness shall exceed the righteousness of the scribes and Pharisees, ye shall in no case enter into the kingdom of heaven" (Matt. 5:20). That was His interpretation. And He had just said: "Till heaven and earth pass, one jot or one tittle shall in no wise pass from the law, till all be fulfilled" (Matt. 5:18). "Heaven and earth shall pass away," he says, "but my words shall not pass away" (Matt. 24:35). God, He says, demands a righteousness beyond the righteousness of the scribes and Pharisees.

And we are just like the Pharisees. We tend to think that as long as we keep a kind of code in a general and external sense, all is well. But our Lord takes this up point by point and shows how utterly wrong that idea is. He says that what matters in connection with the keeping of the law that God gave to Moses is the spiritual character of the law. The law, he says, is not merely interested in actions—it is interested in motives. The law is not only interested in what people do—it is equally interested in what they desire. It does not merely look at the outward appearance—it is very concerned about the state of the heart.

How endlessly did our Lord teach that! He said in essence, "You Pharisees are very careful to clean the outside of the cup and the platter, you wash the outside and you polish it, but the inside is full of ravenous desires and wickedness" (Matt. 23:25). And then He brought that out in detail in the Sermon on the Mount—I am just giving you a summary of His teaching. He said in effect, "You Pharisees say that you have never committed murder; you say, 'I'm all right, I can face the law. The law says, "Thou shalt not kill," and I never have—I've never committed murder.' But wait a minute," says Christ, "have you ever said in your heart about a fellow-man, 'Thou fool!'? If you have, you have murdered that man in your heart, and you are guilty of murder in the sight of God" (Matt. 5:21-22).

And our Lord takes up the same teaching in the case of adultery. The Pharisee stands forward and says, "I've never committed adultery." But our Lord asks, "Are you quite sure? When the law says, 'Thou shalt not commit adultery,' it is not only interested in the action. It is interested in the action, but it is much more interested in the spirit." So our Lord says, "Whosoever looketh on a woman to lust after her hath committed adultery with her already in his heart" (Matt. 5:28). In the sight of God this man is guilty of adultery. He has never committed the act, but he has done it; and God has seen it. So our Lord takes them through these various points of the law, and the moment He exposes the spiritual character and nature of the law, He convicts them all of sin.

And this is what the Pharisees could not see. The members of the Sanhedrin, too, could not see it—they thought they were all right. That is why they objected to the preaching of Stephen and the apostles. That is why they thought this preaching about Jesus Christ was against the law and against Moses and against the temple. This showed their ignorance of the law.

Now the supreme, classic example of this is, of course, none other than the great apostle Paul himself. He tells us that there was a time when he thought he was all right with regard to the dictates and the commands of the law—perfect. He says, "I was alive without the law once" (Rom. 7:9). What was it that convicted him? It was when he understood this phrase, "Thou shalt not covet" (Rom. 7:7). He had never understood it before. And Paul, remember, was an authority on the law of Moses; he had taught it. He was a Pharisee and a brilliant exponent of the law. But he had missed the whole point of the law, which is that to desire is as damnable as to do, and to covet is as reprehensible as to commit. Paul had never seen this. But this is what the law teaches, and that is why you and I must listen to it. The Lord Jesus Christ tells us that it is not enough just to be good in a negative sense, it is not good enough to be moral, it is not good enough to be religious—we can be all these things and yet it is of no value to us.

But the moment the Lord shows us the meaning of the law of God—the law that we say we are so proud of and believe in—the moment our Lord shows us what it really tells us, we see it very differently. But then, in the light of that, he goes on to say: "For the Son of man is come to seek and to save that which was lost" (Luke 19:10). That is why you should listen to Him. He alone tells us the truth about ourselves, and the truth is that we are all lost. Take his three parables in the fifteenth chapter of Luke's Gospel. They are all parables about being lost—lost sheep, lost coin, lost son. "This my son was dead, and is alive again; he was lost, and is found," says the father in the Parable of the Prodigal Son (v. 24).

What does it mean to be lost? It means that we have, as it were, lost our souls. We have lost our real being. We are not what we were meant to be. We are not what we were at the beginning in the original creation. This is a lost world, which means that human beings are not living as God intended. God made man perfect, and that is how he was meant to be. But where is the perfect man? Can you find him? No; he is lost. We are all lost; we have lost ourselves. We do not know who we are; we do not know how to live; we do not know where we are; we do not know what is coming. And that, our Lord says, is the reason why He came.

Have we realized that? Have we ever faced the fact that we are completely lost, that we have lost ourselves and lost our souls? We can have great knowledge of science, we may know a great deal about the atom, but we do not know the truth about ourselves, and our knowledge of science does not help us here at all. We are like persons groping about in the dark. The Bible talks about those who "sit in darkness" (Luke 1:79)—they cannot move; they are paralyzed, helpless. That is the condition of the whole world. And do you not see that this is the only adequate explanation of the present state of the world? Why are people behaving as they are? It is because they are lost. They have lost their way. They do not know where they are. They are baffled, bewildered, straying helplessly, like sheep without a shepherd. That is what our Lord tells us.

But then our Lord goes further—He tells us that we are not only lost but that we are also hopeless. Have you ever listened to this blessed person? Do you know what He says? "Verily, verily, I say unto thee, Except a man be born again, he cannot see the kingdom of God" (John 3:3). We must be "born again." What does this mean? It means that we all by nature are in such a terrible state and condition that we cannot be improved. That which we call *civilization* is simply human beings putting paint and varnish on the rottenness that is beneath. It is like a man whose house is suffering from woodworm or dry rot and who says, "I can't stand seeing this." So he buys some paint, paints over what is there, and puts varnish on top of that. "Now, look," he says, "isn't this marvelous?" That is civilization! That is what people get so excited about. All the music and the literature and the art and the national laws—"look at the world, look at what we have discovered, look at what we are doing, see how we can entertain you!" But put a knife into it, scrape off the paint, and what do you find? You find woodworm, dry rot.

This is the difference between civilization and Christianity. This is the difference between modern faith in educational and cultural movements and the Christian message. It is the gospel message, and this alone, that faces the real cause of the trouble and says, "That is so rotten that nothing can be done with it. It is beyond hope. It is no use painting it and varnishing it; it is no use patching it up—it is rotten. And it is a disease that will spread."

And that is a summary of the last 2,000 years and more of human history, is it not? In spite of all the efforts and endeavors of humanity at its best and at its most brilliant and intelligent, the rottenness is still there. It seems to be covered for a while in certain periods and epochs. The Victorian era was such a period. The Victorians put on the paint and the varnish, and they really thought that the world was going on to perfection. "The Parliament of Man!" "The Federation of the World!" the poets sang. Oh, what blind prophets they were! False prophets.

We are living in a time when rottenness is breaking out again, and the dry rot is manifesting itself. Our Lord said it from the beginning. That is why we should listen to Him and listen to Him exclusively. He alone tells us the truth—"Except a man be born again"! We cannot be improved. We must be regenerated. We need to be created anew. Unless something new is put into us, we are hopelessly, irretrievably lost. That is what our Lord said; and, remember, He said it to a very learned and able Jew, a Jew like these members of the Sanhedrin, a man called Nicodemus.

And that is what our Lord says to everybody today. To the most religious person in the world, He says, "You must be born again. Your religion is valueless; it is filthy rags; it is dung and refuse in the sight of God. If you rely on that, you will go to perdition because you are rotten. It is your pride that makes you do it, and it is your conceit that encourages you to keep on, but it does not count with God." That is His teaching.

This is why, of course, our Lord infuriated the Pharisees and scribes. That is why they killed Him; that is why the Sanhedrin did not like the preaching of Jesus—it convicted them of sin. They knew, of course, that the publican and the harlot were sinners. "Look at them," they said, "obvious sinners." But *they* were not sinners. *They* were good men; *they* were religious. But our Lord said, "You are *all* sinners; there is nobody who is not a sinner." He convicted us all of sin. He said that God sees the heart. "Ye are they which justify themselves before men; but God knoweth your hearts: for that which is highly esteemed among men is abomination in the sight of God" (Luke 16:15). The world does not know us, but He knows us. He sees the truth. He sees the rottenness. We are hopeless; we must be born again.

And then our Lord went on to say that He alone could deliver us—that is why He came. "The Son of man is come to seek and to save that which was lost" (Luke 19:10). But he also made an exclusive claim. He said, "All that ever came before me are thieves and robbers" (John 10:8). They have come into the sheepfold by some other way; they cannot care for the sheep. He called Himself "the Son of man" and the Savior of the world! He said, "Come unto me" and "I am the light of the world" and "No man cometh unto the Father, but by me" (Matt. 11:28; John 8:12; 14:6).

But then—and this is crucial—He tells us that even He can only save us in one way. What is this way? Is it by giving us teaching? No! It is His very teaching that condemns us, as I have shown you. This idea that Jesus Christ saves us by teaching us is, of all the ridiculous misinterpretations, the most ridiculous. If I have nothing but the teaching of Christ about the law of God, I would be groveling in the dust in utter, final hopelessness. The moral teaching of Christ? The imitation of Christ? Trying to live according to the example of Christ? It is impossible. I cannot do it. I cannot please myself, let alone please or imitate Him. That suggestion condemns me.

But He never said that He would save me by His teaching. His teaching is designed only to bring me to see my need of Him. The value of His teaching is that it convicts me, strips me, unmasks me, shows me my rottenness, scrapes off the paint and the varnish and the putty, puts a knife into it, and clears it out, so that I see the running sore of my soul. The only way in which He can save me, He says, and He keeps on saying it, is by giving His life: "The Son of man came not to be ministered unto, but to minister, and to give his life a ransom for many" (Matt. 20:28).

Or listen to Him saying that in another way: "I am the good shepherd"—and then—"the good shepherd giveth his life for the sheep" (John 10:11). "I lay down my life for the sheep," He says (John 10:15). "No man taketh it from me, but I lay it down of myself" (John 10:18). And we are told, "He stedfastly set his face to go to Jerusalem" (Luke 9:51) because "it cannot be that a prophet perish out of Jerusalem" (Luke 13:33). In the Garden of Gethsemane we see Him sweating drops of blood. He said in essence, "Is there any other way?" "O my Father, if it be possible, let this cup pass from me: nevertheless not as I will, but as thou wilt" (Matt. 26:39). These are the different ways in which He tells us that even He can only save us in one way.

In many ways the crucial statement of this teaching came at a place called Caesarea Philippi when our Lord asked the disciples, "Whom do men say that I the Son of man am?" They said, "Some say that thou art John the Baptist: some, Elias; and others, Jeremias, or one of the prophets." Then we read:

> *He saith unto them, But whom say ye that I am? And Simon Peter answered and said, Thou art the Christ, the Son of the living God. And Jesus answered and said unto him, Blessed art thou, Simon Barjona: for flesh and blood hath not revealed it unto thee, but my Father which is in heaven.*
>
> —*Matt. 16:13-17*

And then Matthew says:

> *From that time forth began Jesus to shew unto his disciples, how that he must go unto Jerusalem, and suffer many things of the elders and chief priests and scribes, and be killed, and be raised again the third day. Then Peter took him, and began to rebuke him, saying, Be it far from thee, Lord: this shall not be unto thee. But he turned, and said unto Peter, Get thee behind me, Satan: thou art an offence unto me: for thou savourest not the things that be of God, but those that be of men.*
>
> —*Matt. 16:21-23*

But the disciples could never grasp this, though our Lord constantly told them that the only way even He could save anybody was by giving His life as a ransom, by dying for us, by bearing "our sins in his own body on the tree" (1 Pet. 2:24). He said that was the only way!

That was His teaching. You and I can never keep the law of God or satisfy His demands, and our Lord Himself cannot save us by just teaching us and giving us an example to imitate and to follow, by telling us to make a bigger effort and live a better life—all that is of no value. There is only one way whereby even He can save us, and that is by bearing our punishment in His own body on the cross. He came into the world "not to be ministered unto, but to minister, and to give his life a ransom for many" (Matt. 20:28).

Have you heard Him? Have you heard "that God was in Christ, reconciling the world unto himself, not imputing their trespasses unto them. . . . For he hath made him to be sin for us, who knew no sin; that we might be made the righteousness of God in him" (2 Cor. 5:19, 21)? That is the message; that is what He has to say. He says in essence, "There is no hope for anybody unless he realizes his utter, final hopelessness before God and realizes that I save not by teaching but by dying."

He came to "taste death for every man" (Heb. 2:9). It is in Him, and in Him alone, that we are reconciled to God. That is His teaching. We must listen to Him!

And then we should listen to Him because of what He offers. It is what He alone can offer and what He alone has the right to offer because of the life He lived and because of the death He died and because He has risen from the dead. He has a right to offer all I am going to mention because He was able to say on the cross, "It is finished" (John 19:30)—finished completely and absolutely. He could say to His Father in prayer, "I have finished the work which thou gavest me to do" (John 17:4).

So what does He offer us? Listen to Him! He offers us free pardon for all our sins—it does not matter what we have been or what we have done. It does not matter what we were until this moment. I tell you, in His name, that if we acknowledge and realize our sin and confess it to God and believe that this person is the Son of God and that He has borne our punishment and died for our sins, then our sins from this moment are completely pardoned and forgiven, and God looks at us as if we had never sinned at all. That is called justification by faith. He offers us that. This blessed person offers us free pardon, full pardon, complete pardon of all our sins.

What else? Well, He offers us the very thing He has told us that we must have—a new nature! He does not mock us and say, "You must be born again," knowing perfectly well that no man can give birth to himself. He has come to give us a new birth, to make a new birth possible. He does something infinitely bigger and more important than improving us or renovating us—He gives us an entirely new start, a new life. He makes us "partakers of the divine nature" (2 Pet. 1:4), "born of . . . the Spirit" (John 3:5), new men and women. Paul writes in 2 Corinthians 5:17: "If any man be in Christ, he is a new creature [a new creation]: old things are passed away; behold, all things are become new."

What else does He offer? Power and strength! He Himself will help us—He will put His Spirit within us. He has been in this world, and as we have seen, He suffered temptation, and therefore "in that he himself hath suffered being tempted, he is able to succour them that are tempted" (Heb. 2:18). He will be with us in our trials and our troubles, in all our agony, our pain, and our temptations. We will not be left alone. He offers us this.

And beyond it all, He will take away from us the fear of death and the grave, the fear of the judgment of God, and He will tell us about an eternal glory that is awaiting us.

> *Let not your heart be troubled: ye believe in God, believe also in me. In my Father's house are many mansions: if it were not so, I would have told you. I go to prepare a place for you. And if I go and prepare a place for you, I will come again, and receive you unto myself; that where I am, there ye may be also.*
>
> —*John 14:1-3*

He offers us all this now, so that as we are here in the flesh and in the world, we may become children of God and be heirs of eternal bliss and glory. He offers us all this, and all for nothing.

Have we all realized that? The members of the Sanhedrin had not. They regarded such an offer as blasphemy. They said, "Who is this? What is this teaching that suggests that my morality and my religion and my temple worship are inadequate and that all this has come to an end?" They thought it blasphemy to say, "Christ is the end of the law for righteousness to every one that believeth" (Rom. 10:4). They were furious, and so they killed Stephen. The end of Acts 7 tells us that.

Is that our attitude? Do we feel that He insults us when He tells us that we must be born again? Do we resent this Gospel and its offer? That is what we are refusing—this free grace, this free pardon, this new life, this everlasting hope of the eternal glory. These are the reasons why we should listen to Him.

Have we contemplated the consequences of not listening to Him? "Why should I listen to Jesus Christ?" asks someone. I can tell you: He is God's last word; He is God's final offer. There is nothing after Him—nothing at all. If we reject Him and what He says, we have nothing; we will never have anything. It is no use looking to the future for some new theory, some new teaching, some new gospel—there never will be one. Christ is the one, the only one, the last. He is "the second man"! He is "the last Adam"!

Jesus Christ and all He has done is God's way of salvation. It is not man's. John 3:16, 18 says, "For God so loved the world, that he gave his only begotten Son, that whosoever believeth in him should not perish, but have everlasting life . . . he that believeth not is condemned already, because he hath not believed in the name of the only begotten Son of God." Can we not see this? We cannot save ourselves, human beings cannot save us, civilization cannot save us, but God can. "God was in Christ"—in and through what He has done in Christ—"reconciling the world unto himself" (2 Cor. 5:19). This is God's way, and if we reject this, there is nothing left. God saves us in and through this person whom He calls us to hear. So I repeat that if we refuse to listen to Him, we have rejected our only way of salvation.

This is the great emphasis in the whole of the New Testament. When the apostle Paul was preaching in the great and learned city of Athens, he said, "God . . . now commandeth all men every where to repent"—why?—"because he hath appointed a day, in the which he will judge the world in righteousness by that man whom he hath ordained; whereof he hath given assurance unto all men, in that he hath raised him from the dead" (Acts 17:30-31). That is why you should listen to Him. God has appointed Him as the judge of the whole world.

Or listen to the author of the Epistle to the Hebrews: "How shall we escape, if we neglect so great salvation" (2:3). Here we are, desperately ill, and here is the only cure. If we refuse it, we must die, we are finished. Hence we see the importance of the warning passages in the Epistle to the Hebrews:

> *For it is impossible for those who were once enlightened, and have tasted of the heavenly gift, and were made partakers of the Holy Ghost, and have tasted the good word of God, and the powers of the world to come, if they shall fall away, to renew them again unto repentance; seeing they crucify to themselves the Son of God afresh, and put him to an open shame.*
>
> —*Heb. 6:4-6*

If we reject what Christ has done on the cross for us, there is nothing left. And the writer repeats this in the tenth chapter: "For if we sin wilfully"—he means if we reject the Gospel—"after that we have received the knowledge of the truth, there remaineth no more sacrifice for sins, but a certain fearful looking for of judgment and fiery indignation, which shall devour the adversaries" (vv. 26-27).

But, oh, listen to the Lord Himself! "Hear Him!" He is the one we are to hear, says Moses. Jesus tells us in John 5:22 that God the Father has committed judgment to Him. He says He is coming again to judge the whole world in righteousness. He constantly said that. The people thought He was mad. He told them He was coming back and that they would "see the Son of man coming in the clouds of heaven" (Matt. 24:30). He said:

> *When the Son of man shall come in his glory, and all the holy angels with him, then shall he sit upon the throne of his glory: And before him shall be gathered all nations: and he shall separate them one from another, as a shepherd divideth his sheep from the goats.*
>
> *—Matt. 25:31-32*

Judgment has been committed unto the Son of God, and if we have rejected His offer, we have condemned ourselves to everlasting and eternal punishment. I am not the one saying that. He it was who said it in His story about Dives and Lazarus, where Abraham says to Dives in hell, "Between us and you there is a great gulf fixed" (Luke 16:26). He said that we decide our fate in this world and that we cannot have a second chance when we die. There is no movement from hell to heaven. We decide in this world, and we decide in terms of listening to Him or refusing Him, as the members of the Sanhedrin were refusing Him. This was His own teaching. It was He who talked about the place where "their worm dieth not, and the fire is not quenched" (Mark 9:44) and where "there shall be weeping and gnashing of teeth" (Matt. 8:12).

Our modern world is rapidly becoming a kind of hell, is it not? I am not only thinking of the wars and the bombs and the bloodshed—I am thinking of the filth and the vileness and the noise and the clatter. But that is nothing compared with hell itself! This world is a very pale picture of what hell will be like. And anybody who rejects this message has nothing to look forward to or to anticipate except to spend eternity in that, with all the blasphemy and the foulness of life without God, and to suffer that for all eternity. That is what He says.

Here is His final word to us:

> *I am come a light into the world, that whosoever believeth on me should not abide in darkness. And if any man hear my words, and*

believe not, I judge him not: for I came not to judge the world, but to save the world. He that rejecteth me, and receiveth not my words, hath one that judgeth him: the word that I have spoken, the same shall judge him in the last day.

—John 12:46-48

Why should we hear Him? Why should we listen to Him? Here is the answer: His word offering us all this glorious pardon and renewal, sonship of God, and heirship of eternal bliss—all that will be in evidence against us. We were offered pardon, deliverance from sin, Satan, the world, the flesh, and the devil, and assurance of eternal life. We were offered it all and for nothing. He said, "Whosoever cometh" (Luke 6:47); "whosoever believeth" (John 12:46). Not only good people but the worst people—publicans, the vilest sinners, murderers—must come, listen, repent, "that whosoever believeth in him should not perish, but have everlasting life" (John 3:16).

Have you heard Him? He is saying to us now, "Come unto me, all ye that labour and are heavy laden, and I will give you rest" (Matt. 11:28). Do we know what He is saying to us? "Him that cometh to me"—though he comes in rags and tatters, though he comes as foul as hell—"I will in no wise cast out" (John 6:37). Have you heard Him? Then tell Him so. Turn to Him and say:

I hear thy welcome voice
That calls me, Lord, to thee,
For cleansing in thy precious blood
That flowed on Calvary.
I am coming, Lord!
Coming now to thee!
Wash me, cleanse me, in thy blood
That flowed on Calvary.
Lewis Hartsough

Tell Him that, and He will assure you that it is true.

13

The Character of Unbelief

To whom our fathers would not obey, but thrust him from them, and in their hearts turned back again into Egypt, saying unto Aaron, Make us gods to go before us: for as for this Moses, which brought us out of the land of Egypt, we wot not what is become of him.

—Acts 7:39-40

We are at a kind of turning-point in Stephen's speech. He has dealt in general with the facts that he was anxious to use and now he began to apply them to the members of the Sanhedrin. He had rehearsed the history, but he was not merely content to do that—he was showing its relevance. He now showed clearly the point that he was making, which is that the members of the Sanhedrin were guilty of exactly the same unbelief as their forefathers in the time of Moses, this man whom they claimed to admire and to revere so much. So Stephen was driving this point home and showing them the character of unbelief. They could not see it for themselves. So he tried to make them see it by reminding them of their own history and showing them that they had unconsciously fallen into this same fundamental fallacy and were bringing down trouble upon themselves, even as their forefathers had done.

"But," someone may say to me, "that's all right, but what does it have to do with us? Have you nothing better to say to us with the world as it is? Are we not perhaps on the threshold of a third world war that would probably be the end of civilization? Have you nothing better to tell us on such an occasion than some old story of something that happened back in the first century? Surely," says this critic, "you really should try to be abreast of the times. You should try to say something that's relevant to the days in which we're living and the calamities through which we're passing. Have you nothing better to do than preach a sermon that could have been preached a hundred years ago, when everything seemed to be peaceful?"

Undoubtedly, somebody is thinking thoughts such as that. Let me tell you exactly why I am calling your attention to this question. Here we shall see how the first martyr, Stephen, showed quite clearly the real cause of all the ills of the human race. It is *because* I am concerned about the present situation that I am calling attention to this story. We have here a great principle in operation. Stephen was at pains to show that humanity is always in trouble because it always rejects the voice and the word of God. That has always been the cause of all our troubles. So there is nothing that is more relevant to the present situation than these words of Stephen.

The problem, from the Christian standpoint, of what is happening in the world today will not be solved by going into the niceties of the disputes between nations, nor indeed into the intricacies of the dispute between Arabs and Jews. We have something much more important to do, and that is to discover why there is any trouble between people, indeed between any two individuals—husband and wife, two brothers, two sisters, relatives, friends, associates.

Let us go a step further: we need to discover why there is any trouble in any one of us, for there is a warfare going on in each of us. Life is a struggle; life is a fight; forces are battling within us. So we are concerned with that. We must view these things, you see, on a deeper level than that of politics. I would be insulting you and your intelligence and wasting your time if I simply gave you my opinion as to what should happen in the Middle East and everywhere else. That is not my function. I say again, I have an infinitely more important function to carry out, and that is to get every one of us to see why these things happen, why our world is as it is, why every individual is as he is or as she is by nature. That is the subject that we have here, and Stephen unfolds it and makes it perfectly simple and perfectly plain.

But this is what the world does not understand, and that is why we must call attention to it so constantly. There is nothing new about this. This century is no different at all from any other century. I have often said this, but let me repeat it again because people seem to be so slow to grasp it. "But," they say, "you can't be right. They hadn't split the atom until recently. They didn't have jet airplanes before." I am aware of all that, but what is its importance?

And the answer is just this: the only difference these discoveries and advances make is to the way in which we do things. We are now fighting one another with rockets and bombs, with airplanes and various other machines, and we say that this is quite new, that the problem of humanity is quite new.

But it is not! It is not the way in which people fight that matters—it is the fact that they do fight; and human beings have been fighting throughout the centuries. There is no difference in principle between fighting with two fists and fighting with bombs—not the slightest. It is fighting in both cases. We have merely changed the implements with which we fight—fists, sticks, bows and arrows, spears, gunpowder, cannon balls, and so on, until you come to our present horrible bombs. The world is exactly as it has been throughout the centuries; the troubles are the same—marriage troubles, economic troubles, industrial troubles, capital and labor issues. We are so dull that because we have changed the clothing we think that people are different. They are not; they are exactly the same. "There is no new thing under the sun" (Eccl. 1:9).

So what is needed above everything at the present time is this old treatment, the only treatment that really brings us to the heart and center of the problem. And I say that it is the only one because this alone treats the problem in depth; everything else is so superficial. It is almost pathetic to see how writers, political commentators, and others, with their apparent cleverness, never look beneath the political level. They are incapable of it. With all their cleverness, they really do not get down to the true problem. "It is only this," they say, "or that." But it is all political thinking, and for that reason it misses the point. The Gospel is the only message that really shows us the depth of the problem, and this is important because people reject the Gospel for one main reason—they have never understood the depth of the problem of the human race. If only they knew that, they would be more ready to listen to the gospel message. It is because they fail at this point that their rejection has continued.

So my fundamental contention is that the state of the world and the rejection of the Gospel are inextricably intermixed. The world is as it is because it refuses to listen to the voice of God. That is the very point that Stephen was making. He was a Jew himself, and he was addressing Jews. And Stephen knew that our Lord had prophesied that the Jewish nation, because of its rejection of Him, would itself be rejected and that a terrible calamity would come upon it. Our Lord prophesied the destruction of Jerusalem, which took place in A.D. 70. Read the twenty-fourth chapter of Matthew's Gospel or the twenty-first chapter of Luke's Gospel or the thirteenth chapter of Mark, and there you will see how he described it in detail. "Seest thou these great buildings?" He said. "There shall not be left one stone [of the temple] upon another, that shall not be thrown down" (Mark 13:2). He prophesied it, and it all came to pass.

But our Lord also told the people why this destruction was going to happen; it was because they were refusing Him and refusing His message. "O Jerusalem, Jerusalem . . ." He lamented as He looked down upon the city for the last time, "how often would I have gathered thy children together, even as a hen gathereth her chickens under her wings, and ye would not!" (Matt. 23:37). That was the whole cause of the trouble.

And Stephen was making exactly the same point. He said in effect, "You are charging me with blasphemy. Can you not see that you are the people who are guilty of blasphemy? You are rejecting the message of God through Jesus Christ His Son in exactly the same way as your forefathers rejected it through His servant Moses."

And it is because the world is still doing the same thing today that I am calling your attention to this whole subject. I am not only interested in it in terms of world powers and countries and the possibility of a world calamity—I am much more interested in it as it regards individuals. I have no comfort to offer you as regards this world. This world is under the wrath of God. But thank God, I have a message that can give you all that you need in spite of what is going to happen to the world. I have a message that can tell you something that will avail you not only in this world and in all that may happen to it but will be with you through death and beyond it in the eternity that awaits us all. That is the message of the Gospel.

The members of the Sanhedrin were rejecting this message, throwing it back. Stephen was concerned to open their eyes to what they were doing. So I have tried to analyze Stephen's ideas as he puts them in these two verses in particular. And my first and absolutely vital comment regards the depths of the problem.

Look at it like this. Here were the members of the Sanhedrin. They were not fools; they were intelligent and able men, and they were the leaders of the nation. Why did they reject the Gospel? Why does the world still do so? Why do men and women go on behaving as they do? We must think seriously about this question. And the first thing we must grasp is that this is not a superficial problem; it is the profoundest problem of all.

Now this problem is not just a question of lack of knowledge or the need of a little more teaching and exhortation or an appeal to people to love one another. We have had that until we are sick and tired of it. It leads to nothing; it does not touch the situation. No; the problem is deeper than this—it affects men and women in a total manner. They are in a condition in which they are not merely partly but entirely wrong. Now I defy you to find any other teaching anywhere that says that. And it is obviously basic. The great message of the Bible is that the world is as it is because man has disobeyed God and has fallen. It is a total fall; he has fallen in all his faculties, in every part of his being. He is not what he was meant to be, and every part of him is suffering from this fall.

Now I emphasize that and start with it because there are so many people in the world who reject the Gospel because they say it is a lot of nonsense. This idea that Jesus Christ is the Son of God, this notion of incarnation, that God the Son came down out of heaven and was born as a man and lived in this world and worked miracles and that His death upon the cross somehow or another saves us and that you and I must be born again—this idea, they say, is utter rubbish and nonsense. What men and women need is just instruction, education, and culture, they say. You need to send lecturers around to enlighten the people by showing the horrors of drink and of bombs and of war. Put your lecturers on television, and then the country, having been taught, will change. It is unnecessary to bring in God and incarnation and an atoning death and miracles and being born again.

People say all that because they have never seen the depth of the problem. Their solution is easy because their diagnosis is superficial. They are quite consistent, of course, but they are wrong on all counts; and, of course, history is proving them to be wrong. No people looked more ridiculous than the optimists of the nineteenth century, the politicians and the poets and the philosophers—the whole lot of them. How blind they were! That is why I always find it a little bit difficult to speak with restraint about the so-called "great Victorians." They were, conceivably, the blindest leaders of the blind of any century. They were fool enough to think that they were on the verge of perfection, that evolution was about to reach its acme. It is, I repeat, because people do not realize the depth of the problem that they cannot see the necessity of this supernatural Gospel, this miraculous deliverance, this unique intervention of God.

So, having given you the general principle, let me now put it like this: What does Stephen teach us here about the nature of unbelief? What is the character of this problem in men and women that makes them reject the Gospel, as the members of the Sanhedrin were doing, as the people had done with Moses, and as they are still doing?

Stephen tells us that primarily this unbelief and rejection of the Gospel is due to the state of the heart. "To whom our fathers would not obey, but thrust him from them, and *in their hearts* turned back again into Egypt, saying . . ." The real trouble with men and women, the cause of their unbelief, is in their hearts. Now in Scripture the term *heart* generally means the very center of personality. Particularly it means the seat of the desires. It is that in people that determines what they really want.

Now, you notice, unbelief is not in the mind. This is the first thing that people today must learn, for they fondly think that they are not Christians because of their great brains, because of their understanding, and especially because of all this wonderful modern knowledge that we have garnered. But that is exactly where they go wrong. The trouble with them is not primarily in their head but in their heart. The heart is deeper than the mind.

I can prove this to you quite simply. Here are two men who, as far as you can tell, are about equal in their ability. At school either one or the other was always on top of the class and the other second. Ask those who taught them who was the abler, and they reply, "I really can't tell you; sometimes it was one, sometimes the other." They seem to be endowed in an almost identical manner with the same gifts and powers and propensities. But one is a Christian, and the other is not. Why is that? It cannot be a matter of intellect because it is agreed that there is no difference between them. You can have two brothers almost identical in gifts, and one is a Christian and the other not. If Christianity were a matter of intellect, you would have to come to the conclusion that no one of intelligence ever can be a Christian; but that is not true. Some of the most intelligent people the world has ever known have been some of its greatest Christians.

But I have a still better argument. Take one man, take a genius—Saul of Tarsus. Here is a giant intellect. There was a time in his history when he regarded Jesus Christ as a blasphemer and was not afraid to say so. We will have to consider his story later in this series. There he was, with all his amazing ability, his knowledge of the law. He was a wonderful teacher, a religious genius, and, with his great brain, he said that Jesus of Nazareth was a blasphemer and that Christians were blasphemers too. He was entirely in agreement with the Sanhedrin.

But you and I think of this man not as Saul of Tarsus the blasphemer, the rejecter of the Gospel, but as the mighty apostle Paul, the great preacher and exponent of the Christian faith. The same man, with the same intellect, the same understanding and knowledge, the same everything, changed radically. What changed? The same intellect that wrote the epistles to the Ephesians and Romans formerly had worked with all its devastating power against Christ and His Gospel—the same ability but a different man. The trouble is never primarily in the mind but in the heart. This is what we read of in the third chapter of the Epistle to the Hebrews: "Take heed, brethren, lest there be in any of you an evil heart of unbelief" (v. 12).

What does this mean? Well, let us go right back to the origin of all our present troubles, seen in the third chapter of the book of Genesis. Now I know that sounds ridiculous to the modern sophisticated man or woman, but all I say to them is this, give me another explanation if you can find it. This is a complete explanation. There were Adam and Eve, created in perfection, enjoying the life of Paradise. The world has become as it is because of the heart of man, and the devil knew that the heart was the key. That is why, when he tempted Eve, he appealed to her heart, not to her intellect. He appealed to her pride: "Hath God said?" "Has God told you that you are not to do that? Do you know why He has? He does not want you to be equal with Him. He is trying to keep you down."

The devil knew her weakness exactly, and down she fell, and Adam with her; and the whole of their posterity has gone down with them. That was the original sin, which is in the heart of all men and women. We are told of Eve that she "saw that the tree was good for food, and that it was pleasant to the eyes" (Gen. 3:6). Surely it was going to taste very wonderful, and that was what appealed to her. That was the heart in control.

If you read the story of the children of Israel in the Old Testament, you will constantly find this truth that Stephen is expounding here. Constantly their hearts lusted after something else, lusted after other gods or other women. They were always lusting after something. That was the whole cause of their tragedy. If I had the powers of a dictator, I think I would compel everybody to read the story of the Jews in the Old Testament. There you see men and women behaving like fools, always governed by their wicked hearts.

Indeed, our Lord put it still more plainly and clearly when he said, "For out of the heart proceed evil thoughts, murders, adulteries, fornications, thefts, false witness, blasphemies" (Matt. 15:19). That is where it all comes from. It is "not that which goeth into the mouth defileth a man; but that which cometh out of the mouth" (Matt. 15:11). It is not even the influences that are around us. They only play on what is inherent in us. "Unto the pure all things are pure" (Titus 1:15); but if you are not pure, everything will become impure. It is the human heart that is evil.

So the trouble with the world is not due to the fact that it does not have light and knowledge. Look at the books that have been poured out showing the madness of war and the wrongness of various attitudes that are ruining life. There is no lack of light and knowledge, and the light has come supremely in the Son of God Himself. We have it all in the Sermon on the Mount. So why are the nations fighting? Why are they arming? Why are they on the brink of some abyss? Here is our Lord's answer: "This is the condemnation, that light is come into the world . . ." Why does everybody not turn to it and submit to it? Why do we not all live in the light? Here is the answer: ". . . and men loved darkness rather than light, because their deeds were evil" (John 3:19).

That is why people reject the Gospel. It is because they love evil; they enjoy what they are doing; they are governed by the heart. The apostle Paul sums this up in his customary manner when he writes to the Ephesians:

And you hath he quickened, who were dead in trespasses and sins; wherein in time past ye walked according to the course of this world, according to the prince of the power of the air, the spirit that now worketh in the children of disobedience: among whom also we all had our conversation in times past [what sort of life was it? Here it is] in the lusts of our flesh, fulfilling the desires of the flesh and of the mind [that means, the lusts of the flesh, the body, and the mind]; and were by nature the children of wrath, even as others.

—Eph. 2:1-3

I am talking about the world as it is. Listen to James:

From whence come wars and fightings among you? come they not hence, even of your lusts that war in your members? Ye lust, and have not: ye kill, and desire to have, and cannot obtain: ye fight and war, yet ye have not, because ye ask not.

—Jas. 4:1-2

Is that not the explanation of the whole of history, I do not care which country you may name? This country [England], too, has been guilty of lusting for power, taking over this and that area of the world. We do not like other people to do it, but we have done it—all nations have. "This is mine." "No, it's mine." Lusting! Desiring! Lust is the cause of the troubles of the world. Light is brushed aside because people are not governed by their reason but by their lusts and passions. This is the universal teaching of the New Testament.

The apostle John says exactly the same thing:

Love not the world, neither the things that are in the world. If any man love the world, the love of the Father is not in him. For all that is in the world, the lust of the flesh, and the lust of the eyes, and the pride of life, is not of the Father, but is of the world. And the world passeth away, and the lust thereof: but he that doeth the will of God abideth for ever.

—1 John 2:15-17

These people, said Stephen to the Sanhedrin, their forefathers, had "in their hearts turned back again into Egypt."

But the problem is not confined to the heart—the will is involved. These words in Acts 7 are extraordinary. How accurate is Scripture! "To whom our fathers," said Stephen, "would not obey." A better translation is this: "To whom our fathers did not wish to be obedient." When Adam fell, it was not only his heart that fell—his will fell also. On October 31, 1517 we celebrate that great and momentous day when Martin Luther nailed his Ninety-five Theses to the door of the church at Wittenberg. What had this man discovered? What proved to be the turning-point in so many ways? What Luther saw was "the bondage of the will." The Roman Church did not believe that. But Luther saw it from the Scriptures.

This teaching is fundamental to the whole of Scripture. "They did not wish to be obedient," and this is still the trouble with all people. They do not want to live this life; they do not want to be delivered; they want to have their own way. We can all prove this; we have all known it in personal experience. Have we not found that even when we have been convinced and convicted by the truth, we still fight against it, we do not want to obey it, or, when we see it clearly, somehow or other our will is paralyzed and we do not put it into practice? Our wills have fallen quite as much as our hearts. Our wills are bound and in bondage. We are governed by the god of this world, "the prince of the power of the air, the spirit that now worketh in the children of disobedience" (Eph. 2:2).

"But," you say, "doesn't the mind come in at all?"

Oh, yes, it comes in, but it is in the third place. Everything is affected by the fall of man, and the mind is affected as much as the will and the heart. Man's mind has been perverted; he cannot think straightly; his whole judgment is gone.

Have you not been surprised when you have read the story to which Stephen is alluding or when you have read the words he is quoting from the Old Testament? He is referring to a most amazing and extraordinary incident in the thirty-second chapter of the book of Exodus. There is something so surprising about the behavior of men and women in sin. Look at these Israelites: "To whom our fathers would not obey, but thrust him from them, and in their hearts turned back again into Egypt." There is something almost incredible about this. They had suffered more in the bondage and captivity of Egypt than perhaps any people had hardly ever suffered; they had become absolute slaves; they had been maltreated—Stephen has already taken the Sanhedrin over the history—and were beaten with whips by the taskmasters, forced to make bricks without being given adequate material for this work. They had been in agony, and their children had been murdered. They had only recently been taken out of this in a miraculous manner by God, through His servant Moses. They had crossed the Red Sea and were marching toward the

Promised Land. Then a little thing went wrong, and this is what happened: "[They] thrust him from them, and in their hearts turned back again into Egypt."

Now that, I repeat, is almost incredible. Do you maintain that the sinner, the man who rejects the Gospel, is an intelligent person? But when you have been delivered from a horrible captivity and then a little thing goes wrong when you are in freedom, is it intelligent to say, "Ah, if only we had never come out of Egypt! If only we could go back into Egypt"? Read the story in the Old Testament. They lusted after Egypt and its alleged luxuries (Exod. 16:3). Is that a mark of intelligence? No; it is the clearest proof that the human mind has become debased. People have become fools; they cannot think sensibly. Going back to Egypt, to the captivity? Yet that is exactly how humanity argues. This is irrationality, not reason.

This terrible thing called sin that makes us reject the Gospel not only affects our reasoning power, it affects our memory also. How soon these people forgot the sufferings of Egypt! Consider the statement of Hegel, the German philosopher: "History teaches us that history teaches us nothing." Who would have prophesied on November 11, 1918 that on September 3, 1939 a second world war would break out? Who would have predicted, when we obtained peace in 1945, that in 1967 we would be on the brink of a third world war? What is the matter with man? I say that he has lost his memory. He is a fool! Has he forgotten? Of course he has! That is his great trouble.

Why do people forget? It is because they never face the facts; it is because they are always fooling themselves. When we are in trouble, of course, we cry for relief. The children of Israel had done that. In the bondage of Egypt they had cried out under the lashes of the taskmasters. They had cried out to God, asking for deliverance, asking Him to raise up someone to lead them out of it all. Ah, yes, in their suffering they had cried out, but when they were relieved, they soon forgot their suffering and turned against the man who had led them out.

And that is exactly what the world does. When there is a war and when there is trouble, a nation has days of national prayer and puts on a cloak of religion. And when somebody is desperately ill in the family, or when we ourselves are ill, we become good people and pray to God, and we say we are going to be different. But how soon we forget! What is the matter with us? Our trouble is that we never face the problem. So many of the people who are protesting against war and other things today do not face the real problem; they are interested in the pain, not in the problem. And as long as that is true of us, we will go on suffering. If we are only interested in the pain, when the pain is relieved we will soon forget. Many a man woke up this morning with a splitting headache and said, "I'll never drink a drop again." But he will forget all about it by next Saturday.

All the politicians, philosophers, poets, and sociologists are interested in the pain. They want to give us a life of ease. But "righteousness exalteth a nation" (Prov. 14:34), and nothing else does; and until we come back and face our real problem as it is revealed in Scripture, there is no hope for us. That is what the fall has done to the human mind. Man not only cannot think rationally, he cannot even remember.

And then people are fool enough to blind themselves still further. The children of Israel said, "Make us gods to go before us: for as for this Moses, which brought us out of the land of Egypt, we wot not what is become of him" (v. 40). How clever they thought they were! Having forgotten everything that had happened in the past, they said, "Make us new gods; we will continue this journey in our own way."

That is it. Humanity rejects God; it forgets all that has happened, and then it evolves a new teaching, a new religion, a new philosophy, a gospel adequate to the atomic age and to the great men of the modern world. "Make us new gods!" We have been making them very busily for well over a century. But where have they led us? Here is the madness of men and women.

That is where the intellect comes in, in the third place. And the real use we make of the intellect, as fallen men and women in sin, is this: we use the intellect to cover up and to try to justify what is dictated by our hearts. We like a gospel that allows us to do what we want to do. The trouble with the children of Israel was that this message of God had the Ten Commandments, it had a moral law, it was strict, and it asked for separation from the world. They did not like that, so they said in effect, "Let us make gods that will allow us to do what we want to do, gods that are compatible with our lusts and our desires."

That is exactly what clever men and women are still doing. They use their little intellects to make gods for themselves that have no life and no being, that can give them no comfort when they most need it, and that have nothing to put before them as a solution either for time or for eternity. That is the character of unbelief as expounded and analyzed by this first Christian martyr, Stephen.

But, lastly, let me show you briefly what unbelief makes us do. These are Stephen's words: "To whom our fathers would not obey, but thrust him from them, and in their hearts turned back again unto Egypt, saying unto Aaron, Make us gods to go before us: for as for this Moses, which brought us out of the land of Egypt . . ." That was the way they spoke of this great man—with scorn and sarcasm and derision. They dismissed Moses. This is what unbelief always makes the human race do. It makes them thrust away God's messengers. That was the whole point of Stephen's address. God raises up leaders one after another—and what do the people do? They "thrust him from them"! Remember what Joseph's brothers did to him. They sold him to traders traveling to Egypt—they wanted to get rid of him. The world has done this with all its greatest men and women. That is the tragedy of the human race, and yet it boasts about its intellect! ". . . thrust him from them"! Stephen said to the members of the Sanhedrin, "Can you not see that you have repeated and perpetuated the ancient error, the tragedy of people rejecting the messengers of God? And you have rejected His last messenger—His Son."

But this is what unbelief makes us do; it makes us turn away from God and from His way. I have already reminded you that was the original sin. Adam and Eve had been made in God's image; they had been enjoying the fellowship of God. But at the suggestion of the devil and in their lust for knowledge and authority and power, what did they do? They deliberately turned away from God.

This is madness, sheer irrationality. This is the lunacy of the human race, and it is the whole explanation of human troubles. The world is as it is because of this, and this alone. It has been happening throughout the centuries; there is nothing new about it. Do not be mad enough to think that you are doing something new by rejecting this Gospel. This text alone proves that you are not. You are just repeating what human beings have been doing throughout the centuries.

In Psalm 14:1 we read, "The fool hath said in his heart, There is no God." Perhaps you thought you were a modern man because you say that, but the fool has always said it! You are not original; you are just a slave, repeating what fools have always said. And did you notice where the fool says it? "In his heart," not in his head. He does not want a God. "Life would be so much more comfortable," he says, "if there were no God. I could do what I like; I could have my fill; I could enjoy myself." That is the old argument of the prodigal son. "If only I could get away from my father, then I would . . ."

Throughout the centuries, that has always been the fool's argument. "The carnal [natural] mind," says Paul, "is enmity against God: for it is not subject to the law of God, neither indeed can be" (Rom. 8:7). We have all turned our backs upon God; we are at enmity with Him. And the result is that we have set ourselves up as gods. So I stand here as a god, and there is the line, and the other god stands there, and I am trying to make myself bigger, and so is he, and we will end in a fight. Why? Because we are not both on our knees worshiping the only true and living God. That is the sole explanation. If the whole world were only worshiping God and listening to His law, we would have none of the problems that are troubling us and terrifying us.

But the supreme example of this is what the world did with the Son of God. "God so loved the world, that he gave his only begotten Son." He sent His own Son into it. What did they do with Him? They "thrust him from them," as these people had done with Moses. "Away with Him!" they said. "Take Him out of our sight. Away with Him! Crucify Him." Who did they want instead? A robber!

That is why the world is as it is, and as long as it remains like that, no politician will ever settle it. There will be "wars and rumours of wars" (Mark 13:7). As long as the world prefers robbers to Jesus Christ, we will get what we are getting, and we deserve what we are getting. This is rejection of God and the rejection of Christ! The phrase that Stephen uses is so typical and so perfect: "They thrust him from them, and in their hearts turned back again into Egypt." That is what unbelief makes us do. It always makes us turn back.

Back from what? Well, at the beginning it made man turn back from what God had originally made him to be. How perfect he was: what a spectacle, made in the image and likeness of God and endowed with an original righteousness. What a creature was man—how noble! He was God's representative here on earth and was made lord of creation. That is how God made him. What has unbelief made of him? It has made him turn back from that. To what? Well, to what we see man to be now. It is always a fall, a fall from glory and Godlikeness to shame and misery and contempt and unhappiness and war and wretchedness.

Yes, when men and women thrust God and Christ away from them, they always turn back! Back from liberty and freedom to slavery, from glory to serfdom. Can we all not see that? God made the world perfect, but it is as it is because men and women have turned back from God and turned downward. It is a fall—always a fall, always a lowering. And yet people are mad enough to glory in it and to think they are doing something wonderful in rejecting Jesus Christ and His Gospel.

And that brings me to my last point, which is the base ingratitude of unbelief. Listen to these wretched people: "Make us gods to go before us: for as for this Moses, which brought us out of the land of Egypt, we wot not what is become of him." That is typical of people. This is how they treat their greatest leaders; we have done it in our own country. We will use them when we want them; then we will throw them onto the scrap heap. We care for nothing except our own pleasures, our own ease, our own enjoyment. We will sacrifice a man; we will thrust him out. "This Moses . . ."

"This Moses"? This was the man who had been brought up as the son of Pharaoh's daughter and had the most glittering prospects that a man could ever have. But he forsook it all to make common cause with them. He not only gave up glorious prospects, he risked his life, and he suffered with these people in all the agonies and the terrors of their journeys. He gave himself up utterly, absolutely to them, to save and deliver them. But they turned on him and said, "This Moses . . . we wot not what is become of him." Oh, the sarcasm and the contempt involved in it all!

Yes, but what is that when you consider the attitude of men and women to God and our Lord and Savior, Jesus Christ? They only use His name as an oath and a curse. "This Jesus of yours!" they say. "This Christ of yours!" "This cross of yours!" "This blood of yours!" You hear them with their sarcasm and scorn and derision. They utter their blasphemies not only against God but against the greatest act that God has ever done. They throw it into His face and dismiss it with utter scorn and derision!

Are you guilty of that? Well, if you are not a Christian, you are! And do not talk to me about your scientific problems—I know as much about them as you do! That is not an explanation. You are putting them up as a camouflage to hide your lusts and passions and desires. You are insulting me if you say that your unbelief is because of your intellect, for you are saying that I am a fool; but I am ready to meet with you on scientific grounds whenever you like. Face the facts! Face yourself! Face your world as it is today. Read history, and you will see that it is the story of just this very unbelief, this madness, this being governed by lust and desire rather than by reason and truth. It is the rejection of God. It is spitting into the face of God's love, rejecting His most glorious offer. He is offering you free pardon; He is offering to reconcile you unto Himself, to give you a new heart, a new life, and a new nature. He will take from you the fear of death and will hold before you the prospect of a glory that transcends your highest imagination. He is offering you all that for nothing. Do you say that you are wise in rejecting all that? It is the only solution to your problem and to the problem of the nations; it is the only solution to the problem of the whole world.

May God grant us ears to hear! May God enable us to listen to the argument of Stephen presented of old to the members of the Sanhedrin, and may God give us grace to apply it to ourselves and to see that unless we repent, there is nothing awaiting us but the disaster and the doom that we so richly deserve. Let us listen to Him and yield to Him before it is too late.

14

The Folly of Humanity

To whom our fathers would not obey, but thrust him from them, and in their hearts turned back again into Egypt, saying unto Aaron, Make us gods to go before us: for as for this Moses, which brought us out of the land of Egypt, we wot not what is become of him. And they made a calf in those days, and offered sacrifice unto the idol, and rejoiced in the works of their own hands. Then God turned, and gave them up to worship the host of heaven; as it is written in the book of the prophets, O ye house of Israel, have ye offered to me slain beasts and sacrifices by the space of forty years in the wilderness? Yea, ye took up the tabernacle of Moloch, and the star of your god Remphan, figures which ye made to worship them: and I will carry you away beyond Babylon.

—Acts 7:39-43

We have seen that the whole teaching of the Bible is that the world is as it is because of its rejection of the word of God. This has never been more true than at the present time. You would have thought that with the world as it now, everybody would be very ready to listen to the Gospel. We have exhausted what humanity can do, so you would have thought people would instinctively turn to God and listen to the Gospel. But they do not—they reject it.

Why is this? There are many reasons, but I want to note two in particular. The first is that the whole conception of the message is wrong. Look at these intelligent members of the Sanhedrin. They were deliberately rejecting the message concerning the Son of God as the Savior of the world, and they were going to put a man to death because he preached it. What was the matter with them? Well, it is obvious, is it not, that they had completely misunderstood the message. And it is because men and women still misunderstand this message that they persist in rejecting it.

There are two main elements to this misunderstanding. The first is that people have a curious notion that the Gospel promises to solve and to settle all our difficulties and put the world in order. That is the common idea with regard to the Christian message. It is thought that Christianity will put an end to war and solve all the problems of humanity, and we shall all live happily ever after. That is one element. The second is the mistaken view that it is a message that brings to pass that desired condition by teaching us how to live, by showing us what is wrong, and then by telling us what is right and urging us to act accordingly.

Let us look at these two ideas. The answer to the first is that the Gospel—our Lord Himself in His teaching and all who followed it and repeated it—never promised to reform this world and put it in order—never! Indeed, I could adduce much evidence to show you that our Lord preached and taught the exact opposite. He said, "In the world ye shall have tribulation" (John 16:33). He did not promise that He would banish war and that the nations would all love one another. Rather He said, "Ye shall hear of wars and rumours of wars" (Matt. 24:6). He promised the sort of time we have just been having this last week.[3] It was He who said things like this: "As it was in the days of Noe, so shall it be also in the days of the Son of man. They did eat, they drank, they married wives, they were given in marriage, until the day that Noe entered into the ark, and the flood came, and destroyed them all. Likewise also as it was in the days of Lot . . ." (Luke 17:26-28). They were careless, carefree, drinking, marrying, giving in marriage, planting, building, selling . . . they did not think about God until the calamity came, when it was too late to think. That is our Lord's teaching. He never promised to put this world in order.

Now this is important because many people reject the Gospel because they say it is a proven failure. They say, "Your Gospel has promised to bring peace and to banish war and to put the world in order, and yet look at the world! It has been preached now for nearly 2,000 years, and look at the world. Your Christianity is demonstrably a failure." And that is all based upon the fallacy that Christianity has promised to put the world in order.

So what does the Gospel say? It says that in spite of the fact that the world is under the judgment of God and is facing a final doom, all who listen to the voice of God, and especially to the Gospel of the Son of God, can be delivered out of the world, "translated . . . into the kingdom of his dear Son" (Col. 1:13) and are being prepared for a future glory, which will be evident even on the face of this material earth in some great day that is yet to come. That is the Christian message. It is not about world reform but is a message of salvation for men and women—deliverance out of the world and translation into the kingdom of God. That is the answer to the first misunderstanding.

But take, second, this idea that the Gospel is really just a teaching, a great idealistic and ethical teaching, and that what is needed is that it should be taught and propagated, so that men and women, hearing it, will say, "Yes, that's what we want. We must now go and put this into practice. We must either legislate the kingdom of God into being through the government or, by means of moral persuasion, we must persuade people to imitate Christ and to make a new world." That has been the popular creed. It was taught by men like the late H. G. Wells and many others, men who flourished toward the end of the Victorian and particularly the Edwardian periods. Their whole idea was that the world behaves as it does because of its lack of knowledge. But how completely fatuous such an idea looks now. They said, "People fight and there are wars because humanity is ignorant. If it only thought, if it only used its brains, it would stop." So education was seen as the solution for all our troubles. "An educated people," they said, "will be incapable of war. The moment people think, they will see how monstrous and ridiculous war is; so they will banish it. We must put our faith in education, give the people knowledge and information, show them what war really is, and they will stop fighting."

An amazing amount of energy has been given to the propagation of that teaching in this present [twentieth] century alone. But it has nothing at all to do with the Gospel. The Gospel says the opposite. It says that men and women, far from liking the teaching of God and rising to it and being anxious to put it into practice, hate God and hate His teaching and do not want to have anything to do with it. The Gospel goes even further and says that even if people like the teaching intellectually, they are incapable of putting it into practice. This is the plain statement of the Gospel. This idea that all you need to do is confront men and women with a wonderful teaching and exhort them to carry it out and so make a perfect world is a complete denial of the very essence of the Gospel.

But why are men and women incapable of obeying the teaching of the Gospel? This is the very fact that Stephen makes so plain and clear to us. Since the fall there has been an unbelief in human beings that makes them persist in rejecting the word of God. What is the cause of this? We have seen that the trouble is not in the intellect but in the heart. But that is not all—that is general. Stephen goes on with the analysis, and if we really are concerned about our own condition, if we are concerned about the state of the world, if we are perplexed as to why the world can be as mad as it is, why people should ever think they can settle problems by doing what has been happening recently, if we want to understand that, we must listen to this message. It is the only explanation. We will get no explanation in the newspapers, nor in the clever interviews on television. They do not touch it; they know nothing about it. The cause is not political—it is spiritual, and here Stephen gives a masterly analysis of the problem and lays it open so we can see why the world is as it is today.

The trouble is, I say again, rebellion against God. But why do people behave in this manner? Stephen gives us the answer—and this is the first thing we must grasp: they do it quite deliberately. In other words, the trouble with men and women is not their ignorance, nor is it that they lack information. We know by now that is not the answer to the problem of war and the troubles of the world. In spite of what they know, people have always deliberately chosen to reject God's way and to do it with scorn and sarcasm.

Consider the Bible, one of the oldest books in the world—it has been confronting humanity for many centuries. In 1938 we celebrated the quatercentenary of the giving of the open Bible to the people of England. For 400 years we have had it open. So we cannot plead ignorance. Here is an analysis of your ills, here is an exposure of them, and here is the proffered remedy, the only remedy that works. And there has been preaching. For nearly 2,000 years the message has been sent forth. And there is the great story of the martyrs and confessors. All this has been known.

What, then, is the problem? Why do people reject the Gospel? We have seen that one reason for this rejection is that people misunderstand the Gospel. Here is the second and more fundamental reason: they reject the Christian message because they are fools. I am sorry. I must use plain language because I too am by nature a fool. All men and women, by nature, are fools. It is very difficult to decide, as you read the Bible, which is the more potent factor—the arrogance or the folly of the human race. I think it is the folly because the arrogance arises out of the folly. People would not be arrogant if they were not such fools. They are arrogant because they do not know what they are doing and they do not understand what they are saying. So the ultimate cause of the trouble is their folly, and you will notice that this is what the Bible says most frequently about the sinner.

The Bible has many ways of defining sin. It says that sin is missing the mark. It is like a man aiming at a target and missing it. It also says that sin is a transgression and that it is disobedience. But the ultimate fact about sinners, the men and women who disobey God, is that they are fools. "The fool hath said in his heart, There is no God" (Ps. 14:1). Our Lord told a parable about a rich fool. The man, who was a farmer, was congratulating himself. His harvest was so great that his barns had become too small, and he was planning to pull them down and build larger ones. He was pleased with himself, and he said, "Soul, thou hast much goods laid up for many years; take thine ease, eat, drink, and be merry." But that night God spoke to him and said, "Thou fool, this night thy soul shall be required of thee: then whose shall those things be, which thou hast provided?" (Luke 12:16-20). The fool! And this is the most common charge that is brought in the Bible against men and women in sin and in rebellion against God.

How does this folly show itself? The chief way is that men and women show their folly in fooling themselves, in self-deception. This is the most tragic thing of all. It is bad enough when they fool others, but it is really tragic when they fool themselves. And that is what human beings have been doing from the very beginning, since they first rebelled and turned against God. The original sin—listening to the suggestion of the devil against God, believing that lie—was the greatest act of folly that has ever been committed. It was madness!

So, then, I want to show you the essence of this self-deception, and it comes out very clearly here in what Stephen says about the children of Israel. Moses had led them out of Egypt, and he had gone up onto Mount Sinai to receive the law from God. Then, says Stephen, "To whom our fathers would not obey, but thrust him from them, and in their hearts turned back again into Egypt, saying unto Aaron, Make us gods to go before us. . . . And they made a calf in those days, and offered sacrifice unto the idol, and rejoiced in the works of their own hands."

Here is a perfect picture of this incredible folly of the human race. "Make us . . . [they] rejoiced in the works of their own hands." What is the meaning of this? Well, as is not infrequently the case, Paul has said the final word about it. In Romans 1:22 he makes the most devastating statement that has ever been made about the human race, and it has never been seen more clearly than at this moment: "Professing themselves to be wise, they became fools." If that is not the most perfect description that you have ever heard of men and women in this modern day, then you know very little about life.

"Professing themselves to be wise"—in what sense? In their self-confidence. The self-confidence of men and women is endless. They think there is nothing they cannot do. After all, they have split the atom, they have beaten the law of gravity, they sent men into space . . . can anything stand before them? They think they are the center of the universe. The greatest thing in the universe is the human brain. There seems to be no limit to its capacity, and the first claim men put forward is that they can make God. But there is nothing new about modern man—his forefathers did exactly the same thing. At the foot of Mount Sinai, they turned to Aaron and said, "Make us gods to go before us . . ."

Stephen said, "They made a calf in those days, and offered sacrifice unto the idol, and rejoiced in the works of their own hands." They wanted a god, so they proceeded to make one. They made a god out of gold and then proceeded to worship it. They had no hesitation at all, of course, in doing this. Human beings have never had any hesitation about making gods. There have been pantheons of gods, and people have given them names—Mercury, Mars, Jupiter, and all the rest.

And men and women still do the same. This, of course, has been their most evident and prominent activity for the last hundred years or so. In their cleverness, they have been constructing and making a new god. It is called the higher criticism of the Bible. This approach to the Bible originated in Germany and had its starting point in a great belief in man and the idea that to believe in God was an insult to man.

The way this worked itself out in terms of the Bible was that these men sat in judgment upon it and said, "Of course, there are some things that are right in the Bible, but it also contains a great deal of nonsense and rubbish. So if the Bible says something you don't like about God, it's wrong. Throw it out because it's not true." Who decides what God is like? Man! And that is what they have been doing for a century. They have been constructing a new god; there is no wrath in this God, there is no justice, there is no righteousness. This God does not punish; He is only love and nothing else. They have not hesitated to do this. They have constructed a new Father, a new Son, a new Holy Spirit—if they believe in the Holy Spirit at all—and they have not hesitated to say that man can sit in judgment on this revelation in the Scriptures and that man is competent to define, to describe, and to delineate God. If God does not tally with my ideas, so much the worse for God.

Perhaps you have been guilty of this? Examine yourself. Do you realize that you have been setting up your pygmy intellect as the final authority and that you have not hesitated to deliver your opinions on God—"God is wrong if He does this" or "Why doesn't God do that?" Have you not said these things? That is judging God. Your self-confidence makes you say that you are capable of making and creating a god.

Second, and, of course, it follows from the first point, men and women have been very confident that they know the truth about themselves. They do not like the biblical view of man. That was the original temptation, was it not? "Yea, hath God said, Ye shall not . . . ?" (Gen. 3:1). That is not right; it is not fair; it is not just! In other words, Adam and Eve set up their own opinion against God's opinion of man; they rejected God's and accepted the devil's.

And that is what you find so constantly in the pages of both the Old Testament and the New. People believe that they know themselves, that they understand themselves; and again, never have they done this more assiduously than during the modern age. Men and women today do not accept the biblical view of man; they regard it as insulting. What is their view? Well, some people regard man as a purely economic unit. They believe that he is nothing but the result of the interplay of capital and labor—dialectical materialism, or call it what you like. Others have a biological view of man or a supposedly scientific view, while yet others have what they call a psychological view. But in each case they claim the competence to define man; they think they understand him and reject everything else.

That leads, third, to the fact that they are quite confident that they know how life is to be lived in this world and how this world is to be run and how it is to be ordered. That is what the children of Israel did; they turned their backs on God and said, "Now, then, we are going to do it." That is how they first asked for a king. They were never meant to have a king, but they said, "Other nations have kings—why don't we? This isn't fair—let us have a king too." They were God's people, a theocracy, but they were not content with that; they wanted to be a kingdom like other kingdoms. They always thought they wanted something better than God—that was their whole story. So they pleaded for a king, and God said in effect, "All right, I will give you a king, but this is what will happen to you if you have one" (1 Sam. 8). And all that God said did happen to them.

And that is still the story. Men and women think they know how to live, how to run the world. Oh, the confidence in philosophy and politics during the last hundred years! The people believed that by government acts they could make a perfect world, that they could banish war. They were not dishonest, they really believed it, such was the folly of this delusion of grandeur, this megalomania. They really believed they could make the world perfect by politics and education, sociology, philosophy, science, and so on. And they still believe it! That is the astounding thing.

Now I am simply pointing this out to you because Stephen said it is the only explanation of why the Sanhedrin rejected the Lord Jesus Christ and His salvation; and that is still true today. Why do people reject the revelation of the Bible? Why are they so slow to believe it, even though it is being verified every day and even though the world is proving the truth of its warnings and everything else is being shown to be false? It was not the Bible that said the twentieth century would be the greatest century of all time. The Bible said the exact opposite, as I have shown you. It is the people who deny the Bible who said that. They have been the false optimists. There is no false optimism in the Bible.

So why do people resent this revelation, this teaching that comes to us? It is because they believe they have ability and power. Why, they are research workers, and they can split the atom, so surely there is nothing they cannot do! They do not like to be treated as children. They really believe that if they only set out on the great research, the great endeavor, they must arrive at ultimate truth, absolute reality. So when they confront this Gospel, which tells them, in the words of our Lord, "Except ye be converted, and become as little children, ye shall not enter into the kingdom of heaven" (Matt. 18:3), they feel insulted. They are such fools, such megalomaniacs, they are so deluded about themselves that when God addresses them, they reject Him.

That, then, is the first great manifestation of this incredible folly of humanity in which people say, "Make us gods" and worship the work of their own hands. The first great element in this folly as it is analyzed here by Stephen is self-deception, man's illimitable confidence in his own power and capacity. Stephen said in effect, "Do you not see you are doing the very thing your forefathers did?" And I am now attempting feebly to say the same thing. Do you still have this fatal trust in your own capacity, in your own understanding? Do you understand the world? Do you understand yourself? What do you really know about God? Face it!

But, second, let me prove to you that men and women are fools. The Bible does not stop at assertions—it goes on to give us demonstrations. I know of nothing more devastating—in a kind of literary sense—than the way in which Stephen did it here. I see this awfully, devastatingly, in the world around me at this present moment. Let me show you what I mean. Look at that poor fellow—he is ready to take on anybody in a fight, ready to enter into any competition; there is nothing he cannot do. What is the matter with him? He is drunk! His self-confidence is based on the fact that he is drunk, but he does not see it. And the world is like that at the present time. It does not see its folly. In spite of what is happening, it cannot see the truth because it deceives itself. This is the whole difficulty; this is why the world does not see the essence of its problems even at this present moment.

If you are in any doubt about this, let me demonstrate to you the folly of human beings, let me prove it beyond the possibility of contradiction. First, men and women show that they are fools when you look at what they produce in contradistinction to what they reject. Stephen brought that out at this point by quoting from the thirty-second chapter of the book of Exodus. The children of Israel had rejected, and they had made. What had they rejected? God! What had they made? A calf! Could anything be plainer? They rejected God: "To whom our fathers would not obey, but thrust him from them, and in their hearts turned back again into Egypt, saying unto Aaron, Make us gods to go before us: for as for this Moses, which brought us out of the land of Egypt, we wot not what is become of him. And they made"—they were going to make a god; they were rejecting the true God—"a calf in those days, and offered sacrifice unto the idol."

What else needs to be said! That is humanity at this very moment. In the second half of the first chapter of the Epistle to the Romans, the apostle Paul says:

> *Because that which may be known of God is manifest in them; for God hath shewed it unto them. For the invisible things of him from the creation of the world are clearly seen, being understood by the things that are made, even his eternal power and Godhead; so that they are without excuse: because that, when they knew God, they glorified him not as God, neither were thankful; but became vain in their imaginations, and their foolish heart was darkened. Professing themselves to be wise, they became fools, and changed the glory of the uncorruptible God into an image made like to corruptible man, and to birds, and four-footed beasts, and creeping things.*
>
> —*Rom. 1:19-23*

That is what people did, and that is what they are still doing. They reject God—God the Creator, God the sustainer of the whole universe, God the orderer of all things, the God of providence, the God of history, the holy God, the glorious God. I will tell you about the God whom the children of Israel had rejected. He gave a description of Himself to Moses soon after the incident of the golden calf:

> *And the* LORD *descended in the cloud, and stood with him there, and proclaimed the name of the* LORD. *And the* LORD *passed by before him, and proclaimed, The* LORD, *The* LORD *God, merciful and gracious, long-suffering, and abundant in goodness and truth, keeping mercy for thousands, forgiving iniquity and transgression and sin,*

> *and that will by no means clear the guilty; visiting the iniquity of the fathers upon the children, and upon the children's children, unto the third and to the fourth generation.*
>
> —*Exod. 34:5-7*

That is God! The everlasting and eternal God!

> *Immortal, invisible, God only wise,*
> *In light inaccessible hid from our eyes,*
> *Most blessed, most glorious, the Ancient of days,*
> *Almighty, victorious, thy great name we praise.*
> Walter Chalmers Smith

Paul wrote to Timothy, "[God] only hath immortality, dwelling in the light which no man can approach unto" (1 Tim. 6:16). No man has seen God or ever can see the everlasting God, the God of glory, who is beyond description. And yet He is a God to whom we can pray, a God who is ready to listen to us. He is the living God, the powerful God, the acting God.

> *God in three persons, blessed Trinity.*
> Reginald Heber

That is the God from whom people turn away.

And what do people turn to? What do they make? A calf! Have you noticed, they always do something like this. Of course, they make it of gold, and this is where they show their folly still further. They think that making a calf of gold will be different from making a calf of wood. They do not see that in all cases it is still a calf. But because it is gold, it looks marvelous and is costly, and they think, "This is it—a calf made of gold!" And they bow down before it. And as Paul says in Romans 1, it does not stop with calves—they make "creeping things" (v. 23) and so on.

The people of this country [England], over 90 percent of them, are much too intelligent, they tell us, to believe in God any longer. What do they believe in? They believe in the British lion! He has recently had his tail twisted a bit, has he not? A lion. It is always an animal. The Russian bear! The German eagle! It is always the same. How we give ourselves away! What utter fools we are. We do not believe in God, but we believe in our country. Many people worship their country. Nationalism is ultimately worship of country, worshiping the blood that is in you, worshiping yourself writ large.

Then look at the worship of money! Oh, we are much too intelligent to believe in God, so we go in for sports pools to win money. Or perhaps our god is food, drink, travel, or pleasure. People say, "We can't possibly believe in God," but they literally worship money. I have known people who have worshiped houses—there is no question about it—and cars. I have known many people who have worshiped their own children. They have sacrificed God without a moment's thought for the sake of their children. They will discourage their children from being religious so that they might get on in the world. In all this, as Paul reminds us, man has been worshiping himself. Not only "four-footed beasts, and creeping things" (Rom. 1:23) but man himself. Great man! Scientific man! Man come of age. What is man but a fool! He turns from God and worships a beast.

There, then, is one proof and manifestation of human folly, but let us look at a second. People turn from law to license. The children of Israel turned from the law of God, the law that they had in their hearts, the law that had been given to them in the Ten Commandments, the moral law, all the teaching. Look again at the Ten Commandments. What a body of doctrine, what a body of law—the worship of God! Consider the keeping of God's day. It is a good principle to have a day of rest, one in seven, set apart from the other days. Oh, the wisdom of the Ten Commandments!

And then you come to the second table of the law: "Thou shalt not kill. Thou shalt not commit adultery. Thou shalt not steal. Thou shalt not bear false witness," and so on. I have often said from this pulpit that if only the whole world observed the Ten Commandments, most of our problems would be solved. Add to that our Lord's interpretation of the Ten Commandments in the Sermon on the Mount. If the whole world were only living according to the moral, ethical teaching of the Bible, we would not have wars or divorce or violence or crime; we would not have drug-taking. What a noble law it is! What a pattern for living!

But men and women in their cleverness turn from that—to what? Drinking and dancing. That is what they were doing at the foot of Mount Sinai when Moses came down. They were naked, they were drinking, and they were dancing. And that is what the world is doing today in spite of its troubles and its tragedies—drink, drugs, dancing, sex, promiscuity, diseases, rampant confusion! That is what humanity produces. When people turn from God's holy law, that is what they always produce.

Or let me put it to you in a third form. People invariably turn from a condition in which they have been delivered and set free and given joy to slavery and fear. This, too, is what always happens when they turn from God. Listen to these children of Israel; they made this calf out of gold, and they said, "These be thy gods, O Israel, which brought thee up out of the land of Egypt" (Exod. 32:4). It was a barefaced lie, and they knew it; yet they said it. They gave the credit to the golden calf for having delivered them out of the bondage and the captivity of Egypt! It was God who had delivered them. How soon men and women forget! They had forgotten the slavery and the misery and the taskmasters and the lashes of the whips and their utter, complete impotence. God had sent His servant Moses and had given him miraculous powers. Read the story for yourselves in the early chapters of the book of Exodus. It was God, and God alone, who had brought them out. He had opened the Red Sea before them; He had led them through the wilderness; He had fed them with manna; He had given them water from rocks—it had all been the action of God.

And that is only a picture, an adumbration, of the yet greater and more glorious deliverance that God has brought about in Jesus Christ, His Son, and the salvation that He sent Him into the world to give us. God, at the cost of the death of His own Son, has made it possible for you and for me to be forgiven, to be set free from the bondage and the captivity of sin, to become the children of God and the heirs of eternal and everlasting bliss. That is what people reject.

What did they turn to? It is so obvious in that ancient story, and Stephen analyzed it here. The children of Israel not only made a calf, they not only made idols and bowed down before them, as people are still doing, but did you notice this: "Yea, ye took up the tabernacle of Moloch, and the star of your god Remphan, figures which ye made to worship them." God gave them up to worship the host of heaven. This means that having turned their backs on God, they began to worship the stars and the moon and the sun. In other words, they took up astrology, they went in for spiritism, and people are still doing that.

Modern men and women are much too intelligent to believe in God, but they believe in astrology and in spiritism. Why is that? The answer is simple. When you turn from God, you turn from deliverance and liberty and joy to bondage, serfdom, slavery, the fear of life, and the fear of death, and you do not know where you are, you do not understand life. So you consult the stars, and every day you look at the paper and read the experts on the stars. You say, "What's going to happen to me today?" This is sheer slavery; it is tragedy! Humanity worshiping stars! To fate! To the occult! To spiritism!

People have never been so afraid of life and have never felt so helpless as at the present time. They do not know where they are, and they do not know what to do. But you cannot pray to a calf, you cannot pray to a lion, you cannot pray to man! They cannot help you. Your idols are silent, helpless. The psalmists ridicule them. Look at your idols, look at your god, says the psalmist. "They have mouths, but they speak not: eyes have they, but they see not. . . .They have hands, but they handle not: feet have they, but they walk not" (Ps. 115:5-7). You have created a god, but you have to move him about. He cannot move; he is helpless. And the result is that in your agony, in your trouble, in your moment of greatest need, when you yourself need help from outside, there is nobody there, there is nobody to pray to. The idol does not care. He is deaf and dumb; he cannot give you a word of comfort or consolation. He cannot tell you what to do. He is completely silent, and he leaves you to yourself. That is what happens when people turn from God.

That is why men and women go in for astrology and spiritism. They will clutch at anything to give them help. They are in a wilderness. They are frightened by what is happening, and they have no idea what is coming to them. They are already terrified of the future—what is going to happen? They do not know how to live; they do not know how to die; they do not know what lies beyond death. They are fumbling, stumbling in the dark, trying to find a bit of knowledge. It is all because they have rejected the word and the law of God.

But, finally, the ultimate folly is seen in this: "And they made a calf in those days, and offered sacrifice unto the idol, and"—and then—"rejoiced"—"rejoiced"!—"in the works of their own hands." When Moses and Joshua were coming down from that mount, they heard a noise, and Joshua in his ignorance said, "There is a noise of war in the camp" (Exod. 32:17).

"No, no," said Moses, "it is not. It is the noise of singing."

Can you imagine this among an intelligent people, especially a people who had just been delivered from the bondage and the captivity of Egypt and had seen the marvel and the miracle of the dividing of the Red Sea? Can you believe it of them, that having made a god for themselves, a golden calf, they were rejoicing, they were dancing, they were singing, they were making merry, they were drinking? They were having a marvelous time. They thought they had done something glorious. They had dismissed this fellow Moses: "We wot not what is become of him." They had made a great advance. Having dismissed the servant of God, having dismissed God, they were happy and were congratulating themselves. They said this was progress.

And that is the modern world, this modern world that glories in the fact that man was not made in the image of God but has evolved from some primitive slime and is just a highly developed ape! They are glorying in it; they think it is marvelous. It is marvelous to deny God and to worship man or some creature, some idol. It is marvelous to think that we are not made upright and righteous in the image of God but are just intelligent animals. People are glorying in this, and they are pouring ridicule upon the Son of God and His glorious Gospel. There is only one thing to say about people who do that—they are mad, they are unutterable fools, they are drunk, they are drugged. They are not awake; they cannot think. They cannot see; their world is not open to them. In the name of God, I plead with you, wake up! Let history speak to you. Let this summary of the history of the children of Israel speak to you. Awake to righteousness! Be sober.

And the moment we become sober, we will say, in the words of Hosea, "What have I to do any more with idols?" (Hos. 14:8). Such a life is monstrous! Have we been bowing down to a graven image, to an idol, to a calf, to an animal? It is incredible. Or take the words of the prodigal son when he eventually came to himself in "a far country" and said in effect, "What am I doing here in this condition? What a fool I've been! How many servants, paid servants, are there in my father's house who are in a better condition than this? I'm mad! I'm a fool! I will arise and go to my father" (Luke 15:17-18).

If you, too, are conscious that you are away from home in a far country, away from God, surrounded by swine and animals and four-footed beasts and eating the husks on which swine feed, if you realize that you are there and that you are a fool to be there, that you were made for God and meant for communion with Him, I say to you, "Arise! Go home! Go back to your Father." And blessed be His holy name, if you do that, you will find that He is waiting for you. He will come to meet you, and He will embrace you. He will say, "Son, daughter, your sins are forgiven you. I have already punished them in the person of My only begotten, dearly beloved Son. Come! Enter in! Let us rejoice and make merry."

15

God Gave Them Up

Then God turned, and gave them up to worship the host of heaven; as it is written in the book of the prophets, O ye house of Israel, have ye offered to me slain beasts and sacrifices by the space of forty years in the wilderness? Yea, ye took up the tabernacle of Moloch, and the star of your god Remphan, figures which ye made to worship them: and I will carry you away beyond Babylon.

—Acts 7:42-43

We are interested in Stephen's account of the children of Israel because these people and their behavior and what happened to them is a great object lesson of God's relationship to the entire human race. It is most important to observe that Stephen was not dealing with theory, he was not expressing an attitude or a point of view, but he was dealing with history. You need only read this chapter to see that quite clearly. More important still, he was dealing with history that had not only happened but had been foretold. The history that we have in the Bible is history that had been previously prophesied, and in addition to that, this history is itself a prophecy. It tells us of what will come if we persist in behaving in the same way as the Sanhedrin or as the children of Israel had done under the Old Testament dispensation. So my assertion is that it is only as we understand the principles that were taught here by Stephen that we can possibly understand the past history of the human race and indeed the very condition in which we find ourselves as a world of people at this very moment.

Look at the state of the world. Look at the things that are happening.

Look at this [twentieth] century and the two world wars and the possibilities that are looming upon the horizon. Now there is only one way to understand all this—it is to grasp the principles that were taught here by this first Christian martyr, Stephen, as he reviewed the history of Israel and worked out what I venture to call a philosophy of history.

Why are we in the situation in which we find ourselves nationally, internationally, as members of society, and as individuals? Why is the world as it is? Many, of course, looking at this problem, blame God for it, and it is their great reason for not believing in Him. "Why does God allow this?" they protest. "If He is a God of love, if He is omnipotent, why does He allow these things to happen? Why doesn't He stop it all?" That is the argument, and I'm sure you are familiar with it, but I must point out in passing how inconsistent people are in their reasoning. Their main objection to God is that they believe in freedom, free will, man's freedom to determine his life and his future. God is regarded as someone who is inimical to that. So people reject God because they feel that He is holding them down. And yet the moment they get into trouble, they want God to handle them as if they were machines. "Why doesn't God stop it?" they say. They boast about their freedom, and yet they complain when God continues to regard them as free individuals who are responsible for their actions and the results that follow from them.

But as for the question of why the world is as it is, let me give you the full answer as it is given here. Stephen made it abundantly clear that the state of the world is all due to the fact that men and women turn away from God and His holy laws. We have begun to consider this, and we have seen that they do that because they are fools, because they are self-confident. But that is not all. Stephen went on. Another most important principle is taught here—and if this is not relevant to the situation that we are in, then I do not know what is. This is what I call the true philosophy of the history of the world.

Let us look at it like this. If we take a bird's-eye view of the history of the world, what do we find? We see clearly that nothing has so characterized the history of the human race as a strange kind of periodicity. There have been certain times and epochs when things seemed to be getting better, when the human race seemed to be improving, when men and women seemed to be really ascending and going upward. But those times have been followed by periods of decline and retrogression.

The nineteenth century appeared to be a period of ascension. It was a time when peace reigned, and though there was an occasional war here and there—the Crimean War, for example—there was nothing commensurate with the Napoleonic Wars. There was the great *pax Britannica*, which looked as if it was going to last forever, an empire on which the sun never set. Science was making great advances, knowledge was growing, and the whole world seemed to be going right up into the heavens. Some were quite sure that the twentieth century was really going to be the grand climax for which the whole of civilization had been waiting. But, alas, the twentieth century turned out to be very different; it was a century of calamity, a century of disaster, a century of horrors. The great question is, why is this? How do you explain the periodicity—an apparent improvement, then a terrible declension in which the human race faces the abyss and the end of all things—what is the cause?

The world simply cannot understand this periodicity at all and admits that it cannot. It is completely baffled by it. This is because the world postulates development. The world believes in evolution and says that there is a "force" working in the direction of goodness that lifts up the entire human race—the *élan vital* of Henri Bergsen and others. That is what the world believes, and it believes it very firmly; it has rejected belief in God in favor of this. Now, obviously, if that is what you believe, you have no explanation for what is happening at the present time. Indeed, it seems to be a reversal of all the progress of the last [nineteenth] century. So the world does not understand and is completely bankrupt in its thinking because it has this fatal belief in a steady, inevitable, constant development and evolution. The world does not know what to say and is turning to drugs and drink and pleasure for some temporary relief.

And the world does this because men and women forget God and the fact that this world is God's world. They think of this world solely in terms of themselves—their own activities and their own efforts. Their idea of history is this—man fighting, being born, getting married, dying, wars, increasing knowledge, science and its discoveries. They think of everything always and exclusively in terms of themselves and their activities. That is why they are baffled when they live in a period such as this. And the only answer to this problem is the answer that was given here by Stephen in his extraordinary statement to the members of the Sanhedrin. The answer to men and women and their baffled condition is that what matters in this world, ultimately, is not what people do but what God does, and it is the failure, I say, to grasp and to understand this that accounts for all the bewilderment about the present situation.

Here is the biblical case. God made the world, and He made man. He made the world perfect, and He made man perfect and put him into this perfect world. So why are things as they are? The answer is, man fell. He disobeyed God and rebelled against Him. Man asserted himself and said, "I will take charge." That is the fall. And because man fell, God punished him; and remember, a part of the punishment was that God, because of the rebellion and the fall of man, even cursed the ground. Nature and creation are not what they were as God originally made them; briars and thorns and diseases came into existence as a result of the fall. These things were never intended to be in the universe; this is all a part of the punishment of the sin of man.

But still more serious, of course, is that as the result of his folly and his conceit and his rebellion and his blasphemy against God, man became the slave of the devil and the slave of sin and evil. Again, take a bird's-eye view of the history of the human race, and what do you find? In the main it is a history of misery—troubles, problems, illnesses, wars, earthquakes, calamities, pestilences, and death. But it was never meant to be like that. This is all a part of God's punishment of sin, and man has been unhappy because he has become the slave of the devil. The devil has become "the god of this world" (2 Cor. 4:4); he governs men and women, and they have become creatures of lust and desire and passion and evil.

But—and this is an essential part of the biblical message—God has controlled even that. He did not abandon the world but decided to keep evil and sin under control. One of His ways of doing that, the Bible tells us, was by appointing government. Government is not a human invention; it has been introduced by God. We talk about kings and princes and emperors and governors and so on, as if man brought them into being. But he has not. This is God's device. Paul says:

> *Let every soul be subject unto the higher powers. For there is no power but of God: the powers that be are ordained of God [Paul is talking about magistrates and governments]. Whosoever therefore resisteth the power, resisteth the ordinance of God. . . . For rulers are not a terror to good works, but to the evil. . . . [The magistrate] beareth not the sword in vain: for he is the minister of God, a revenger to execute wrath upon him that doeth evil.*
>
> —*Rom. 13:1-4*

This all means that God has not given unrestrained freedom and activity to man in sin. He has brought in government and order and system to keep it all in bounds, to keep it in check. This is an essential part of the biblical teaching. God did this when man fell. He punished him, and certain consequences happened, but God put a limit and a control upon it all.

The world turns against God and says, "Why does God allow these problems and this suffering? Why doesn't He stop it?"

I will give you the answer to that, and it is Stephen's answer, not mine. Here is the principle: God controls sin and evil and their effects upon the human race. And He does it in this way: whenever men and women abuse God's goodness, whenever they become exceptionally arrogant and vile, God acts, and He acts in a specific manner. This is the only explanation of what has happened in the twentieth century.

I suggest this because men and women have been exceptionally arrogant and vile. People have ridiculed God, laughed at Him, made a joke of Him, and dismissed Him. Science has come in and convinced human beings that they can do everything. Man has said he can control the universe, that there is nothing he cannot do, and he has been setting out to do it. And when man behaves like that, God invariably acts in the manner that is taught here by Stephen.

Let me put it to you in the form of principles. At such times God punishes men and women. And, said Stephen, the first element in the punishment is that God turns away from them. Did you notice this? "Then God turned, and gave them up to worship the host of heaven." We have just been told that these children of Israel would not listen to Moses: ". . . but thrust him from them, and in their hearts turned back again into Egypt." This is the typical arrogance of man. The people said in effect, "This Moses—we don't know what's happened to him. Who is he? He's gone up onto a mountain. Shall we ever see him again? Let's make a god for ourselves." They turned away from God, and they thought they were clever. So as part of the punishment God turned away from them! The most awful thing that I can think of is that God should turn away. But this is what He does at certain periods of exceptional arrogance on the part of man.

Oh, how little we know about God, and how little we understand Him! Though men and women had sinned against Him, God did not turn away from them. He brought powers, governments, magistrates, kings, order into society, and also into the family, the home, and so on. These are God's way of controlling and keeping sin within bounds. Not only that, "He maketh his sun to rise on the evil and on the good, and sendeth rain on the just and on the unjust" (Matt. 5:45). How good and kind God is to us; He looks at us still. But there are times when He turns away. Men and women in their arrogance turn away from God and think this is marvelous and wonderful. But they forget that God can turn away from them, and I suggest to you that if you want to understand the twentieth century, there is the first key to it. This is a century in which God is turning away—deliberately.

Now let us be clear about this. God never turns away from people until He has first of all blessed them and given them every chance and every opportunity. Oh, the blessings that God has given to the human race! God blessed the children of Israel. He had only just brought them out of the captivity and the bondage of Egypt; He had just brought them miraculously through the Red Sea. Then they became arrogant, and He turned away from them

I will tell you more. God never turns away from people without first of all warning them that He will do so. Read the story of these children of Israel—Stephen was really just giving a summary of it here—and this is what you will find. God, when He speaks to them, says every time that there will be "a blessing, if ye obey the commandments of the LORD your God." But He always adds, "And a curse, if ye will not obey the commandments of the LORD your God" (Deut. 11:27-28). This happened at the very beginning when God made Adam and Eve. He made them in His own image; He surrounded them with everything they could desire. It was Paradise. But God gave a warning: "There is one tree from which you must not eat. 'For in the day that thou eatest thereof thou shalt surely die'" (Gen. 2:17). They were warned. God never turns away without first of all warning us that if we disobey, there will be certain consequences. From the beginning until now it has been the case that when we ignore the goodness of God and ridicule His warnings, God turns away from us.

This is a terrible thing. The prophet Amos, who lived in a similar period to the one in which you and I are living, put it in his own graphic manner. God's message through Amos to the people was: "Behold, the days come, saith the Lord GOD, that I will send a famine in the land, not a famine of bread, nor a thirst for water, but of hearing the words of the LORD" (Amos 8:11). And that is the most awful thing that could ever happen. We are then left with nothing but the humanists, the scoffers, and the unbelievers and their supposed wisdom, and nothing else. Can you imagine what such a world would be like, a world in which God does not speak and just leaves us? God's turning away from them is part of His punishment of man's exceptional arrogance and vileness.

But that is not all. "Then God turned, and gave them up"—"gave them up"!—"to worship the host of heaven." Now the real exposition of this is in Romans 1. "God gave them up . . ." Paul says that three times. God gave them over to "a reprobate mind," He gave them up to this, He gave them up to that (vv. 24, 26, 28). What does this mean? As I have said, when man fell and brought calamity upon himself and his world, God did not just leave him. God did not say, "All right, I have finished with you; carry on." No; God in His great kindness—it is what we call common grace—put limits and restraints upon sin. But the second way in which God punishes the exceptional arrogance of man is that He withdraws these controls. "God gave them up." "God gave them over." God allows people to do what they like and withdraws all His restraining influences. I would be baffled about the present state of the world but for this; this is the whole key to it.

Let me put it like this: People hold God responsible and blame Him for what is happening in the world today and for what happened during the twentieth century—the two world wars, concentration camps (Belsen and Buchenwald and all the rest of them). But the answer to that accusation is this: all that is merely God allowing people to have their own way. Normally God does not allow that; He sets limits. There is a kind of decency that He produces even in the unregenerate, and by means of laws and a general moral teaching He restrains evil. But when men and women have displayed this unusual, exceptional arrogance and vileness, God takes away the restraints and just allows them to do anything they like.

And that is what is happening in this modern world of ours at the present time. Men and women have turned their backs upon God. They have said, "We don't need you. You are unnecessary. We can do it all."

"Very well," God is saying, "get on with it! Let us see what you make of it; let us see what you produce."

God does this quite deliberately. As people deliberately turn from God, God deliberately turns from them. And now we are seeing the world as it is without the restraints of God. God is no longer keeping evil in check; He is allowing it to have its fling and its full course. "He gave them up." "God gave them over to a reprobate mind" and all that follows from it. That is the second principle.

The third is this: "And I will carry you away beyond Babylon." That means that in addition to turning His face from them and not smiling upon them, in addition to withdrawing His restraints and His controls, God actively punishes. This is part of the biblical teaching. God sent the Jews to Babylon. In other words, He allowed their enemies to conquer and control them. If you read the story of the children of Israel, this is what you will always find: when they were obedient to God, they could conquer any enemy that came along. It did not matter who it was—they were always victorious. But when they turned their backs upon God and trusted in their generals, in their own powers, or in their own armaments or skill, they were invariably defeated. God just left them to themselves. And He did so when the Chaldeans raised a great army against them. God allowed the Israelites to suffer defeat. He withdrew all His power and all His help, and they were carried into captivity by Babylon. This was deliberate punishment given by God.

What happened to the children of Israel in the matter of going to

Babylon is just a picture of what happens to the whole human race: God punishes sin. Try to defy that if you like. Perhaps you laugh at that; you may scorn God's laws; maybe you say, "I don't care. I don't believe that sort of rot. I'm going to do this and that." Very well, do it. But I will tell you what will happen to you—you will suffer. "There is no peace, saith my God, to the wicked" (Isa. 57:21). And you know that is true, do you not? You have been wicked. You do not believe in God. You say you are going to live your own life. Have you found peace? Of course not. You will not be allowed to have peace. God makes it impossible. That is a part of your punishment.

Of course, you would not think that from today's novels and films, would you? But follow the end of the story in real life. The sinner is always found out. "Be sure your sin will find you out" (Num. 32:23). "The way of transgressors is hard" (Prov. 13:15). You will get misery, you will get unhappiness, you will get agony, and you will get remorse. If you sin against God, you will be made to pay for it. I am simply giving you hard facts; this is history. God does this deliberately. He said He would, and because He has warned us we have no excuse.

And according to Stephen's exposition, this is how God dealt with the children of Israel when they were recalcitrant and refused Moses and refused God's law. Stephen says in essence, "You members of the Sanhedrin, you are refusing God's Son—not His servant but His Son. So this is what will happen to you. Listen!"

The last principle is this: Why do you think God behaves in this manner? God turned away from the children of Israel. He delivered them up; He gave them up. God punished them by sending them into the captivity of Babylon. Why did God do this? Can I justify God's ways? Of course I can; there is no difficulty. The whole of the Bible gives us the justification. Here is the answer: God does this in order to reveal to men and women their true state and condition. For a hundred years people have been ridiculing belief in God. It is said: God is unnecessary—man is perfect. Man is wonderful, and he can make a wonderful world. The people who do not believe in God generally tell you themselves that what they believe in is "the dignity of man and the capability of man." If you reject God, that is all they have to offer you. But what is that? You can read a description of man in the first chapter of Paul's Epistle to the Romans.

> *Wherefore God also gave them up to uncleanness through the lusts of their own hearts, to dishonour their own bodies between themselves [so much for the dignity of man or the capability of man!]: who*

> *changed the truth of God into a lie, and worshipped and served the creature more than the Creator, who is blessed for ever. Amen. For this cause God gave them up unto vile affections: for even their women did change the natural use into that which is against nature.*
> —*Rom. 1:24-26*

That is the dignity of man! This is how capable men and women are of controlling themselves and life and the whole world! The dignity and the capability of man—what is it? It is the modern world, sexual perversions, drugs, drink, pilfering, dishonesty, the vileness of life.

In our cleverness we have rejected belief in God. Of course, we know far too much, we are scientific, we cannot possibly believe in God! Very well, then, that means that we are capable of running the universe. Of course it does! We are quite capable of doing so. So what is happening in the modern world? Do you see what God is doing? He is showing us what man makes of himself and of the world when he is given free play. We are seeing today what life is when God withdraws His restraints and His controls. "God gave them up." "God gave them over." He abandoned them. He said in effect, "All right, I will leave you alone. You have told Me to leave you alone; you say you do not believe in Me; you say you can stand on your own. Very well, I will act as if I were not there. Carry on!"

See what we are doing. Civilization is but a veneer, and men and women are seeing what their supposed dignity and capability are producing. Are we proud of it? That is what God is doing. He wants us to see the vileness, the rottenness of human nature. What produces Buchenwald? Human nature! What produces infidelity and divorce and rape! Human nature in sin and degradation rebelling against God. This is the supposed dignity of man. There it is revealed to us today. The world that rejects God proves God to be right—that human nature is rotten, it is vile, it is putrid, just as our papers are proclaiming to us day by day. God deliberately turns away and abandons us, gives us up, in order that we may learn the truth about ourselves.

Second, God does this to show His own holiness and His hatred of sin. He does it to justify His own punishment of sin. He wants us to see why He has ever given us the Ten Commandments and the moral law and the Sermon on the Mount. He wants us to see why He tells us that we must obey Him. It is because if we do not, that is the result. He is proclaiming His holiness and His hatred, His abomination of sin.

What else is He doing? He is teaching by all this, is He not, that He normally controls the world because it is His world. By abandoning it occasionally He is asserting his control. He gives us up, He gives us over for a period in order to bring us to our senses, in order to convince us, in order to make us see that we are completely helpless and hopeless and vile and utterly impotent and can do nothing; and in the meantime He is asserting His holiness. He says, "You would not come My way; so see where you are going. I am a holy God. 'Be ye holy; for I am holy'" (1 Pet. 1:16).

What else? He does this in order to warn us of an ultimate and final judgment. The particular judgments of God in history are but prophecies of a final judgment. God brings down particular judgments upon men and women. As a result, they see the folly of their ways and turn to Him. There is a good period, but then they go back again. Then there is another judgment. These judgments come one after another: the Flood, the tower of Babel, captivity in Egypt, captivity in Babylon, the destruction of Jerusalem in A.D. 70. God warned the Jews that if they did not obey Him, He would drive them out of their land, and their city would be sacked. It was all prophesied centuries before it happened. And then it happened, a punishment of sin.

But all this is nothing compared with what will happen in the final judgment. Our blessed Lord Himself, in prophesying the destruction of Jerusalem in A.D. 70, was clearly prophesying the final judgment, when He will come back to judge the world in righteousness. A day is coming when the end will arrive, and the Son of God will come back to judge the whole universe. Then God will finally turn His back upon those who have continued in rebellion against Him, and they will be cast into the sea of destruction. He will never look at them again; He will never smile upon them. They will never receive mercy, and they will go on living in a real hell forever. They will have the world they say they want, and they will never be able to get out of it. That is hell!

So God "gives [us] over" in order to warn us of the coming of that great and terrible day of judgment. How near it may be, I do not know, but I know it is coming, and I know that Buchenwald and all these other horrors, life as it is being lived today, the poor drug addicts and the victims of other ills and diseases and all the unhappiness and the misery—I know that this is going to be multiplied a thousandfold, a *millionfold*, and it will go on forever. God will have abandoned men and women in sin forever, and there will be no hope for them.

That is why God gives people over. But can you not see that the object of it all is love? God wants people to see what He is doing. God is trying to awaken the human race. People will not listen to the Gospel; they laugh at it and ridicule it. They make fun of Jesus Christ and blaspheme His holy blood shed on the cross on Calvary's hill. But "God so loved the world" that He is trying to open their eyes to the inferno they are creating. This is God's way of calling men and women to repentance. As Paul puts it in Romans 2:4: "The goodness of God leadeth thee to repentance."

Or as Peter says in the third chapter of his second epistle, "There shall come in the last days scoffers, walking after their own lusts, and saying, Where is the promise of his coming? for since the fathers fell asleep, all things continue as they were from the beginning of the creation" (vv. 3-4). And Peter has his answer. Why does God tolerate the world as it is? Why has He not blasted it to destruction long since? Here is the answer: "The Lord is not slack concerning his promise, as some men count slackness; but is long-suffering to us-ward, not willing that any should perish, but that all should come to repentance" (v. 9). Can you not see that God, by allowing men and women to reap the consequences of their own folly, is just trying to awaken us, to make us see our wretchedness, our rottenness, our vileness, our hopelessness, our utter helplessness? He is awakening us, calling us to repentance before it is too late. It is God's love that allows this. We will not listen to His appeals, so he tries another method, but it is all in love.

But let me put this to you in its final and most glorious form. Why is God permitting these things to happen? Why is God giving humanity up to its own way of living and its own devices and the reaping of the consequences? It is not only to call us to repentance—it is also to proclaim His wonderful offer of salvation in Jesus Christ, His Son. What do the bread and wine in the Communion service remind us of? They remind us of a cross on Calvary's hill and the death of the Son of God. What was happening? Was that just human activity? Of course, that is what men say, is it not? They explain the death of the Son of God in terms of the activity of man. They regard Jesus Christ as a pacifist, a good man who was not understood—good men never are—so men killed Him. It was a great tragedy, they say, a great pity.

What utter nonsense! Do you know what was happening on the cross on Calvary's hill? It was not man acting—it was God! This is how Peter put it in his sermon on the Day of Pentecost: "Him, being delivered"—handed over, given up—"*by the determinate counsel and foreknowledge of God . . .*" (Acts 2:23). God had planned His Son's death on the cross before the foundation of the world. It was the holy God acting on the cross. Look at this blessed person, Jesus Christ, Son of God. Look at Him; see His agony. What was the matter? God had turned away from Him, the very thing that Stephen tells us He did with the children of Israel, as we have seen. What was happening there on the cross was that God was averting His face. God was turning away from His own Son! Why? Because the Son had made Himself responsible for sinners and for the sin of humanity.

Not only that, God delivered Him up. These are the steps. God turned away. "God gave them up"; "God gave them over to a reprobate mind" (Rom. 1:24, 26, 28). And here is the astounding thing—that is just what I read in Romans 8:32: "He . . . spared not his own Son, but delivered him up for us all." It is exactly the same word that we have in our text in Acts 7. God gave up His only begotten, dearly beloved Son. He abandoned Him. What for? So that the full wrath of God against sin might fall upon Him. He spared Him nothing. "He that spared not his own Son, but delivered him up for us all, how shall he not with him also freely give us all things?"

Can you not see, then, what God is saying? He is turning away at this present time. He is "giving [us] over to a reprobate mind." He is punishing us actively in our modern Babylon, and He is doing it in order that He may call us to look at and to consider and to think of what happened to His own dearly beloved Son. He made Him to be sin for us, and then He could not look at Him; He turned away from Him. He "gave him up"; He did not spare Him anything. He left Him to Himself! And so the Son cried out in His agony, "My God, my God, why hast thou forsaken me?" (Matt. 27:46). "Why do You give Me up? Why have You turned away? I cannot find You."

God punished Him for our sins. He did to Him there on the cross the three things that He always does to sin. He did it once and forever in order that He might turn to you and say, "If you realize that you have rebelled against Me and that I am going to turn My face against you through eternity and abandon you and give you up and leave you to yourself and to your hell and to the punishment you so richly deserve, if you realize that and turn to Me and acknowledge and confess your sin and repent of it, I will tell you something: I have already done all that in My only begotten, dearly loved Son for you. He has suffered it all to the last dregs in order that you might never experience it. Come unto Me! Look unto Me! I am turning toward you. Turn to Me. 'Look unto me, and be ye saved, all the ends of the earth'" (Isa. 45:22).

There, it seems to me, is the philosophy of history as taught by the martyr Stephen to the members of the learned Sanhedrin. They were blind to it, and they put him to death. Are we able to read the signs of the times? Are we seeing what God is doing in the modern world? Can we hear him speaking to us through wars and alarms and terrors? He is calling us to repentance before it is too late. It is not too late yet. The door of grace is still open; the day of grace is still here. Why should you perish? Repent. Believe the word of God concerning Jesus Christ, the Savior of the world.

16

Religion

Then God turned, and gave them up to worship the host of heaven; as it is written in the book of the prophets, O ye house of Israel, have ye offered to me slain beasts and sacrifices by the space of forty years in the wilderness? Yea, ye took up the tabernacle of Moloch, and the star of your god Remphan, figures which ye made to worship them: and I will carry you away beyond Babylon. Our fathers had the tabernacle of witness in the wilderness, as he had appointed, speaking unto Moses, that he should make it according to the fashion that he had seen. Which also our fathers that came after brought in with Jesus [Joshua] into the possession of the Gentiles, whom God drave out before the face of our fathers, unto the days of David; who found favour before God, and desired to find a tabernacle for the God of Jacob. But Solomon built him an house. Howbeit the most High dwelleth not in temples made with hands; as saith the prophet, Heaven is my throne, and earth is my footstool: what house will ye build me? saith the Lord: or what is the place of my rest? Hath not my hand made all these things?

—Acts 7:42-50

In these verses Stephen came to what is in many ways the climax of the case that he had been building up against the members of the Sanhedrin. He had been reminding them of their history, and here we reach the point at which he was now applying it to them. He applied the lessons of their history along three lines—Moses, the law, and the temple—and we are now dealing particularly with the whole question of the temple. Again, to anyone who wonders what all this has to do with us, I would say that if there is anything really relevant to what is happening in the world today, it is this. I will go further: you cannot understand history apart from the message of the Gospel. You cannot understand past history, you cannot understand what is happening now, you cannot understand the future without it. The understanding we need is here in this analysis, this teaching of Stephen, which is representative of the teaching of the whole of the New Testament in particular and also of the whole Bible. It is only as we grasp the principles given here that we shall begin to understand the situation in which we find ourselves.

Now this applies not only to the world situation—though it is illuminating on that in a most amazing manner—but still more to our own situations. It is the only thing that will ever give us any light on our own personal problems. What happens on the world's scale is no different from what happens in the case of the individual. We are so foolish. We do not see that there is no difference in principle between two nations fighting and two men or two women fighting.

That is what children do, is it not? "I'm not giving in—you must give in. I'm not going to make a move—you must make a move." Each person is a sort of microcosm; what the individual does is true of the whole world. So the Gospel covers the world and the individual, and that is why we must start with the individual. It is no use talking about what nations are going to do. Nations consist of individuals: nations are governed by majorities, and statesmen are only interested in numbers. They will not listen to the Christian until Christians are in a position to make them listen. So we start with the individual, and here in Acts we are given an insight into our own personal positions and the only way whereby we can ever find liberty and release and healing.

We have already seen that man is a fool and that he is ignorant and blind. But his ultimate trouble is that his whole idea of worship and of God is so completely wrong. And this is the most important factor of all because man is seen at his highest in worship. Religion should be the highest expression of himself that man can ever achieve. So if he goes wrong at this point, it is the greatest tragedy of all. But that was the very tragedy of the Sanhedrin.

Here, therefore, is a teaching that receives great attention in the New Testament writings. I want to show you the essential trouble with the Pharisees, because the leaders on this council were, after all, Pharisees and Sadducees. As we read the four Gospels, we notice that much of our Lord's time and attention was taken up in argument and disputation with the

Pharisees and the scribes and the Sadducees. He had great trouble with them, and thus much of the Gospels had to be devoted to them. Here were men who believed they were serving God and were proud of it, and yet they rejected their own Messiah.

The Jews, let us never forget, were the greatest nation in the ancient world because they, and they alone, had the knowledge of the one and only true and living God. Whatever you may say about Greek philosophy and about Roman law and culture, the Romans and Greeks were polytheists; they had not arrived at the knowledge of the one and only God. That is what makes the nation of the Jews unique and so remarkable, but that also constitutes their greatest tragedy—the greatest tragedy of all history—because it was this people, of all people, who rejected God's greatest act. The very guardians and custodians of the faith, as it were, were the ones who rejected their own Messiah.

And that is what Stephen dealt with here. Our Lord Himself dealt with it, and the apostle Paul, as a Jew and a Pharisee, dealt with it also, in his own expert way. But Stephen here gives us all the essential principles, and you and I must examine them because there is nothing so fatal to true Christianity as a false religion. The greatest enemy of the Christian faith has generally been the Christian church when she has misunderstood and perverted her own message and has behaved as the members of the Sanhedrin were behaving on this particular occasion. Now this is tragic, and yet we must say it. I do not preach Christendom. I do not preach the church or religion. I preach salvation in and through the Son of God, the Savior, the Lord Jesus Christ.

So let us follow Stephen's argument—he puts it perfectly. He first of all shows us the characteristics of false religion. What are they? Oh, may God give us grace to examine ourselves! Do we think you are Christians? If so, are we enjoying life in Christ? Are we happy in it? Are we rejoicing in it? Are we like the New Testament Christians? Is this a power in our life? If not, I wonder whether we have the true thing or whether we merely have religion. The greatest enemy of the Christian faith is religion. So let us look at its characteristics.

The first characteristic noted by Stephen is *hypocrisy*. He puts it like this: "Then God turned, and gave them up to worship the host of heaven; as it is written in the book of the prophets, O ye house of Israel, have ye offered"—notice this—"*to me* slain beasts and sacrifices by the space of forty years in the wilderness?" The children of Israel did offer "slain beasts and sacrifices in the wilderness," but God asks them, "Were you really doing that for *Me*?" They had done it; He does not dispute that. The hypocrite does do what he says. If he did not, there would be nothing to be said against him. So we must not dispute the facts. People often do this when they consider the Pharisees. Consider the Pharisee who said, "I fast twice in the week, I give tithes of all that I possess" (Luke 18:12). People think he was a liar, but he was not. He was speaking the literal truth. But God asks, "Did you do it for *Me*?"

This is a very searching question; this is the whole point that each of us must face. Did those people really believe in God? What was the value of this action of theirs in offering slain beasts and sacrifices? The fact that people do these things does not prove that they are really worshiping God. It can all be a substitute for the worship of God, and that is the truth that Stephen brings out here. You find this repeatedly in the Old Testament. We read in the second book of Kings, "So these nations feared the LORD, and served their graven images." Ah, yes, they feared the Lord—they had good reason for doing so; He had just been dealing with them, and they had been defeated. "These nations feared the LORD, and served their graven images, both their children, and their children's children: as did their fathers, so do they unto this day" (17:41).

The children of Israel too kept up the appearance of worship, but their real worship was not given to God—it was given to their own gods. And that is what Stephen was saying here to the members of the Sanhedrin. He said in effect, "You are a religious people, and you say that you alone are religious, and you regard what I am standing for as blasphemy. You say you are the worshipers of God, but are you really worshiping Him?" You and I, too, must answer his searching question.

So one of the characteristics of this false, hypocritical religion is that we pretend to be something that we are really not, that we are only concerned about appearances, that we are fundamentally dishonest, that we are really doing something that we do not actually believe in our hearts and are guilty of this kind of double action—fearing God and serving something else. Or to put it more simply, the trouble is that we always think we can balance the wrong and the evil in our lives by the good that we do. We know about that, do we not? We have all done it. We think that if we do a bit of good, it somehow balances the other. We are experts at accountancy; we all keep our balance sheets. Ah, there is a lot against us on this side—very well, let us do a bit of good here and give a donation there and show a bit of kindness. This is the essence of false religion—it is sheer hypocrisy.

But it is even worse than that, and this is where men and women show their unutterable folly. Why did the children of Israel offer these slain beasts and sacrifices for forty years in the wilderness? Why did they go on doing it? It was because they thought that God could be bought; they thought that He could be deceived, that He could be fooled. They said, "As long as we take the burnt offerings and sacrifices, God will be placated. We can put Him at rest and peace; we can settle our accounts with Him." And they persuaded themselves that this was clever and was succeeding. So God put his question to them: "Did you offer those sacrifices to *Me*? Were you really concerned about making your offerings to *Me*?"

In other words, the trouble with men and women who have a false notion of religion is that they have never understood the truth either about God or about themselves. It is to such people that God says, in the words of the psalmist, "Thou thoughtest that I was altogether such an one as thyself" (Ps. 50:21). That is what we do, is it not? We cover things over, we balance, we fool one another and ourselves, and we think that God is like us. We really think we are clever, that we can placate God with our cleverness. We think we can treat God in the same way we treat other people. And that only means one thing: we know nothing about God. It is ignorance of God that ultimately accounts for all our troubles and all our tragedies.

It is no use being governed by fear and self-interest. What matters is this: is there a genuine desire on our part to know God and to honor Him, to obey Him and serve Him? Half-and-half does not work with God; He demands total allegiance. "Thou shalt love the Lord thy God with all thy heart, and with all thy soul, and with all thy mind, and with all thy strength" (Mark 12:30). He wants it all. Our Lord Himself has said the final word about this: "This people honoureth me with their lips, but their heart is far from me" (Mark 7:6). To imagine that your lip service is enough with God is tragic; it means you do not know Him.

Or take what is written in Matthew 23. There our Lord finally exposed the hypocrisy of the Pharisees: "Ye make clean the outside of the cup and of the platter, but within they are full of extortion and excess" (v. 25)—or "ravening and wickedness," as it is sometimes translated. How typical that is of men and women and of their worship. They put on a good appearance, clean the outside of the cup and the platter, but inside there is filth and rottenness. That is the essence of hypocrisy. You put up a good appearance to the world, modify yourself in certain respects, but what about your inside, what about your heart? What is the condition of the vitals of your being?

Or, again, our Lord puts it like this, and what a perfect exposure this is: "Ye pay tithe of mint and anise and cumin"—these trivialities, these little minutiae and details of the law; oh, the Pharisees were punctilious about these things—"and have omitted the weightier matters of the law, judgment, mercy, and faith: these ought ye to have done, and not to leave the other undone" (Matt. 23:23). But that is what we all tend to do instinctively. We begin to become concerned about these things, and we say, "Well, yes, I've been wrong. I've not done this and that. I'll put this right, and I'll put that right. I'll drop this and take up that." And we think we are pleasing God. But that is "mint and anise and cumin"! We have not faced the ultimate questions of God and ourselves and His knowledge of our hearts and our relationship to Him.

So, then, we can sum it all up like this: The characteristic of this hypocritical religion is that it is always an external religion, something that people put on as if they were putting on a coat or a garment. It is outside, it is appearance—the outside of the cup and the platter, not the inside. That is the first point.

The second characteristic of false religion is that it is always very keen on what we must call *institutionalism*. I mean something like this: these people in the Sanhedrin actually worshiped the temple—and here Stephen really came to the point. They were putting up temple worship against Christianity. Stephen said in effect, "You accuse me of saying that the temple is no longer necessary, that Jesus has done away with it, that He has finished with all the sacrifices and the burnt offerings, and that now it is all in Him." To these leaders the temple was everything; that was their whole trouble. The temple had become an idol. And that is always a characteristic of false religion.

God had allowed the people to build the temple; but, as the record tells us here, He had never asked them to do so. David had conceived the idea, and Solomon had put it into practice. God was not very pleased with all that. That way of worshiping Him was not the way He chose; it was man's suggestion. Men and women always want to institutionalize everything; they are never happier than when they are organizing, and they do so supremely in the church by making it an institution. They harden, they petrify, everything; they turn the spirit into stone and into buildings. They think this is marvelous, and they tend to worship what they have made.

This is the tendency, and these Jewish leaders were saying that people could only worship in Jerusalem and that they could not worship apart from the temple. This was always the attitude of the Jews, but this has continued to be true throughout the centuries. This is one of the great lessons of history. This attitude puts form in the place of substance. It pays attention to the letter, not to the spirit. It begins to think in terms of "holy places," consecrated places; it believes that God is confined to buildings and that you can really only worship Him in those certain buildings.

There is a wonderful illustration of this in John 4, where we have an account of our Lord's meeting and discussion with a woman of Samaria. Her words were typical of this view of worship. Here was a woman living in terrible sin, but she was a religious woman. She was doing this balancing act; she was expert at using religion to balance out her adultery. This is the sort of thing she said: "Sir, I perceive that thou art a prophet. Our fathers worshipped in this mountain; and ye say, that in Jerusalem is the place where men ought to worship" (vv. 19-20).

You see the argument: she, as a Samaritan, said, "It is on this mountain that God is to be worshiped. You will only find Him here."

"No, no," said the Jews, "you do not find Him there. You find Him in the temple in Jerusalem."

God is confined to places, we think, and each one argues for his particular place—Mecca, Rome, Canterbury, wherever it may happen to be. This is hardening, institutionalizing. So if you destroy the temple, it is the end of worship.

This attitude always manifests itself, and it is something on which we can test ourselves. The characteristic, I repeat, of false religion is always that its worship is controlled by buildings. If you walk into a cathedral, you walk quietly and speak softly. Why? That shows reverence for God! But does it? Why do you not revere God anywhere else? You see how ridiculous this is! The same people who are so concerned about decorum and order and dignity and worship when they are in cathedrals behave very differently when you put them in a public hall. They claim to be worshiping the same God on the two occasions, so why do they behave differently? It is because their worship is governed by buildings, not by the Spirit. This is institutionalism; this is temple worship; this is feeling that God is confined to temples. And, of course, with that you get all the notions of men and of hierarchies, high priests, priests, underlings, assistants—all these great offices; that is the church, and that is worship, and you really cannot worship apart from this, it is said.

Now this year is the 450th anniversary[4] of that great day when Martin Luther nailed his Ninety-five Theses to the door of the church at Wittenberg. This was the beginning of the Protestant Reformation, and it was a part of the battle that he had to fight. Roman Catholicism has confined worship not only to certain buildings but to certain people. You cannot worship without the priests—they are absolutely essential; you cannot find God without them. And you must have the sacraments and the Virgin Mary and the saints, these intermediaries. The church building and all its organization are essential. That is the very charge that Stephen was bringing against the members of the Sanhedrin. He said, "You are worshiping the temple; you are regarding it as absolutely essential, and thereby you are going against what God Himself has revealed concerning these matters."

And then, of course, you add to that *tradition*, the tradition of men. "You," said our Lord in effect to the Pharisees, "are setting aside the law and the teaching of God, the commandments of God, for the traditions of men" (see Matt. 15:3-6). The Pharisees always asked, "What have the great authorities said?" They would quote the authorities, bringing out their books—"So-and-so said this"—the traditions of men. And the church has continued doing that, quoting men and church tradition, making these their authorities. Where have many of these beliefs come from? They have been invented by men; yet they are held as stumbling-blocks, and people cannot go to God without them. This is the way that throughout the centuries men and women have been denying God and His law while believing that they are serving Him.

The final characteristic of this false religion, always, is *self-righteousness*. We read concerning the Pharisees, "which trusted in themselves that they were righteous" (Luke 18:9). You find it all in the statement made out of a broken heart by the apostle Paul (Rom. 9:2-4; 11:1) and in his letter to the Philippians where he describes what he was like as a Pharisee, proud of the fact that he was a Jew: "Circumcised the eighth day, of the stock of Israel, of the tribe of Benjamin, an Hebrew of the Hebrews; as touching the law, a Pharisee . . ." (3:5). He was living on that, relying on it. What makes a man a Christian? False religion says it is his good deeds, his good works, his acts of kindness, the fact that he does not do this or that and that he does do other things. This is a tragedy. That was the trouble with these Jews.

Our Lord, again, dealt with this finally and exhaustively in his parable about the publican and the Pharisee who both went up to the temple to pray. This is his picture:

> *Two men went up into the temple to pray; the one a Pharisee, and the other a publican. The Pharisee stood and prayed thus with himself, God, I thank thee, that I am not as other men are, extortioners, unjust, adulterers, or even as this publican. I fast twice in the week, I give tithes of all that I possess.*
>
> —*Luke 18:10-12*

That is pharisaism. You are relying on your good life, your good works, your good actions, your prayers, your fasting, and all the good you are doing. It is false religion.

What is true religion? It is the exact opposite of all this. Our Lord was put to death because He exposed that kind of belief, and here Stephen was on trial for his life because he was exposing it also in his own way. What are the characteristics of true religion?

First, true religion is based entirely and exclusively on *God's revelation and teaching*. The forty-fourth verse is so vital here: "Our fathers had the tabernacle of witness in the wilderness, as he [God] had appointed, speaking unto Moses, that he should make it according to the fashion that he had seen." God called Moses up onto the mount and gave him the exact details, specifications, and plans concerning this tabernacle of witness. And then he said to him at the end, "And look that thou make them after their pattern, which was shewed thee in the mount" (Exod. 25:40). Stephen was just repeating that command.

This is the very beginning of Christianity. What does it mean to be a Christian? How do we find God? How do we know our sins are forgiven? What is true worship? How do we find out? Here is the first and the basic principle: we must submit utterly and completely and absolutely to the revelation that we have in the Bible; if we do not, we will be wrong. We must start with this—that all our ideas about worship are entirely wrong.

The children of Israel were constantly going astray at this very point. On one occasion there was a rebellion, called the rebellion of Korah. Korah, Dathan, and Abiram were three of the princes of Israel, and they were able and outstanding men. They met together one afternoon and began to talk, and they said, "Why should we submit to the leadership of this man Moses and his brother Aaron? Who are they to be authorities?"

These three men had forgotten the fact that God had chosen Moses and Aaron and had given Moses the revelation. "We are as good as they are," they said in effect, "and that's not our idea as to how these things should be done. We don't think this is necessary." So they held a public meeting, and of course it was very popular, as most public meetings are, and it was carried with acclamation that Moses and Aaron should be put to one side and that the new method of Korah, Dathan, and Abiram should be put into practice (Num. 16).

If you read the story, you will find out how God dealt with that rebellion in a most terrifying manner and finally gave a memorial of the event to the children of Israel through Aaron's rod that budded. But this is the principle: it is God who determines how He is to be worshiped. If you tell me that you are going to be taught about this by the modern philosophers or by the modern religious leaders or by the modern scientists, I will tell you, in the name of God, that you are wrong, that you are in the position of the Sanhedrin and will receive the punishment that you deserve. It is all of God—"their pattern which was shewed thee in the mount" (Exod. 25:40).

This is the very point that our Lord made to Nicodemus on the famous occasion when Nicodemus went to see him at night. "Rabbi [Master]," Nicodemus said, "we know that thou art a teacher come from God: for no man can do these miracles that thou doest, except God be with him" (John 3:2). "I have been listening; I have been intrigued; I have been most interested. I am a teacher myself, but you have something extra. Tell me, what is it?"

Our Lord looked at him, interrupted him, and said to him, "Verily, verily, I say unto thee, Except a man be born again, he cannot see the kingdom of God" (v. 3). It does not matter that you are a teacher; it does not matter that you are a religious man; it does not matter that you are a great man. All that is of no value to you: "Ye must be born again" (v. 7).

Our Lord said the same thing to the woman of Samaria. "Ye worship ye know not what: we know what we worship: for salvation is of the Jews" (John 4:22). And, again, as he put it to Nicodemus, "No man hath ascended up to heaven, but he that came down from heaven, even the Son of man which is in heaven" (John 3:13); and, "Verily, verily, I say unto thee, We speak that we do know, and testify that we have seen" (v. 11). It is through Christ and in Him alone that we worship God; we must listen to Him. True worship must be Christ's way; it is the only way. He says, "All that ever came before me are thieves and robbers" (John 10:8). And above all He said, "I am the way, the truth, and the life: no man cometh unto the Father, but by me" (John 14:6).

"Look that thou make them after their pattern, which was shewed thee in the mount" (Exod. 25:40). We do not decide how God is to be worshiped. People have their modern ideas: "Sit in a comfortable chair and relax," says one, "and you will be talking to God and listening to God." No; that is not true. And the other world religions say this and that. They are lies; they are not true. There is only one way. You must receive it from God. You do not follow your own ideas; you do not vary the specification; every detail must be exact. That is why we are given all the details in the books of the Old Testament.

The second element is *honesty and sincerity*. David found this out. David is so like us, a religious man; yet lust and passion came in. Then he committed adultery and murder. He was quite happy; he had done very well afterward. He went on worshiping God. We do not stop worshiping God when we do what we want to do. This is a balancing act. We go on paying our respects to God; we still attend a place of worship; we do what we want to do and think all is well. Oh, but God is displeased, and David cried out in his agony, "Thou desirest truth in the inward parts" (Ps. 51:6). And in another psalm he said, "If I regard iniquity in my heart, the Lord will not hear me" (66:18). He means that if we are shielding some favorite sin, if we are saying, "Yes, I will do everything He wants, but I'm holding on to this," then we are regarding iniquity in our heart; we are shielding it.

God will not tolerate that; He will not hear us. We do not decide, God decides, and He demands absolute honesty. Listen to our Lord putting it to the Pharisees in devastating words: "Ye are they which justify yourselves before men; but God knoweth your hearts: for that which is highly esteemed among men is abomination in the sight of God" (Luke 16:15). God sees the heart, and He demands inwardness, honesty, sincerity, wholeheartedness. "Unite my heart to fear thy name," cried the psalmist (Ps. 86:11).

And then next, of course, worship must be "not of the letter, but of the spirit" (2 Cor. 3:6). Our Lord put it in this way to the woman of Samaria: "You are talking about worshiping in this mountain or in Jerusalem. You are wrong. 'God is a Spirit: and they that worship him must worship him in spirit and in truth'" (John 4:24).

Stephen brought this out, it seems to me, in a most marvelous manner in addressing the members of the Sanhedrin: "Our fathers had the tabernacle of witness." The right translation there is, "the tent of witness." God never wanted the temple; what God ordained was a tent, just a movable tent. But man says, "Oh, no, a tent is not good enough for God—we must have a great temple. It must be ornate, there must be gold and silver, precious metals, and it must have a certain height." But God says, "No! I ordered a tent."

Thank God, He did. What you put against institutionalism is the freedom of the Spirit, a movable tent. God is not to be worshiped only on a certain mountain or only in the temple in Jerusalem. There is nothing more wonderful than this in the universe—God can be worshiped anywhere, wherever you seek Him truly. It does not matter where you are. You need not go to St. Peter's in Rome; you need not go to St Paul's Cathedral in London. Wherever you are, wherever your heart is longing and yearning for God and you have cried out to Him, He is there, and He will meet with you. He lives in a tent! He is not institutionalized. It is freedom that matters here, not forms. The apostle Paul had to say this same thing to the learned philosophers, the Stoics and Epicureans, in Athens, and this is the message that is needed and has been needed throughout the centuries: God is to be worshiped not in the letter but in the spirit; he wants the heart and its freedom. Tent, not temple! The freedom of the Spirit, not institutionalism.

And that brings me to the last and most vital characteristic of true religion, which is *truth* itself. God, I say, must be worshiped in His way, and He can only be worshiped in His way. What is it? Well, God's way is quite clear in the New Testament. Peter had already said it: "Neither is there salvation in any other: for there is none other name under heaven given among men, whereby we must be saved" (Acts 4:12). "God was in Christ, reconciling the world unto himself" (2 Cor. 5:19). This is God's way.

"But," you say, "I can get to God without that. I don't believe in that teaching about shed blood and the atonement. I'm not interested in doctrine and dogma. I just want to meet Jesus Christ and all will be well."

No; that is *your* way, not God's way. God says that you must go via the cross, and there is no other way, and we must not substitute our ways for God's ways: "whom God hath set forth to be a propitiation through faith in his blood" (Rom. 3:25). The Gospel is God's way of salvation, and it is the only way.

> *God, who at sundry times and in divers manners spake in time past unto the fathers by the prophets, hath in these last days spoken unto us by his Son, whom he hath appointed heir of all things, by whom also he made the worlds; who being the brightness of his glory, and the express image of his person, and upholding all things by the word of his power, when he had by himself purged our sins, sat down on the right hand of the Majesty on high.*
>
> —*Heb. 1:1-3*

That is the Gospel. There is no other. "Having therefore, brethren, boldness to enter into the holiest"—how?—"by the blood of Jesus . . ." (Heb. 10:19).

We may say that modern people are not going to be interested in the blood of Jesus, that they regard it as immoral and cannot accept this substitutionary atonement, but neither could the members of the Sanhedrin. We must not forget that! If we reject the Gospel, it is not because we are modern—it is because we are like them. This is what they objected to; this is what the world has always objected to. It has nothing to do with our learning, as I have already proved to you. It is because of our blindness, our hardness of heart; it is because we do not realize the holiness of God and our own vileness and lost condition.

There is only one way whereby anyone can ever find God, and that is through "Jesus Christ, and him crucified" (1 Cor. 2:2). It is "by the blood of

Jesus" and by that alone that anyone can ever enter into the presence of God. This is God's way, and you and I must accept it. "And look that thou make them after their pattern, which was shewed thee in the mount" (Exod. 25:40). We may object to this way; we may reject it. But I will tell you what will happen. We will continue in sin. We will continue to be the failures that we are. We will be afraid of life; we will be afraid of death; we will be afraid of war; we will be afraid of judgment. The cross is the only way; it is God's way.

The other principle that is emphasized here is that salvation is entirely the free gift of God. Listen to the way in which Stephen puts it: "Which also our fathers that came after brought in with Jesus [Joshua] into the possession of the Gentiles"—he is referring to their tent—"whom God drave out before the face of our fathers, unto the days of David." This is the picture. How did the children of Israel ever possess the land of Palestine, the land of Canaan? Did they win it by their own prowess, by their own ability or military superiority? Not at all. There was the land, "a land flowing with milk and honey," but the Gentiles were there, giants, the Anakim. How did this little people ever possess the land? There is only one answer: God drove out the giants and gave them the land.

And that is the principle still. All our goodness and righteousness are of no value at all; they are filthy rags, dung and refuse and loss. "By grace are ye saved through faith; and that not of yourselves: it is the gift of God" (Eph. 2:8). God keeps the law for us in Christ Himself. He conquers the devil and all his powers. He drives out our enemies; he gives us the land. Salvation is the free gift of God's grace, and what He offers us now is forgiveness. Though we may have sinned our way to the very gate of hell, He will offer us free pardon and forgiveness at this moment without our doing a single thing, without our doing a single good deed. He will give us new life, new birth, a new beginning, a new nature, new everything. He will give us the Holy Spirit with power over all our enemies, and He will make us more than conqueror.

That is God's way. Not your morality and mine, not our intellectual understanding, not our superiority to every generation that has ever lived before us. No! It is altogether the free gift of God and is all in His dear Son, on whom He laid our iniquities and punished them in Him once and forever.

So what does the Gospel call us to do? Simply to repent, simply to think again, simply to realize the holiness of God and the vileness of our hearts, which is "full of ravening and wickedness." We must repent, confess our sin, realize we can do nothing about it, and become as "little children." "Verily I say unto you, Except ye be converted, and become as little children, ye shall not enter into the kingdom of heaven" (Matt. 18:3). If we think that because we are adults and have read philosophy or know something about science it is necessary for us to understand before we believe, then we will remain outside. We, like everybody else, must become as little children. We must repent and believe the Gospel! The temple will not save us; the hierarchy cannot save us; the law cannot save us. Nothing can except "the Lamb of God, which taketh away the sin of the world" (John 1:29).

Have you believed in Him? Or are you like the members of the Sanhedrin? God forbid that your religion should be the cause of your damnation.

17

MIND, WILL, AND HEART

Ye stiffnecked and uncircumcised in heart and ears, ye do always resist the Holy Ghost: as your fathers did, so do ye. Which of the prophets have not your fathers persecuted? and they have slain them which shewed before of the coming of the Just One; of whom ye have been now the betrayers and murderers: who have received the law by the disposition of angels, and have not kept it. When they heard these things, they were cut to the heart, and they gnashed on him with their teeth . . . they cried out with a loud voice, and stopped their ears, and ran upon him with one accord, and cast him out of the city, and stoned him: and the witnesses laid down their clothes at a young man's feet, whose name was Saul. And they stoned Stephen.

—Acts 7:51-54, 57-59

Stephen was a true Christian preacher. He had shown the members of the Sanhedrin that not only had they grievously misunderstood the law, the temple, and Moses himself, in all of which they took such great pride, but they had also completely misunderstood the great message of the Old Testament. Then, having dealt with these points one by one in the historical manner that is displayed in this chapter of Acts, having argued and presented facts, having reasoned and shown the Sanhedrin their position, Stephen had now come to the point of application—a sermon that does not apply the truth is of no value—and said, "Ye stiffnecked and uncircumcised in heart and ears, ye do always resist the Holy Ghost: as your fathers did, so do ye." Then we see the reaction of these leaders of the Jews, their violence, which eventually led them to stone him to death. So we are now looking at the conclusion of this famous scene in which Stephen, the first Christian martyr, addressed the Sanhedrin.

This is a remarkable picture with a very striking contrast. On the one hand, we see these members of the Sanhedrin, and there standing before them we see Stephen. This is a perfect and dramatic portrayal of the difference between unbelief and belief; it shows the essential contrast between the non-Christian and the Christian. Here were men who were aware of the same facts, and yet their attitudes toward them were diametrically opposite. To Stephen, these truths were the only things that mattered; to the Sanhedrin they were something that caused them to be filled with fury, so that they "gnashed their teeth" and "were cut to the heart."

Now we are, I say again, not concerned simply with this as ancient history, interesting though it is in and of itself, but we are interested in it because it is preaching to us. The world is still in the position it was in when these events happened, and there is great confusion at the present time as to what a Christian is. The passage we are now looking at is a wonderful portrayal of the essential nature of unbelief.

Here is the big question: Why did the members of the Sanhedrin reject Jesus of Nazareth? And this is still the great question and the great problem. With the world as it is, why do people go on rejecting this Savior and this Gospel? To me, as I have said so many times in working through this chapter, this is the greatest problem of all. If only the whole world lived according to this Gospel and the teaching of this book, you would not have your world problems or your private problems. But the world will not listen. It will pin its faith on almost anything else, but it rejects the Gospel with scorn.

And we are told here exactly why this is so. The analysis of the whole mentality of the members of the Sanhedrin, as given by Stephen, plus what they did, gives us a complete statement of the nature of unbelief. Someone may say, "Ah, yes, but the account of what happened to Stephen is a very extreme case. Are you going to say that this is true of every unbeliever?" My answer to that is quite simple. The members of the Sanhedrin were very learned men; they were great men; they were leaders of the nation. They were not ignoramuses. Many of them were trained in the law, others were trained as priests, and others were men in responsible positions. And yet they behaved like this! So though this is in many ways an extreme case, the principles that are taught here are of universal validity. These are always the characteristics of unbelief.

Of course, we are all different. Some men do things violently; others do them quietly. Indeed, what one often finds is that people who appear to be so quiet can become very violent and vicious where our Lord and the Gospel are concerned. What really matters, however, are the principles that are taught here, principles concerning the nature of unbelief. These are very important principles at a time like this when people have such strange ideas as to what it is to believe or not to believe the Gospel.

What is the difference between the Christian and the non-Christian? Some people think it is merely a matter of conduct. Well, it is a matter of conduct and behavior, but that, in many ways, is not the important aspect of the difference. Other people think that the unbeliever is merely someone who chooses not to believe, while the believer, on the other hand, chooses to believe. They think they can decide one way or the other, and there it is. But this is hopelessly inadequate as an understanding of belief and unbelief, and such superficiality with regard to these matters is the tragedy of the present time.

What, then, is the essential nature of unbelief? It is this. It involves not only what a person does—it involves, in a total manner, that person's entire relationship to God and to truth. There is no greater or more profound distinction than that between a Christian and a non-Christian. This is most important. The term used in the New Testament by our Lord Himself, and then by the apostles and others, is *new birth* or *regeneration*. To become a Christian means to become a new being. This is radical and very profound.

The biblical teaching is this: unbelief results from man's original rebellion against God. And in that rebellion man fell to the depths. The fall affected the whole of his being. There was a radical change. He became something that was quite different from what he had been. And I want to show you how what happened to man as the result of his original rebellion and fall is perfectly illustrated in the teaching given by Stephen and by the behavior of the members of the Sanhedrin. What can be more important than this? Do we realize the real problem of men and women in the world? Why do they not believe the Gospel? Why is this solution to the problem so constantly dismissed completely, as it was by the Sanhedrin? And the answer is that they have become sinners, and as sinners they are the slaves of the devil. They are in a condition of slavery, which affects the whole of their being. It affects the mind, the will, and the heart.

Listen to Stephen's exposition of this—let us start with the mind. He puts it like this: "Ye stiffnecked and uncircumcised in heart and ears, ye do always resist the Holy Ghost." He was addressing religious Jews, people who were interested in the temple, in Moses, in the law, and in the worship of God, and what he said of them is that they were "uncircumcised in heart and ears." Now that is an amazing thing to say. Stephen was really saying that though the Sanhedrin were Jews in name, they were actually heathen. The difference between the Jew and the Gentile was that the Jew was circumcised while the Gentile was not, and Stephen was saying in effect, "Though you are Jews, in your thinking you are uncircumcised. You are thinking like heathen; you are thinking and behaving like people who are unbelievers and not like the people of God. You are boasting that you are the people of God, but you are not."

In other words, Stephen was saying that before men and women can receive this truth, they must undergo a process that is represented by circumcision. The ears are to be circumcised, and the heart must be circumcised; a radical operation has to be performed upon them. The principle is that men and women by nature, as the result of the fall and of sin, are incapable of receiving the truth of God. Now this is a very profound matter. Why did these members of the Sanhedrin reject the Gospel of Christ? It was because as they were, they could not do anything else. They were incapable of believing it. They were uncircumcised in heart and in ears.

So what it comes to is that by nature men and women cannot even listen to the truth properly. They have no contact with truth. They are incapable of recognizing it. Now I am not the one saying this. Stephen said it here, and if you read 1 Corinthians 2 you will find that there the great apostle said it much more plainly and explicitly. Paul's central statement was this: "The natural man receiveth not the things of the Spirit of God"—why not?—"for they are foolishness unto him: neither can he know them"—and why does he not know them?—"because they are spiritually discerned" (1 Cor. 2:14). That is why, Paul says, "None of the princes of this world knew"—the Son of God had appeared before them, but they did not recognize Him—"for had they known it, they would not have crucified the Lord of glory" (1 Cor. 2:8). They were incapable of recognizing Him.

This is one of the most profound things we can ever grasp. Our Lord had said it all already: "Take heed therefore how ye hear" (Luke 8:18). There are people who "seeing see not; and hearing they hear not" (Matt. 13:13). In other words, people can be sitting and listening to truth even from the lips of the Son of God, and yet, though they hear the words, they do not perceive what He is saying. There were many people like that in Stephen's age and generation, and he was saying that was the trouble with the members of the Sanhedrin. Some people look at things, they really look at them, but they do not see them.

This is something that we must grasp as a principle. What Stephen was saying about the Sanhedrin, what Paul said about all natural men and women, is that they cannot, as they are, hear this message. Why? Because they are lacking in spiritual apprehension. This is how Paul puts it in 1 Corinthians 2:12-13:

> *Now we have received, not the spirit of the world, but the spirit which is of God; that we might know the things that are freely given to us of God. Which things also we speak, not in the words which man's wisdom teacheth, but which the Holy Ghost teacheth; comparing spiritual things with spiritual.*

Let me use an illustration that may explain what I mean. A man is reading poetry to an audience. Some of those listening find it the most thrilling thing they have ever heard in their lives; to others it is meaningless gibberish. That often happens, does it not? Or you can take people to see great paintings. Some rave over them; others see nothing at all in them. Or play some of the great musical masterpieces. Oh, the music delights the hearts of some people; to others it is just noise. And yet others regard mere noise as music! Or others may be great poets, but science is nonsense to them, and they cannot begin to follow it. So people are looking at or hearing the same things but responding differently. It all depends upon whether there is within them a faculty that corresponds to what they are hearing or seeing.

Both Stephen and Paul were saying that we need a spiritual faculty before we can appreciate these spiritual things because, as Paul says, "they are spiritually discerned." Therefore, unless we have the corresponding spirit in us, we will not be able to appreciate them. They will be foolishness to us. As we are by nature, we cannot appreciate the things of the Spirit of God. Our nature is twisted; it is perverted; it is fallen. We are "uncircumcised in heart and ears." We cannot believe!

This is a very important message for the unbeliever. Have you ever realized this, my friend? Perhaps you have taken the position that you can believe this Gospel whenever you like, but you have decided not to believe it. I am telling you that the trouble with you is that you *cannot* believe it, that you are "dead in trespasses and sins" (Eph. 2:1). Have you ever realized the truth about yourself? Can you sit and listen to this Gospel about the Son of God and what He has done and not be moved? What a terrible condition you are in! Have you realized that?

But let me apply this to the Christian believer as well. I find that many Christian people are troubled and upset because it seems that the great philosophers and scientists reject the Gospel. As a result, many Christians are afraid of the charge of being unintellectual or obscurantist or of having undergone a psychological change of some kind. But you must never be worried by that again. There is only one thing to say about these people: they are "uncircumcised in heart and ears." They are "natural" men and women, and as such, even if they had the greatest brains in the universe, they simply would not be able to hear this message truly. It would be impossible.

Unbelievers make fools of themselves. They criticize the Gospel. They say they do not understand it. They are always asking questions and talking about their difficulties. Why? Because they are ignorant as to their whole condition. They lack the essential faculty and ability that enables anybody to believe this great and glorious Gospel. "The natural man receiveth not the things of the Spirit of God: for they are foolishness unto him: neither can he know them, because they are spiritually discerned" (1 Cor. 2:14); they are "uncircumcised in heart and ears." What a devastating thing the fall was! The minds of men and women have been so affected that they have no appreciation at all of God and the things pertaining to God. In the first creation this was everything to Adam and Eve. They were made in the image and likeness of God. They enjoyed communion and fellowship with Him, and these were the things that ravished their hearts. But human beings have lost their appreciation of God and the things of God.

But not only that—this in turn leads to blindness. Again, we have this statement by Stephen: "Which of the prophets have not your fathers persecuted?" He said in effect, "What you are doing is nothing new. You go on repeating the errors of your forefathers. 'Which of the prophets have not your fathers persecuted? and they have slain them which shewed before of the coming of the Just One; of whom ye have been now the betrayers and murderers.'" That was Stephen's way of talking about the blindness of the unregenerate, the incapacity of unbelievers, their inability to see the truth that is held before them. It is there, but they do not see it.

The apostle Paul, in writing his second letter to the Corinthians, put this in unambiguous language. We think we are free. But Paul says, "If our gospel be hid, it is hid to them that are lost: in whom the god of this world hath blinded the minds of them which believe not, lest the light of the glorious gospel of Christ, who is the image of God, should shine unto them" (2 Cor. 4:3-4). Unbelievers are slaves. They are not allowed to believe.

Now listen to Stephen working this out. He said in effect, "Your fathers were visited. God had raised up a series of marvelous men, the prophets. He gave those men the ability to write and to speak. He gave them the ability to expound the condition of the nation, to call the people to righteousness, to expound the law and to prophesy things to come—a succession of mighty men of God. But," says Stephen, "your fathers disliked and persecuted these men."

And that is the story we read in the Old Testament. The children of Israel generally preferred the false prophet and persecuted the true prophet. Why was this? Well, the false prophet always prophesied smooth things to them; it was all light and easy. Speaking about the false prophets, Jeremiah said, "They have healed also the hurt of the daughter of my people slightly, saying, Peace, peace; when there is no peace" (Jer. 6:14). The false prophet put it all so simply, and it was so nice that people were always ready to believe him. But the true prophet probed, he analyzed, he condemned, he showed them themselves as they were, and they hated him and persecuted him. The nation had been blind to the message of these messengers of God and had always withstood them. The real trouble was that they could not see this. They did not merely act like this for the sake of doing so; they were blind.

And then Stephen went on to point out how the Sanhedrin were infinitely worse. He said in essence, "You are not only doing what your fathers did before you—you cannot see that what has happened in this Jesus of Nazareth is nothing but a fulfillment of the prophecies of your great prophets: 'They have slain them which shewed before of the coming of the Just One.' You are interested in religion; you are the religious leaders. You are interested in the writings of the prophets. You say you are superior to all other nations because you have the prophetic writings, but have you read your prophets? Have you seen that the prophets prophesied that a 'Just One' was going to come? Some of them prophesied where He would be born, the circumstances, the poverty, and so on. The prophets tell you of the coming of this Jesus whom you rejected and murdered."

Is this not extraordinary? Here are learned men, religious men, who have the writings of the prophets before them. They study them, they are interested in them, and yet they have never seen the message. Here is the phenomenon that we must recognize: this is the essential nature of unbelief, that people can look with their eyes at the message and not see it, that they can hear it and yet not hear it. The Sanhedrin had completely missed the astonishing way in which Jesus of Nazareth was a fulfillment of the prophecies of the prophets.

Not only that, these members of the Sanhedrin had actually looked at Him, they had heard Him, they had seen His miracles, and still they had never seen Him. John could say, "The Word was made flesh, and dwelt among us, (and we beheld his glory, the glory as of the only begotten of the Father,) full of grace and truth" (John 1:14). But these men, these religious authorities, could look into the face of the Son of God, they could look into those eternal depths of love in His eyes and see nothing but "this fellow, this carpenter."

We, too, must come face to face with the nature of this unbelief. What is it that renders men and women incapable of recognizing what they see standing before them? Is unbelief merely intellectual, something light and superficial, something within human control? It is obviously deeper. The Jewish leaders missed the glory of the person; they missed the perfection and the wonder and the amazement of His life. They could see the miracles and just for a moment be affected but then dismiss them and go into some legalistic dispute as to whether or not He should do them on the Sabbath and who had given Him the right and the authority. They missed the essence!

What makes people behave in such a manner? They had heard His teaching about God. Some guards had said, "Never man spake like this man" (John 7:46), and yet these authorities could not get it, they could not see it. His exposition of the law as given in the Sermon on the Mount was without equal, and yet they did not see it! They were annoyed simply because, according to them, He had no right to speak. They were so concerned about their own decorum and their own dignity as the appointed teachers that to them He was an upstart. They did not listen to what He said. They were interested in the surroundings, in the degrees, the qualifications, as it were—who had appointed Him, who He was. And so they never heard His message at all. This is unbelief in its very essence.

And then there was what our Lord said about the object of His coming into the world: "For the Son of man is come to seek and to save that which was lost" (Luke 19:10). He was the friend of publicans and sinners. He gave hope to the downcast, the downtrodden, the hopeless, the vile, the refuse of society. His amazing offer was free forgiveness: "Son, be of good cheer; thy sins be forgiven thee" (Matt. 9:2). But all this meant nothing to them.

And on top of that Stephen was saying in essence, "Are you completely blind to what is happening to these men among whom I now live, these apostles, as we call them? You know what happened on the Day of Pentecost; you have seen the miracles since then; you have heard their preaching. Can you not see the significance? Can you really explain all this away? Is all this nothing? You are seeing facts, but are you *seeing* them? The fact is, you *cannot* see them; you are blind, just like your fathers. All this is happening before you, yet you see nothing in it. Look at me! Who am I? How am I capable of doing these things? Can you not see it?"

In other words, fallen human beings in sin are not only incapable of hearing, they are incapable of seeing and understanding. They are blinded by "the god of this world" (2 Cor. 4:4). That, then, is the explanation of the rejection of the Gospel with regard to the mind.

Let's put it now in terms of the will. "Ye stiffnecked and uncircumcised in heart," says Stephen. Men and women, as the result of sin, are not only in terrible trouble in their minds and rendered incapable of appreciating God and the truth of God and the most glorious things that have ever happened in this universe, but they are also in terrible trouble in the realm of their wills. "Stiffnecked"! Stubborn! The trouble with unbelievers is that they not only cannot, but they are not ready. They will not even allow themselves to listen. Their whole approach is antagonistic, and they are determined to resist.

Oh, have you seen the true nature of sin? The only explanation of why people do not believe on the Lord Jesus Christ is that they are so totally fallen that they have never seen the problem and the depth of sin. They have never seen that it is such a profound problem that it takes the coming of the Son of God from heaven and His dying and resurrection, this miraculous action, to save them. Here they are in the realm of their wills. They are never neutral. Oh, I know people like to think that when they sit and listen to the Gospel, they can accept or refuse, whichever they like. They think their response is all within their own control; and sometimes, alas, preachers seem to agree. But that is not the case. People are never neutral and open-minded; they are always, by nature, antagonistic to the truth.

Listen to Paul on this: "The carnal mind is enmity against God"—it is not neutral—"for it is not subject to the law of God, neither indeed can be" (Rom. 8:7). And that is simply the truth about every one of us by nature. We are instinctively opposed to God's message; everything that is in us is against it. We do not listen with an open mind. We reject the Gospel. We have never read the Bible. We know nothing about the history of Christianity and the Christian church; we have never really investigated it. We all start by thinking that we are very clever. In adolescence, or somewhere around that age, we think the cleverest thing we can ever do and the proof that we are adults is to say, "The Gospel is nonsense! Christianity is ridiculous, an insult to the intelligence!" That is what we believe. But what is this? It is just violent prejudice. "Stiffnecked"! Stubborn!

But it is even worse than that. "Ye stiffnecked and uncircumcised in heart and ears, ye do always resist the Holy Ghost: as your fathers did, so do ye." This means that men and women are not passive in their refusal to listen to the Gospel; there is a terrible and a malign activity about their rejection. "Ye do always resist the Holy Ghost," said Stephen. These members of the Sanhedrin had not merely listened to a kind of academic or theoretical statement of the message but had listened to preaching in the power and demonstration of the Holy Spirit. "Stephen, full of faith and power, did great wonders and miracles among the people" (Acts 6:8). He spoke to them, and they could not answer him, they could not say a word against him, they could not make any reply to what he was saying. And yet they would not believe.

They stirred up the people and set up false witnesses, but "they were not able to resist the wisdom and the spirit by which he spake" (Acts 6:8).

The same was true of the preaching of Peter on the Day of Pentecost and also of his addresses before the Sanhedrin. They had already arrested Peter and John more than once, as we read in the earlier chapters of Acts, and Peter had spoken, "filled with the Holy Ghost" (Acts 4:8). Peter did not give an academic and detached statement. Oh, no; the Holy Spirit was operative. The power of the Spirit was present, and these men on the Sanhedrin had felt something of it. When a man is speaking under the power of the Holy Spirit, even the natural man knows there is something unusual, and he cannot help feeling it. The message comes not only in word, it may come in circumstances, and yet people deliberately resist the Holy Spirit.

Let me give you one obvious example from the book of Acts itself. Later on we read that the apostle Paul was called one day to speak before the Roman governor Felix and his wife Drusilla. Paul, filled with the Holy Spirit, "reasoned of righteousness, temperance, and judgment to come." And as Paul spoke, "Felix trembled" (24:25). What made him tremble? It was not merely Paul speaking—it was the Holy Spirit speaking through him and using him, and the power was such that Felix was literally trembling. But he deliberately stopped the preaching and sent Paul back to prison. That is "resist[ing] the Holy Ghost."

If you are an unbeliever, do you not know something about this? Have you not felt at times something of the power of these words? Have you not felt something suddenly moving your heart and spirit, something about the inevitability of this truth, and knew that you had been coming under its influence? But you did not want to do so, and you deliberately turned away. You were deliberately resisting the Holy Spirit. And why did you do it? You did it because your will is the slave of the devil and is opposed to God.

Not only that, this opposition makes a person deliberately twist the very law of God. "Who have received the law by the disposition of angels, and have not kept it," says Stephen. And this is what the Pharisees had been doing. They had been evading the law of God and had been twisting it to suit themselves. They had been glorying in it and praising it, unlike men who seemed to criticize it, and yet they had never kept it, and they had been quite deliberate in what they were doing. Hypocrisy!

The last consideration concerns what sin and the original fall have done to the human heart—and this is the most frightening and alarming and astonishing thing of all. Have you ever realized how utterly irrational unbelief is? Listen to these words describing the Jewish leaders:

When they heard these things, they were cut to the heart, and they gnashed on him with their teeth. . . . Then they cried out with a loud voice, and stopped their ears, and ran upon him with one accord, and cast him out of the city, and stoned him: and the witnesses laid down their clothes at a young man's feet, whose name was Saul. And they stoned Stephen, [as he was] calling upon God, and saying, Lord Jesus, receive my spirit. And he kneeled down, and cried with a loud voice, Lord, lay not this sin to their charge.

—Acts 7:54, 57-60

Here we have an extraordinary demonstration of the effect of sin upon the heart. Unbelief, which likes to pride itself on its rationality and its intellectuality, is nothing but sheer irrationality; it is madness; it is sheer emotionalism. It is not the believer who suffers from emotionalism—it is the unbeliever! It starts with a kind of irritation against the truth, a general annoyance against it. "This Christianity!" unbelievers say with derision and scorn. Have you not seen the mocking and the jokes? You can see it almost whenever you like on television; you can see it in the papers—these clever intellectuals who are always poking fun at the Gospel. This is pure emotionalism. They do not argue in rational terms; there are innuendoes, suggestions, sneers, sarcasms, dismissal. This is irritation, which moves on to annoyance, then on to hatred and ends in some shape or form in violence.

Now here is a graphic description of unbelief: "Then they cried out with a loud voice, and stopped their ears." They did not want to hear it; they would not hear it; they must not! Have we not done this ourselves—pushed our hands into our ears, as it were, because we did not want to listen? This is the end of argument; it is the end of reason; it is the end of demonstration; it is the end of understanding. This is people deliberately abandoning themselves to violence and emotion. This is characteristic of unbelief. Have you not noticed how people who often start with an argument about religion and the Christian faith with supposed great intellectuality, if you go on quoting the Scriptures and explaining them and answering their objections, will soon begin to lose their temper and become impatient and get annoyed with you and walk away saying, "You are utterly unreasonable"? They will not listen, and they treat you with sarcasm and derision. Is that not true?

Read the four Gospels. Here is the very Son of God, "the meek and lowly Jesus"—how approachable, how ready to listen, how ready to help. But look at the attitude of the Pharisees and scribes and Sadducees, always trying to trap Him, always trying to trip Him and to be clever, then taking up stones and throwing them at Him, conspiring together against Him and finally putting Him to death. What made them do that? What harm had He done? What wrong had He done? What was wrong in His speech or actions? Nothing. This was irrationality! They hated Him without a cause, and they crucified Him without any charge that they could bring against Him. And here were these members of the Sanhedrin doing exactly the same thing with this man Stephen: "They suborned men" (Acts 6:11). There was nothing to be said against Him; so they bribed men to tell lies, anything to put down this Christianity. Is this rationality? No; it is sheer emotionalism and sheer irrationality.

But we also have the suggestion here of a still more remarkable example of the irrationality of unbelief. "[They] cast him out of the city, and stoned him: and the witnesses laid down their clothes at a young man's feet, whose name was Saul." Who is that? Well, that is the man who becomes the mighty apostle Paul! But at this point he is an unbeliever, and do you want to know what an unbeliever is like? Here he is, this outstanding genius, this brilliant intellect, one of the greatest minds the world has ever known—Saul of Tarsus, later Paul the apostle.

Listen to how unbelief makes a man behave:

> *And Saul, yet breathing out threatenings and slaughter against the disciples of the Lord, went unto the high priest, and desired of him letters to Damascus to the synagogues, that if he found any of this way, whether they were men or women, he might bring them bound unto Jerusalem [so that they might be put to death].*
>
> —*Acts 9:1-2*

This giant intellect is "breathing out threatenings and slaughter." What is this? It is madness; it is irrationality. It is not intellect. It is a man moved by his emotions; he is mad! Mad against God and His Son and the eternal truth.

As you read the story of the Christian church down the running centuries, you will find a constant repetition of this selfsame madness. You see it in the way, for example, simple men were treated in Britain at the time of the Protestant Reformation simply because they had come to believe the truth. They had never wronged anybody—indeed, they had been helping everybody; yet they were maligned, persecuted, put to death—even burned at the stake. The Puritans, the Covenanters, the early Methodists—look at the way they were treated; look at the hatred, the malice. Simply because they had become better people, because they had stopped getting drunk, because they had stopped swearing, because they were living new and holy lives and were trying to help others, that was the treatment they got. Was this rationality? It was sheer irrationality; it was nothing but terrible emotion.

I officiated at a certain man's wedding service when he and his wife got married, one of the first I ever did. Neither of them was a Christian, and I would not take that wedding now, but I took it then because I was not aware of what I was doing. Not long after he got married, this man was converted. He was completely changed, and because of that, of course, he loved coming to the meetings of the church. Church was everything to him.

His wife was a quiet woman, unusually quiet. I will never forget this man coming to tell me one day that he had gone home from the prayer meeting to be greeted angrily by his wife, with bitterness not only in her heart but in her face. She said, "You've been to that prayer meeting?"

"Yes!" he said.

She said, "You know, I would rather that they carry you home drunk from the Working Men's Drinking Club than see you coming home from this prayer meeting."

What causes this kind of thing? Why this bitterness? Why this vituperation? Why this gnashing of the teeth? Why this stopping of the ears? She did not want to hear the truth. Thank God, she was later delivered from the thralldom of sin and Satan, and she herself became a Christian. But at that point, there it was. She was an unbeliever; nothing that her husband said, nothing that anybody else said, availed. She did not want to hear about it. She thought it was all a lot of nonsense! She would have preferred him to be a drunkard; anything but this.

This is the nature and the character of unbelief, and this is the position of every unbeliever in the world today. It is that which leads people into this condition, where the mind and the will and the heart are enslaved and are incapable of recognizing the truth of God as it is in the face of Jesus Christ. Here He is, the blessed Son of God, "who, being in the form of God, thought it not robbery to be equal with God: but made himself of no reputation, and took upon him the form of a servant . . ." (Phil. 2:6-7). Jesus is the eternal Son of God. He is the Creator of the universe. He has come to earth. He has divested Himself of the signs of His eternal glory, and He has come down into poverty and has humbled Himself. What for? In order to save us!

Because He bore the punishment of our sins in His own body on the cross, He stands before us and says, "Look unto me, and be ye saved" (Isa. 45:22). He says in essence, "Come to Me, and I will assure you that your sins are blotted out. I will give you new life, new hope, everything you stand in need of and infinitely more." Here it is: "Come unto Me!" But people's response by nature is, "Away with him, away with him, crucify him" (John 19:15).

There is only one explanation for this. It is the condition of men and women as the result of the fall, human beings in sin, under condemnation, under the dominion of the devil and hell. Apart from Christ, we cannot think rationally; that is why we see nothing in the Gospel. We do not want it. Why not? Can we not see that there is something twisted in us? We are perverted! We prefer the ugly and the twisted to the pure and the clean and the holy and the lovely and the divine. Can we not see that this is utter irrationality? And does that not lead us to the conclusion that if we are in this condition, there is only one hope for us, and that is that we be born again? We cannot do anything as we are except cry out to God to have mercy upon us.

Have you seen yourself? Have you seen the state of your mind, the state of your heart, the state of your will? Are you not horrified? Are you not terrified? If you are, cry out to God to have mercy and to have pity. You cannot do anything else. You cannot believe as you are. You must simply ask for mercy, and He will give it to you, and He will put His Spirit within you, and you will see the truth, and then you will believe it. "We have received," says Paul. That is why we believe these things, the things that the princes of this world have rejected. We believe because "We have received, not the spirit of the world, but the spirit which is of God; that we might know the things that are freely given to us of God" (1 Cor. 2:12).

My dear friend, is there something in you at this moment that makes you feel, "Oh, I wish I could believe that"? Ask Him to change your nature, to give you a new mind, a new heart, a new will. And then to your astonishment you will see the truth. Your mind will rejoice in believing it, your heart will gladden at the sound of it, and your will from henceforth will be anxious to obey Him. You will give yourself to Him to live the remainder of your life in this world to His glory and to His praise.

See unbelief as it is depicted in the members of the Sanhedrin. It is in you as well, and God alone can deliver you out of it and from it. And that is precisely what the Lord Jesus Christ has come into this world to do. Look unto Him! Cry unto Him to have mercy, and He will work in you to give you new life and all that accompanies it.

18

Lord Jesus

When they heard these things, they were cut to the heart, and they gnashed on him with their teeth. But he, being full of the Holy Ghost, looked up stedfastly into heaven, and saw the glory of God, and Jesus standing on the right hand of God, and said, Behold, I see the heavens opened, and the Son of man standing on the right hand of God. Then they cried out with a loud voice, and stopped their ears, and ran upon him with one accord, and cast him out of the city, and stoned him: and the witnesses laid down their clothes at a young man's feet, whose name was Saul. And they stoned Stephen, [as he was] calling upon God, and saying, Lord Jesus, receive my spirit. And he kneeled down, and cried with a loud voice, Lord, lay not this sin to their charge. And when he had said this, he fell asleep.

—Acts 7:54-60

We come now to the conclusion of this extraordinary chapter. This is not only a great but a very vital chapter in the understanding of the Christian faith and of the Christian church. The great question today is, what is Christianity? It is not surprising that people outside the church find it difficult to know what it is when there are so many different voices within. My suggestion is that the most important need at the present time for all of us as individuals, and for the church as a whole, is to know what the Christian faith really is and what it means. And in this chapter I think we are shown that very clearly. We are now at the climax of this story. It is the account of the death of Stephen, this first Christian martyr. This is not a judicial trial. Stephen's death was murder.

Stephen had been arrested because he was a Christian, because he was an official in the church, because of his preaching, and because of his miracles. The Sanhedrin had put him on trial and charged him with blasphemy. When they asked him what he had to say for himself, Stephen, as we have seen, gave a kind of review of the history of the children of Israel, picking out in particular three persons. He began with their father Abraham, of whom these religious leaders were so proud, and he showed them that they had never really understood the story of Abraham. Then he took up the case of Joseph, and there, very simply, he was able to show that their treatment of the Lord Jesus Christ was nothing but a repetition of the way in which Joseph was treated by his brothers. And then he came to the crucial case of Moses, the great lawgiver. Stephen told the story of Moses and thereby worked out its real meaning.

Finally, Stephen applied his message to the Sanhedrin themselves. He said to them: "Ye stiffnecked and uncircumcised in heart and ears, ye do always resist the Holy Ghost: as your fathers did, so do ye . . . the Just One; of whom ye have been now the betrayers and murderers: who have received the law . . . and have not kept it" (Acts 7:51-53). What did they do then? "When they heard these things, they were cut to the heart, and they gnashed on him with their teeth." They threw him outside the city and stoned him to death.

We have finished with Stephen's exposition and will look at what happened next. It is a very dramatic incident, the climax to this great speech of Stephen, the first Christian martyr. It is important that we know all about this historically, but what always seems to me to be of special value is that it gives us a very wonderful picture of what a Christian really is. If we want to know what Christianity means and what it does for a human being, we will see it in this passage. Here it is put before us in a most astonishing manner.

I want to show this to you in terms of a contrast, which is always a good way of looking at something, and here it is all done for us. We see the tremendous contrast between the members of the Sanhedrin and Stephen. This is how it is put in the record: "When they heard these things, they were cut to the heart, and they gnashed on him with their teeth. But he . . ." "But he"! Immediately there is a remarkable and an amazing contrast. The very word "but" immediately puts that before us in a very dramatic manner. Indeed, I never read this great chapter without always being struck by this contrast. Stephen went through this history and made his analysis of it, and it was one that was full of unhappiness and disappointment. How sad the record of the children of Israel is! What a miserable people these members of the Sanhedrin were! Then suddenly it is like passing out of a cloud and a storm into the most glorious sunshine. There is a beam of light, and everything is transfigured and transformed. You look at Stephen, and there you see a Christian in contradistinction to the non-Christian, and you are amazed at the difference.

This is the first point that I want to establish. This difference concerns the most profound truth in the universe; there is no bigger contrast than this. And it is because so many have not realized this that the Christian church is as she is. It is very difficult to tell who is a Christian today because the church and the world are so similar, and that is because the world has come into the church. There has been a lowering of all the standards in belief, in deportment, in behavior, in appearance, and in everything else—this foolish notion that you can win people by being like them! That idea is a complete fallacy, a denial of the whole Gospel. There was never a being more different from the world than the Lord Jesus Christ, but He attracted "publicans and sinners" unto Himself. Why? Because He was like them? No! Because He was eternally different from them. But today what is a Christian? Nobody seems to know. The standards have been lowered, and everything has been muddled; the lines are no longer distinct. But when we look at this book of The Acts of the Apostles, what strikes us immediately is the amazing and absolute contrast between the Christian and the non-Christian.

Paul says in 2 Corinthians 5:17, "If any man be in Christ, he is a new creature"—a new creation. The Christian is not someone who has been improved a bit, polished a bit, given a new suit. No! Christians are born again; they are made anew. Something entirely different has come into being as the result of the action of God. And here we see that difference in the contrast between Stephen and the members of the Sanhedrin. It is shouting at us. You might protest that this was an extreme case, but it was not. It was a very dramatic one, and the difference is heightened here, but the elements of the truth concerning this matter are true in every single case. The Christian is not just a good person, someone who is better than someone else; he is "new." And here it strikes us at once. So let us look at it.

First of all, let me ask a question: What is it that produces or accounts for the difference between the Christian and the non-Christian? In this record we are told exactly what it is: it is simply our relationship to the Holy Spirit. This difference is not something natural. Nobody is born a Christian, and men and women do not become Christians because they happen to have a certain temperament. They do not become Christians because they are good by nature or because they have particular qualities. No; that is a fallacy. Becoming a Christian is in no way dependent on what we are.

Let us thank God for that. If this were only a Gospel for good people, I would stop preaching it. It is a Gospel for anybody; it is a Gospel for everybody. That is the wonderful thing about it. We are all "shapen in iniquity" (Ps. 51:5), and no good will ever come of us until the Spirit of God has dealt with us. That is the Christian position. It does not depend upon us at all. It is entirely a question of the Holy Spirit.

Here is the contrast: Stephen, looking at the members of the Sanhedrin, says, "Ye stiffnecked and uncircumcised in heart and ears, ye do always resist the Holy Ghost." That is why they were what they were. But Luke writes of Stephen, "But he, being full of the Holy Ghost . . ." (v. 55). Do you see the difference? There was no Holy Spirit in them. They had resisted the Spirit; they had fought against Him; they were devoid of Him. They were "natural" men—men as they are by nature, with nothing of the Holy Spirit in them. "But he"—the Christian—is filled with the Spirit. He is a man who is dominated by the Holy Spirit, and all that he is is produced by the Holy Spirit. He is being led and guided and influenced by the Holy Spirit. Could this be clearer? *They* resisted the Holy Spirit; *he* was filled with the Holy Spirit. This is absolutely basic and fundamental. This is a factor that comes from the outside. This is the activity of God.

People resent this, and that is what always amazes me. We ought to rejoice. If I did not believe that the whole situation depended upon the activity and the intervention of God, I would have no message to give at all. My whole message is this: God "hath visited and redeemed his people" (Luke 1:68). It is the action of God—God the Father, God the Son, and God the Holy Spirit. And here we are looking in particular at the activity of the Spirit.

Having seen, then, that what makes the difference between the Christian and the non-Christian is our relationship to the Holy Spirit, let us go on, in the second place, to ask: What is the nature or the character of this difference? Here I shall confine myself to what we have before us in this immediate context. The first thing we notice—and it is very evident, both throughout this great chapter and here in the climax—is that the Holy Spirit makes all the difference in the world to our understanding. And that means, first of all, that the Holy Spirit makes an entire difference to the way in which we think.

This is a most glorious aspect of the work of the Holy Spirit. Christians not only differ from, and disagree with, non-Christians with regard to certain details, but, much more importantly, their whole thinking is different. The apostle, putting it to the Corinthians, says, "We have the mind of Christ" (1 Cor. 2:16). That is it! We look on everything in a different way. "Old things are passed away; behold, all things are become new" (2 Cor. 5:17). If you are still thinking as the world thinks, you are not a Christian. Christians look at the same facts as everybody else, but they do not see them or think about them in the same way. The whole climate, the whole realm, of their thinking is different.

But this change to our understanding brought about by the Holy Spirit also works itself out in details, and this is something that comes out in an extraordinary manner in this great chapter. These members of the Sanhedrin, as we have been seeing, were so wrong, especially where they thought they were so right. That is the tragedy of men and women in sin: they are so proud of themselves, and yet they are fools. Here are the members of the Sanhedrin, rejoicing in Moses, in the law, and in their temple, boasting of them, but, as Stephen had shown them, they entirely misunderstood them. Where they thought they were so right and so expert, they were ignorant, they were fools, they had completely misunderstood.

What do I mean? Well, one way in which there is a difference in the understanding of the Christian and the non-Christian is with regard to the Scriptures. These people had their Scriptures, some of them were authorities on them, and they prided themselves on their knowledge, but they had not understood the Scriptures. Paul, again, told the Corinthians that the tragedy of his fellow-countrymen, the Jews, was that Moses was read and expounded in the synagogues every Sabbath, but they did not understand—a veil was there (2 Cor. 3:13-14).

And Stephen brought out exactly this same point. The natural man can read a Bible, but he does not understand it; he reads the words, he reads the letters, he reads the sentences, but he does not get the meaning. The truth is spiritually understood, and he is not capable of that. This is not criticism—this is simply description. Those of us who know the two positions know exactly what this means. To the natural person, the Bible can be the most boring book in the world; to the Christian, it is the book of life, the manual of the soul, the textbook of salvation, the most precious thing in the whole universe.

But this applies not only to the Scriptures in general. These members of the Sanhedrin were wrong in their understanding of the history that is recorded in their Scriptures. The very thing they boasted of they had completely misunderstood. They would not have boasted as they did about Abraham, Joseph, and Moses if they had really understood what their forefathers had done with regard to these men and what they themselves were doing without knowing it. So they did not understand the history, and they did not understand the teaching.

I would take this and put it into a larger context. No one understands the history of the world except the one who sees it with eyes enlightened by

Scripture. Professional historians are increasingly admitting that they do not understand it. Scientific humanists, classical humanists, and others are admitting that they do not understand the history of the world. I am not boasting when I say that I *do* understand it! Not because I have some exceptional ability, but because I have the solution in the Bible. Here is the explanation of the whole story of humanity, its unspeakable folly in war and fighting, its drunkenness, its immorality, its vice, its lust, its passion, the hell it has made of the world. Here, and here alone, we understand it.

If we are interested in the future, the more we study this book, the more we will know about that too. If we read this book, we will not pin our faith on the United Nations any more than, in the past, we trusted the League of Nations. No; we will realize that this is a doomed, a damned, an evil world and under the judgment of God. We will know that nothing but the return of the Lord will produce order out of it. And since we know that, we will not waste our time with the foolish idealism of men who think they are preaching the Christian Gospel but are simply mouthing their own philosophies and their own ideas.

This comes out here so plainly. These members of the Sanhedrin had completely misunderstood God's purpose for the Jews. Of course, they were very proud of themselves as Jews, and they were proud of their national history, but they had never understood it. They always materialized everything and missed the spiritual element. They could not see that God was only using their history as a temporary plan, a method and expedient, to produce a great blessing for the whole world. He had said so to Abraham, the first person Stephen took up to illustrate his case: "And in thy seed shall all the nations of the earth be blessed" (Gen. 22:18). But the Jews resent this; they cannot understand it. In other words, they completely misunderstand God's whole purpose in the formation of a nation out of this one man Abraham. Christians, by contrast, understand this; they see it.

But the Sanhedrin's misunderstanding of their history led to further misunderstandings. They were charging Stephen with blasphemy. They said that he had spoken against the law: "We have heard him speak blasphemous words against Moses, and against God. . . . This man ceaseth not to speak blasphemous words against this holy place [the temple], and the law" (Acts 6:11, 13). They thought they understood the law, but they did not. One of the great differences between the Christian and the non-Christian is that the Christian understands the meaning and the purpose of the law. The non-Christian never does; the non-Christian always believes that God gave the law so that people might save themselves by it. Non-Christians think they can make themselves Christians by living a good life, by keeping a certain code of morality and behavior. They think they can justify themselves before God.

But Christians, as Stephen has been showing so plainly and so clearly, see that the purpose of the giving of the law was to bring us all under condemnation. "[The law] was added because of transgressions" (Gal. 3:19), so that sin might be multiplied. The law came in on the side, as it were—what for?—"that sin by the commandment might become exceeding sinful" (Rom. 7:13). That is its object. It was never meant to save; it could not save. "What the law could not do, in that it was weak through the flesh . . ." (Rom. 8:3).

The Christian understands this. The Christian realizes that the main function and purpose of the law is to show us our absolutely lost, helpless, hopeless condition and to lead us to Christ. "The law was our schoolmaster to bring us unto Christ" (Gal. 3:24). What is the law saying in its commandments, and especially in its ceremonies, in its burnt offerings and sacrifices? Is it saying that if we live a good life and regularly take our offerings and sacrifices to God, we can save ourselves? No! It is saying that nothing we can ever do will save us. The law with its ceremonies is but a picture of how God is going to save us. God will provide a lamb; God will provide a sacrifice and an offering. "For Christ is the end of the law for righteousness to every one that believeth" (Rom. 10:4). He is "the Lamb of God, which taketh away the sin of the world" (John 1:29). The Christian understands this. But the men on the Sanhedrin were blind to it. They had rejected Christ, and they were persecuting and putting on trial this man Stephen who had been preaching this message.

A further change in the understanding is that only the Christian perceives the true meaning of worship and the purpose, place, and function of the temple. In a sense these members of the Sanhedrin were worshiping the temple: they believed you could only worship there. That is why Stephen in his defense went back to Abraham. He said in effect, "How do you think your father Abraham worshiped? He did not have a temple. He was a pagan living in Ur of the Chaldees. And God called him out from paganism, not through a temple, not through a tabernacle—they had not yet been built. This man met with God, and he knew Him." He was "the Friend of God" (Jas. 2:23), and he worshiped him. When Stephen said, "The most High dwelleth not in temples made with hands" (Acts 7:48), he demolished the whole institutional idea of the Christian church and showed that worship does not depend upon buildings or places or ceremonies or ritual or a priesthood, but on one thing, and one thing only, and that is our relationship to the Lord Jesus

Christ. "We are the circumcision, which worship God in the spirit, and rejoice in Christ Jesus, and have no confidence in the flesh" (Phil. 3:3).

Stephen knew all this, but the Jewish leaders did not. We read of Stephen here that he called upon the Lord (v. 59). Now the Authorized translation says, "Stephen, calling upon God, and saying, Lord Jesus . . ." But the word "God" should not be there; it has been added by the translators. Rather, this verse should read: "Stephen, calling upon, and saying, Lord Jesus, receive my spirit." Stephen was worshiping Jesus. He was offering Him worship and adoration because he had made the grand discovery that there is only "one mediator between God and men, the man Christ Jesus" (1 Tim. 2:5). Stephen had believed the words of the Lord, who said, "I am the way, the truth, and the life; no man cometh unto the Father, but by me" (John 14:6). Stephen knew this. He did not rely upon the temple—we can worship God without it. He was saying, "We must not worship the temple and say it is essential. It will soon be demolished," as indeed it was in A.D. 70.

So in this immediate context we see the essential difference that the Holy Spirit makes to the understanding.

Notice, in the second place, the entire difference that the Holy Spirit produces in the spirit of Christians. Christians have a different spirit from the spirit of non-Christians. Look at verses 54, 57-58—could anything be plainer? "When they heard these things, they were cut to the heart, and they gnashed on him with their teeth. . . . Then they cried out with a loud voice, and stopped their ears, and ran upon him with one accord, and cast him out of the city, and stoned him." That is their spirit. I need not dwell upon this; we have seen this in all its horror and all its vileness. That is the spirit of the natural man; that is the character of man without the Spirit of God in him. That is his heart; that is his nature. What a terrible, horrible, foul thing it is! These members of the Sanhedrin were utterly unjustified in their actions, utterly wrong, violent, insensate, mad.

But look at this other man: "But he, being full of the Holy Ghost . . ." (v. 55). Oh, what a contrast he presents! He is a humble man, a man with a heart of compassion. He is like his blessed Lord; he has sympathy and understanding. Our Lord Himself said in His teaching that the people He was going to produce would be people like Himself. He had said that His followers must be perfect: "Be ye therefore perfect, even as your Father which is in heaven is perfect" (Matt. 5:48), and here is a man exemplifying this. Our Lord had said, "Blessed are ye, when men shall revile you, and persecute you, and shall say all manner of evil against you falsely, for my sake" (Matt. 5:11).

What else had our Lord said?

> *Ye have heard that it hath been said, Thou shalt love thy neighbour, and hate thine enemy. But I say unto you, Love your enemies, bless them that curse you, do good to them that hate you, and pray for them which despitefully use you, and persecute you; that ye may be the children of your Father which is in heaven: for he maketh his sun to rise on the evil and on the good, and sendeth rain on the just and on the unjust. For if ye love them which love you, what reward have ye? do not even the publicans the same? And if ye salute your brethren only, what do ye more than others? do not even the publicans so? Be ye therefore perfect, even as your Father which is in heaven is perfect.*
>
> —*Matt. 5:43-48*

Here was Stephen, being stoned to death just because he was a Christian. He had done no harm to them or to anybody else. He was doing great good, he had worked miracles, he was preaching a Gospel of love and of salvation, and they stoned him and gnashed their teeth. They hated him. "And he kneeled down, and cried with a loud voice, Lord, lay not this sin to their charge." He was sorry for them, though they were killing him. He had a heart full of mercy and compassion toward them. He grieved for them; he interceded for them; he prayed that they might not be punished for this, that this would not be added to the account that was already against them. He asked God to have mercy upon them because he knew that they did not know what they were doing. He did exactly, you remember, what his Lord and Master had done from the cross: "Father, forgive them; for they know not what they do" (Luke 23:34).

This is Christianity! It not only gives people a different understanding and outlook—it changes their whole spirit and nature. The natural person says, "You hit me, I'll hit you! I must have my rights!" Christians no longer live in that way. They have an entirely different view. There is a new spirit within them, a spirit that can enable them even to love their enemies.

But the third difference, and one of the most momentous of all, between Christians and non-Christians is the way in which they face death. "And when he had said this, he fell asleep"—even as he was being stoned to death. This is a very beautiful expression, is it not? "He fell asleep." That is how the Christian dies. In the fifth chapter of Acts we read about the deaths of Ananias and Sapphira—what a different account we are given of their dying! They had cheated, they had lied to the Holy Ghost, and we are told, "And Ananias hearing these words fell down, and gave up the ghost" (v. 5). Exactly the same thing happened to Sapphira, his wife: "Then fell she down straightway at his feet, and yielded up the ghost" (v. 10). But this man Stephen "fell asleep."

Now let us be clear about this. The ultimate test to apply to every one of us and to any theory of life that we may happen to hold, the ultimate test, is this: How does it help us face death? It is no use beating about the bush. It is all very well to talk cleverly when we are young and have health and everything is going well with us, but here is the great question: What are we like when we are face to face with death, whether our own or somebody else's? And this is the special glory of this Christian message, this Christian faith. People think this is mere theory, but nothing in the world is more practical than this Gospel and this Christian life. Here is something that enables a man or woman to live and to die. Here is something that always shines out most gloriously and brilliantly in the great crises of life. The way you test any view of life is by finding out what it is like in difficulties, in crises, in agony, in heartache, in heartbreak, and especially in the face of the "last enemy," which is death. And here in Stephen is our answer.

Now this is the value of history, is it not? "Ah," you may say, "it's all very well for these men to write eloquently about the Christian facing death. I wonder what they are like when they themselves have to face it?" Here is your answer; here is a man facing death—this is literal history. And Stephen was only the first of many, remember. He was the first Christian martyr, and what we see in this man Stephen is what we see in all true Christians. Whether they are martyred or whether they die in their own beds does not matter—this is how they face it. Here is a perfect picture, as if God sets a great example at the very beginning. Oh, what a crowd have followed this man! The glorious army of martyrs! They come down the running centuries, and in different ways and forms they but repeat what this man Stephen did then.

What do we find here? Well, the whole essence of it is this: there was no fear, there was no terror, there was no alarm. Stephen was not excited or frantic, not knowing what to do. Not at all! Oh, how calm the man was! What serenity he displayed in contrast with the gnashing of the teeth and the fury of these wretched members of the Sanhedrin! But what is it that enables the Christian to die like this? Well, we are told here very simply.

The Christian can face death as Stephen faced it because he can differentiate between the spirit and the body. They stoned Stephen as he was "calling upon God, and saying, Lord Jesus, receive my spirit." Here is one of the most fundamental points we can ever grasp in this life. The whole tragedy about non-Christians, natural men and women, is that they regard themselves as virtually nothing but bodies, and, of course, when the body comes to the end, everything is lost; they have nothing else. If I die, well, I have lost everything; if I am killed, it is the end. So I am nervous. I am frightened. I am apprehensive. Oh, there is nothing as terrible as death. Death is a horrible thing; it is a specter approaching me. In its terror of death, the world does its utmost to forget about it.

But the Christian knows that such an outlook is a fallacy, that it is an error to think that the body is all there is. Christians know that when the body dies, there is that within them that goes on—the spirit. They do not say, "Lord Jesus, receive my body," they say, "receive my spirit." The biggest discovery we can ever make is the discovery that the most precious, the most valuable, the most glorious thing about us is that we have a soul and a spirit within us that is imperishable and goes on and on and on without end.

So Stephen believed and was obviously exemplifying in his life what his Lord had taught in the days of His flesh. When our Lord was sending out His disciples to preach, these are the words that He addressed to them: "And I say unto you my friends, Be not afraid of them that kill the body, and after that have no more that they can do. But I will forewarn you whom ye shall fear: Fear him, which after he hath killed hath power to cast into hell; yea, I say unto you, Fear him" (Luke 12:4-5). Do not be afraid of people who can only kill the body. They may kill you, but they cannot do any more than that. They cannot touch your spirit; they cannot touch your soul; they cannot touch that which is eternal. Do not be afraid of them; there is a limit to what they can do. There is only one to fear, the one who can determine the eternal existence of your soul and spirit.

Christians start with that, and it affects the whole of their thinking. They know that the most important thing about them is not that they may have a wonderful body or a wonderful brain, but that they have a soul, and although the body may be destroyed by men—and it does not matter how, whether by bombs or anything else—it makes no difference to the soul.

And then, of course, that leads Christians to take an entirely different view of life in this world. To non-Christians, this world is not only the only world, it is everything, and to go out of this world means the end of all things, and of course they are therefore terrified. But Christians know that this is a sinful world, a fallen world, a temporary world. Christians always have a great contrast in their minds—the apostle Paul uses it so often. He talks about "now" and "then": "For now we see through a glass, darkly; but then face to face" (1 Cor. 13:12). Christians see that this world is a passing world: "For here have we no continuing city, but we seek one to come," says the writer to the Hebrews (13:14). This was the secret of Abraham, the secret of Joseph, the secret of Moses—all these men. Why did Moses give up that brilliant prospect that was there before him in Egypt and ally himself with these miserable, wretched people? Ah, he had his eye on the "recompence of the reward" (Heb. 11:26). "He endured, as seeing him who is invisible" (v. 27). These men all "looked for a city which hath foundations, whose builder and maker is God" (Heb. 11:10). They viewed life in this world as transient, evanescent, a preparatory school—nothing more.

But still more wonderful is this: "He, being full of the Holy Ghost, *looked up* stedfastly into heaven" (v. 55). Christians can do this; they can look up. They do not merely look at the world; they know another dimension, another realm—the unseen, the spiritual. "He . . . looked up." And then Stephen said, "Behold, *I see the heavens opened* . . ." Only Christians know this. They know this by faith. Here is Stephen realizing what he already knew. And therefore Christians, even in this life and in this world, can look ahead and say:

> *Heaven's morning breaks, and earth's vain shadows flee;*
> *In life, in death, O Lord, abide with me.*
> Henry Francis Lyte

Christians know there is another realm.

> *There is a land of pure delight,*
> *Where saints immortal reign.*
> Isaac Watts

They know there is a realm in which "the spirits of just men made perfect" (Heb. 12:23) are dwelling with the Father, the Son, the Holy Spirit, and the glorious angels. They know that this is a reality and that they are going to it—to the glory that awaits them. "But he, being full of the Holy Ghost, looked up stedfastly into heaven, and saw *the glory of God*." Oh, what a difference! What is death when you see the glory of God! What is the malignity of men, what are stones, what is anything compared to the glory of the everlasting God! And Stephen knew he was going to it. He would see it in all its fullness and enjoy it for all eternity.

But the other thing we are told is this: "But he, being full of the Holy Ghost, looked up stedfastly into heaven, and saw the glory of God, *and Jesus standing on the right hand of God*." I agree with all the old commentators who notice that we see here not, as we are often told, that our Lord is "sitting at the right hand of God," but that he is "*standing* at the right hand of

God." And I agree with that interpretation of this that says that our blessed Lord is getting up, as it were, to look at his suffering servant and is waiting to receive him. A hymn puts this very well; let me quote it to you:

Though now ascended up on high,
He bends on earth a brother's eye;
Partaker of the human name,
He knows the frailty of our frame.

Our fellow Sufferer yet retains
A fellow feeling of our pains:
And still remembers in the skies
His tears, his agonies and cries.

In every pang that rends the heart,
The Man of Sorrows has a part;
He sympathizes with our grief,
And to the sufferer sends relief.
Michael Bruce

In other words, Stephen was seeing a fulfillment of one of the last promises that our Lord gave His faithful followers. At the beginning of John 14, our Lord says:

> *Let not your heart be troubled: ye believe in God, believe also in me. In my Father's house are many mansions: if it were not so, I would have told you. I go to prepare a place for you. And if I go and prepare a place for you, I will come again, and receive you unto myself; that where I am, there ye may be also.*
>
> *—vv. 1-3*

Our Lord stands waiting to receive Stephen, this blessed servant who was following in His footsteps so gloriously, even praying for his enemies as he died, and who committed the keeping of his soul into Christ's safe and glorious hands.

That is the kind of difference the Holy Spirit makes to us. He not only gives us a different understanding and puts a different spirit in us, He changes our attitude toward the whole of life, and especially He changes our attitude toward death. He turns death into just a little rivulet standing between this world of sin and shame and evil and sorrow and that glorious land that awaits the people of God.

But let me just make one last point, and it is the greatest and the most glorious of all. We have been considering the great difference between Christians and non-Christians, and we have seen, first, that this difference is brought about by the Holy Spirit. Second, we have looked at the nature or the character of this difference. Now, third and last, we come to the secret or the explanation of the difference.

What is it? Well, it is the very reason Stephen is on trial. He is facing the Sanhedrin because of what he believes concerning the Lord Jesus Christ. What is the work of the Spirit, the Spirit who is resisted by the natural man but to whom Stephen, the Christian, has yielded and with whom he is filled? Understanding? Yes! But of what? It is of life, of history, of the Scriptures; but above all, it is of the Lord Jesus Christ. Our Lord said, did He not, that the Spirit would glorify Him. He said, "He shall not speak of [or from] himself. . . . He shall glorify me" (John 16:13-14). The supreme work of the Spirit is to display the Lord Jesus Christ to us, to enable us to see Him and to know Him.

And that is exactly what happened to Stephen, and that is why he was able to face death as he did. This account is so marvelous. "He, being full of the Holy Ghost, looked up stedfastly into heaven, and saw the glory of God"—that might have crushed him, but—"and Jesus standing on the right hand of God, and said, Behold, I see the heavens opened, and the Son of man standing on the right hand of God." Oh, this is a most wonderful thing! He saw Jesus!

Why did Stephen call the one whom he saw, "Jesus," "the Son of man"? It was because this was the one who, though He is the Lord of glory, became man. "Thou shalt call his name Jesus" (Matt. 1:21). The one Stephen saw here was the one who was once lying as a little helpless babe in the manger in Bethlehem. Jesus! The one who, when He started on His public ministry at the age of thirty, constantly referred to Himself as "the Son of man." This was the name He applied to Himself, and Stephen saw "the Son of man."

What does this mean? Well, Stephen saw a human form, the representative of humanity. The man! He in whom everything is represented, in whom all of man is represented, the one who delighted to call Himself "the Son of man." He has authority; He has power. Human affairs are in His hands. And, oh, the comfort and the consolation of knowing that! It means that we are not left to ourselves: "For we have not an high priest which cannot be touched with the feeling of our infirmities" because He "was in all points tempted like as we are, yet without sin" (Heb. 4:15). And there in the glory Stephen saw

Him, this Jesus, this Son of man. And the moment he saw Him, everything he had ever believed about Him was verified. Why? Because he saw Him standing at the right hand of God.

What does this mean? Well, Stephen had probably seen Jesus many times, as had most people who had been in Jerusalem—Jesus of Nazareth, the prophet, the preacher, the one who was arrested, the one who staggered up Golgotha, the one who was nailed to a tree and died between two thieves. Jesus! The one whose body was taken down, dead, and laid in a tomb, then the stone rolled in front of the entrance. Jesus! Yes, but now he sees Him standing! What does this mean! He has risen from the dead. He has conquered death and the grave. He has ascended on high, and He has been given the place and station of highest honor, even in the presence of God Himself, at the right hand of God!

What a confirmation of Stephen's faith! You and I may not have such a blessed confirmation, but we have exactly the same faith as Stephen. Stephen did not have this confirmation until this point, but he had believed and had gone on in the strength of his faith. That is what made him dare to look at these men who had his life in their hands and to say, "Ye stiffnecked and uncircumcised of heart." He knew that would infuriate them. It did not matter; he knew these things, and now he was given a confirmation of them.

And every one of us will get a confirmation. We shall not be left to ourselves in the agony of death. I remember standing at the bedside of a dying man who had been converted at the age of seventy-seven. He had lived one of the vilest lives a man could possibly live. He had been a drunkard, an adulterer, a wife-beater, even possibly a murderer; he had lived a life of vice and sin. I saw that man converted at the age of seventy-seven, but what I saw by that man's bedside was much more wonderful. It was his going, like Stephen's. I will never forget it! His poor face was a mass of scars as the result of his fightings, quarrelings, and battles, but as I looked at him his face was transfigured. It began to shine with something of the glory of heaven. And then—I will never forget this—just as he was going, a smile broke over his face, angelic, beatific, and he just held out his arms. What was happening? I have no hesitation in answering that question. He saw Jesus waiting to receive him, and he stretched out his hands.

That is it! Jesus is "on the right hand of God." And then Stephen prayed to Him and called Him "Lord Jesus." He is "Jesus," He is "Son of man," He is "on the right hand of God," He is "Lord." This means that He is the conqueror of all our enemies. He has conquered Satan and all his powers. And He has conquered "the last enemy"—death (1 Cor. 15:26). Death itself has been vanquished. He has triumphed over it; He has taken the sting out of it. And now He says, "All power is given unto me in heaven and in earth" (Matt. 28:18). He is at the right hand of God.

What is He doing? He is waiting "till his enemies be made his footstool" (Heb. 10:13). He is the Lord of history; everything is in His hands. He, and He alone, was big enough and strong enough to take the book that was sealed "within and on the backside"; He alone could tear the seals. He is "the Lion of the tribe of Judah" (Rev. 5:1, 5), the one who has triumphed over all the enemies of man and of God, and He is in heaven's highest place. And whatever He may be permitting in the world today—and He permits things we do not understand, He permits tyrants to rise—He always sets their limits, and down they go. Hitlers never last. All the great tyrants of history have gone down, and so will any future tyrants. He, and He alone, is King, and He will reign universally.

Moreover, He is the coming King. He is the one who will return to wind up the affairs of this world and cast evil and sin into hell, and hell itself into destruction. And he is "Lord of all" (Acts 10:36). Because He came and made Himself so low, because He "became obedient unto death, even the death of the cross," because of that

> *God also hath highly exalted him, and given him a name which is above every name: that at the name of Jesus every knee should bow, of things in heaven, and things in earth, and things under the earth; and that every tongue should confess that Jesus Christ is Lord, to the glory of God the Father.*
>
> *—Phil. 2:8-11*

Stephen saw Him, and he "fell asleep."

Those who believe this message concerning the Lord Jesus Christ have nothing to fear in death. They can say with the apostle Paul, "For to me to live is Christ, and to die is gain" (Phil. 1:21). Why? Because it means "to be with Christ; which is far better" (v. 23). Paul knew Him so well, and as an old man at the end of his life, this is how he faced death:

> *I have fought a good fight, I have finished my course, I have kept the faith: henceforth there is laid up for me a crown of righteousness, which the Lord, the righteous judge, shall give me at that day: and not to me only, but unto all them also that love his appearing.*
>
> *—2 Tim. 4:7-8*

This crown is not reserved only for special saints and martyrs. John Wesley used to boast, "Our people die well." That is the distinguishing mark of Christian men and women. They know that though they now see Him only as "in a glass, darkly," they shall then see Him "face to face" (1 Cor. 13:12) and spend their eternity in the glorious presence of God.

How do you face the prospect of death? Are you ready for it? Which of these two positions are you in? You are in one or the other. You have either resisted the Spirit of God, or else He is in you. Which is it? Do you have an understanding of these things? What spirit is in you? How do you face death or the prospect of death? What if you had to die tonight? This is a very uncertain world—there are many accidents and diseases. Are you ready?

Stephen has been reviewing Israel's great history, starting with Abraham. Can you join Thomas Olivers in saying something like this (words that were written by a converted tramp and drunkard)?

The God of Abraham praise,
Who reigns enthroned above;
Ancient of everlasting days,
And God of love.
Jehovah, great I AM!
By earth and heaven confessed;
I bow, and bless the sacred Name,
Forever blest.

That is good. But can you say this—here is the test:

The God of Abraham praise,
At Whose supreme command
From earth I rise and seek the joys
At his right hand.
I all on earth forsake—
Its wisdom, fame, and power;
And him my only portion make,
My shield and tower.

And can you say this?

He by himself hath sworn,
I on his oath depend;

I shall, on eagles, wings upborne,
To heaven ascend;
I shall behold his face;
I shall his power adore,
And sing the wonders of his grace
Forevermore.

Can you say that? Well, then can you join in saying this:

The whole triumphant host
Give thanks to God on high;
"Hail! Father, Son, and Holy Ghost,"
They ever cry.
Hail! Abraham's God, and mine!

Can you say that? Is He your God? Have you ceased to resist the Spirit? Have you given yourself to God? Can you say, "Hail! Abraham's God, and mine!"?

Hail! Abraham's God, and mine!
I join the heavenly lays;
All might and majesty are Thine,
And endless praise.

My dear friend, is Abraham's God your God? Is Joseph's God your God? Is the God of Moses your God? Have you listened to these men? They all foretold His coming, and He came. Have you recognized Jesus to be the Son of God? Have you seen Him as the Lamb of God taking away your sins? Have you laid your sins upon Him? Have you surrendered yourself, your life to Him? Is He the end of all to you, and is your trust entirely and only in Him? If so, you have a new understanding, you have a new nature and spirit, you are not afraid of death. You know that you will be upborne on eagles' wings and ascend into His glorious presence, and you are ready to join the heavenly lays and say:

Hail! Abraham's God, and mine!

If you have never done this before, do it now. Call on Him, and be saved in time, through death, and for all eternity.

NOTES

1. In Studies in the Book of Acts, Volumes 1—4, published by Banner of Truth and Crossway Books.
2. This is the teaching that says, “Every day and in every way I am getting better and better.”
3. The Middle East crisis of 1967.
4. This sermon was preached in June 1967.

OTHER CROSSWAY BOOKS BY
MARTYN LLOYD-JONES

Alive in Christ: A 30-Day Devotional

The Assurance of Our Salvation (Studies in John 17)

STUDIES IN THE BOOK OF ACTS:

Authentic Christianity

Courageous Christianity

Victorious Christianity

Glorious Christianity

Life in Christ (Studies in 1 John)

The Cross

Great Doctrines of the Bible: God the Father, God the Son; God the Holy Spirit; The Church and the Last Things (Three Volumes in One)

The Kingdom of God

My Soul Magnifies the Lord

Out of the Depths

Revival

Seeking the Face of God

True Happiness

Truth Unchanged, Unchanging

Walking with God Day by Day: 365 Daily Devotional Selections

Why Does God Allow Suffering?

Why Does God Allow War?